Vietnam:
Conflict
and
Controversy

Vietnam: Conflict and Controversy

PAUL ELLIOTT

ARMS AND
ARMOUR

ARMS & ARMOUR PRESS
An imprint of the Cassell Group
Wellington House, 125 Strand, London WC2R 0BB

Distributed in the USA by Sterling Publishing Co.
Inc., 387 Park Avenue South, New York, NY 10016-8810

Distributed in Australia by Capricorn Link (Australia) Pty Ltd, 2/13 Carrington Road, Castle Hill, New South Wales 2154

British Library Cataloguing-in-Publication data:
A catalogue record for this book is available from the British Library.

ISBN 1 85409 320 7

Edited and designed by Roger Chesneau/DAG Publications Ltd

Printed and bound in Great Britain by
Hartnolls Limited, Bodmin, Cornwall

CONTENTS

PREFACE

To a younger generation, Vietnam evokes a sense of desperate tragedy. The word conjures up images of failure, waste and folly. But for those old enough to remember, the war was a complex and almost unfathomable conflict that was wrought by unending controversy. That controversy rages on even today. As this book was being prepared, the memoirs of Secretary of Defence Robert McNamara were published and threatened to re-open the searing wound of Vietnam. McNamara, often called 'The architect of the Vietnam War', has apologised for the wartime failures of the Kennedy and Johnson administrations and expressed his regret that deeper political and military debates were not held. And in April 1995, while the United States held a Vietnam retrospective, Vietnam itself held relatively low-key celebrations marking the twentieth anniversary of the end of the war.

Vietnam: Conflict and Controversy is a detailed look at the forces within the American military that contributed to its defeat in the Vietnam War. While other books look at the larger political background of the war or at specific aspects of the US military machine, this book catalogues the controversial decisions of the war, some of which were good and many that were bad. The use of Agent Orange, the implementation of the secret assassination programme called 'Phoenix' and the one-year tours of duty that shattered unit morale are just some of the controversial issues that will forever mar the history of US involvement in Vietnam. Other decisions, although controversial at the time, proved to be highly effective and remain in being today. The central question—whether or not the United States should have intervened in (some say invaded) this small Third World nation—remains unanswered and unasked. Morality, Cold War politics and the perplexing relationship of colonialism, nationalism and self-determination confuse the issue and broaden the scope of any argument. Although other subjects, such as America's support of the Diem dictatorship in South Vietnam and the role that the media played in helping turn the public away from the war, are mentioned, the book concentrates on the military reaction to this most unique of wars. *Vietnam: Conflict and Controversy* is primarily a military critique.

The war has an unshakeable 1990s presence. When President Bush committed US troops to the Gulf War, he promised that this would not become 'another Vietnam'. He did not mean that America would not lose this war as it had in South-East Asia, but that its troops would have no artificial restrictions placed upon them. He said American soldiers would not be expected to 'fight with one hand tied behind their backs' as critics had often remarked about the prosecution of the Vietnam War. *Vietnam: Conflict and Controversy* looks at how the American military fought this 'one-handed war'. Self-imposed limitations and the use of the wrong kind of military machine for the task resulted in defeat. But was this defeat inevitable, as some have suggested?

All wars include a process of learning and adaptation for the forces involved, but, for America, Vietnam was a system shock that saw the traditional role of the military turned upside down. Changes were hastily implemented that were long overdue, and then tested and experimented in an ever deepening foreign war. Today we see US forces participating across the world in various theatres—operating with the foresight of the Vietnam experience, and ever mindful of the pitfalls of unpreparedness. Whether lessons have truly been learned from the war is a question that remains to be answered.

As a writer who is fascinated both with the modern military and with military history in general, I cannot ignore the huge impact that the lesson of Vietnam has had on the US armed forces, and by extension on global politics. It was a deadly lesson, with deadly errors of judgement—but who can name a war without such errors? Warfare is a constant struggle to adapt to a threatening and ever-changing situation in which the most able and quick-witted gain the advantage. What seem to be errors of judgement are often circumstances whereby a defeated force has clearly been outwitted or unable to adapt. I want to show that these errors were the combined result of White House mismanagement and the Pentagon's more general failure to transform the military system speedily enough and in the right directions.

The Vietnam conflict caught everyone by surprise. Consider for a moment the F-4 Phantom jet, of which the US Navy, Marine Corps and Air Force took delivery in the early 1960s. Throughout the skies of Indo-China the Phantom proved to be a valuable and effective aircraft, capable of a wide variety of missions. Fast, agile and 'high-tech', it faced enemy fighters with only a handful of air-to-air missiles. These missiles were designed to be utilised at long range, without the need for a close approach to an enemy MiG, and this meant that the pilots were unfamiliar with dogfighting. In addition, when the missiles were spent, pilots were forced to return to base, frustrated that they had no on-board gun with which to carry on the fight! It was a high-technology miscalculation, and one that typified the approach to 'modern war'. With long-range radar, supersonic missiles and computer-equipped aircraft, a new era in air combat had been predicted. But Phantom losses over North Vietnam illustrated that this prediction had been a false one: air-to-air combat was just as short-range, dirty and deadly as it had always been, but now the Phantom pilots were crippled without a gun. The clamour from fighter pilots forced a re-think, and in 1967 the F-4E flew for the first time, a modified Phantom that included an on-board 20mm Gatling gun. Following the Vietnam War, the Navy's concern about the lack of previous dogfight training resulted in the establishment of its now famous Top Gun air combat school.

The way in which the American military machine was forced to come to terms with such inadequacies was what made the Vietnam War so unique. Planners in the United States, including McNamara, were unprepared for a war of this kind, and they seemed unable to understand it even as it was being fought. In the strategic parlance of the time, it was not even a war but 'half a war', a guerrilla conflict that could be fought alongside two future 'real' wars (probably in Central Europe and the Persian Gulf). And meanwhile, as problems were being evaluated or ignored, servicemen were being killed and wounded in Vietnam. It is not my role to castigate the military planners in Washington or Saigon, the combat troops fighting in South Vietnam or Cambodia, or the pilots flying missions over Laos and North Vietnam. I write as an Englishman who did not participate in the conflict, and the danger of using the advantage of hindsight to judge one side or another, this decision or that, is very great. My objective is to observe with measured dispassion the failure of the American military to come to terms with its first 'modern' war and to examine the errors it made while doing so.

In the following pages we shall explore the tearing apart of established US military thought as new ideas were implemented, either to founder or succeed, while some of the old traditions were stubbornly retained in the face of overwhelming pressure for change. I have striven to remain neutral throughout, and this neutrality is fuelled by a knowledge that every war is to some extent a catalogue of errors. It is also fuelled by a vivid sense of 'it could have been me'—a feeling that I have never been able to shake off since I read Robert Mason's autobiography of his tour in Vietnam as a helicopter pilot. Roughly Mason's age when I first read his gripping, roller-coaster ride of a narrative, I deeply felt that Vietnam was the first war of the modern generation, a generation of anti-establishment, anti-war rock 'n' rollers—a war fought mostly by teenagers plucked from the street, whether they wanted to fight or not. At the lowest level in the chain of command, these draftees and the regular soldiers who fought with them bore the brunt of the Pentagon's experimentation, intransigence and ignorance. *Vietnam: Conflict and Controversy* concerns itself with the painful evolution of the US military machine into the modern world through the trauma of its involvement in South-East Asia. From the wreckage of the war came many things of value for each of the armed services—new ways of recruiting, of fighting, of equipping and of winning.

Today, all Western armies have benefited from the American experience. Up until the mid-1960s, the only war realistically contemplated was one against the Soviet Union, either in a huge conventional stand-up fight in Central Europe or in a four-minute frenzy of atomic annihilation. There seemed to be nothing in between. Vietnam taught our military planners, just as Afghanistan should have taught those of the Eastern bloc, that a different *kind* of warfare existed, and that the methods and equipment employed against the *Wehrmacht* and the Imperial Japanese Army were no longer valid.

Although in historical terminology the war is technically divided into two separate conflicts, the First Indo-China War (an anti-French, anti-colonial war), and the Second Indo-China War (a war of reunification), I shall be using wording that is probably more familiar to the reader: the French struggle against the Viet Minh (1945–54) is here known as the Indo-China War, while the fight to defend the South from North Vietnam (1965–75) is known just as the Vietnam War.

ACKNOWLEDGEMENTS

I would like to acknowledge the help of others in the preparation of this book. Some provided very useful information, others critiqued parts of the work, while still others argued at length with me over the differing standpoints of the controversies. They are, in no particular order, Staff Sergeant Jesse Mendez, Staff Sergeant Edward Quichocho and a number of other US Army servicemen both active and retired; Kevin Ruane, lecturer in Modern History; Michael Lemish, of the Vietnam Dog Handlers' Association; Harvey Waring; James Lawrence, formerly of the Royal Navy; Philip Elliott, formerly of the Royal Armoured Corps; Michael Lowe; and Sue Cotton. I must also thank my wife Christine for her constant support and encouragement, and for her diligent proof-reading of manuscripts. Finally, special thanks must go to my father Philip, who shed first-hand light on the Malayan insurgency and whose love of books these past few years has been my salvation.

Paul Elliott

ABBREVIATIONS

ACAV	Armoured Cavalry Assault Vehicle
APC	Armoured Personnel Carrier
ARVN	Army of the Republic of South Vietnam
CAP	Combined Action Platoon
CIA	Central Intelligence Agency
CIDG	Civilian Irregular Defence Group
CORDS	Civilian Operations and Revolutionary Development Support
COSVN	Central Office for South Vietnam
CT	Communist Terrorist (Malayan)
DEROS	Date Eligible for Return from Overseas
DMZ	Demilitarised Zone
DRV	Democratic Republic of Vietnam (South Vietnam)
FSB	Fire Support Base
GVN	Government of South Vietnam
H&I	Harassment and Interdiction
JCS	Joint Chiefs of Staff
K-Bar	Marine combat knife
KIA	Killed In Action
LZ	Landing Zone
MAAG	Military Advisory Assistance Group
MACV	Military Assistance Command Vietnam
MAT	Mobile Advisory Team
MIA	Missing In Action
NLF	National Liberation Front (the Viet Cong)
NVA	North Vietnamese Army (US name for the PAVN)
OSS	Office of Strategic Services
PAVN	People's Army of Vietnam (the official title of the NVA)
PFs	*See* RFs, PFs
POW	Prisoner of War
REMF	Rear Echelon Mother F—er
RFs, PFs	South Vietnamese Regional and Popular Forces
RPG	Rocket Propelled Grenade
SAM	Surface-to-Air Missile
USAF	United States Air Force

VC	Viet Cong (derogatory name for the NLF)
VCI	Viet Cong Infrastructure
I Corps	First allied military tactical zone (universally referred to as 'Eye' Corps)
II Corps	Second allied military tactical zone
III Corps	Third allied military tactical zone
IV Corps	Fourth allied military tactical zone

CHRONOLOGY OF THE WAR

1945 The Allied war against Japan ends and, in Vietnam, Japanese forces surrender. In northern Vietnam the Viet Minh nationalist movement (dominated by Ho Chi Minh and the communists) proclaim an independent government on 2 September. This is the August Revolution.

1946 French troops and Viet Minh resistance fighters clash in the city of Haiphong. The Viet Minh take to the mountains and begin their guerrilla war against the French.

1950 Both the USSR and China recognise Ho Chi Minh's government. American military aid begins to flow to the French war effort in Vietnam.

1954 French forces are defeated at Dien Bien Phu. France pulls out of Vietnam, and the Geneva Accords temporarily partition the nation into North and South Vietnam along the 17th Parallel. Elections are expected in 1955 to settle Vietnam's future. Ngo Dinh Diem becomes President of the Republic of South Vietnam with full American blessing.

1955 Diem represses the political and religious sects ranged against him. The Geneva Accords are ignored and elections indefinitely postponed.

1956 The Military Assistance Advisory Group (MAAG) initiates the training of South Vietnam's armed forces.

1957 Guerrilla activity begins in South Vietnam. Communists in Laos attempt to seize power.

1959 The Hanoi leadership begins its support of the southern insurgency movement. Construction of the Ho Chi Minh Trail is begun, and arms, material and troops are sent south. Laotian communists receive aid from North Vietnam.

1960 The Viet Cong (officially the National Liberation Front) is established in South Vietnam.

1961 Viet Cong attacks in South Vietnam are frequent and destructive. President Kennedy is inaugurated. The American struggle against wars of communist-inspired aggression is reaffirmed. Kennedy begins a massive increase in military aid and personnel to South Vietnam. A new command, MACV, is set up to organise the effort (beginning operations in February 1962). US troop numbers have jumped from 760 (at the start of 1960) to 3,205.

1962 Start of the 'Strategic Hamlets' programme. US troops number 11,300

1963 Battle of Ap Bac is a resounding defeat for the fledgeling Army of South Vietnam (ARVN). President Diem's generals overthrow and murder him on 2 November. President Kennedy is assassinated on 22 November and is succeeeded by Lyndon B. Johnson. US troops number 16,300.

1964 General William Westmoreland replaces General Harkins as commander of MACV. The USS *Maddox*, sailing off the North Vietnam coast, is attacked by torpedo boats. Retaliatory (and pre-planned) air strikes are ordered immediately against the North. Congress passes President Johnson's Tonkin Gulf Resolution, granting him full power to make war on North Vietnam. US troops number 23,300.

1965 'Rolling Thunder' bombing of North Vietnam begins. US Marines land at Da Nang and begin operations against Viet Cong. Ia Drang battle is first major confrontation between US Army and communists. US troops number 184,000.

1966 B-52s begin bombing targets in North Vietnam. Operation 'Masher'/ 'White Wing'. Further troop build-ups. US troops number 385,000.

1967 Operations 'Cedar Falls' and 'Junction City' comb communist base areas. North Vietnamese troops initiate large-scale border battles. US troops number 486,000.

1968 Khe Sanh is besieged. The Tet Offensive erupts across South Vietnam. My Lai massacre takes place. President Johnson declines to run for the Presidency. He also halts 'Rolling Thunder' in October. General Creighton Abrams succeeds Westmoreland as chief of MACV. Both American government and public are disenchanted with the war. Peace talks begin in Paris. US troops total is 536,000.

1969 President Richard Nixon begins the secret bombing of Cambodian sanctuaries whilst simultaneously pulling US troops out of South Vietnam. Policy of 'Vietnamisation' is unveiled. Ho Chi Minh dies in September. US troops in Vietnam total 474,000.

1970 South Vietnamese combat forces engage communist units in Cambodia. The Cambodian premier calls for American aid in resisting the Cambodian communists. National Guardsmen shoot four protesters at Kent State University. President Nixon announces further troop withdrawals from Vietnam. US troops number 335,000.

1971 Operation 'Lam Son 719', the advance into Laos. Release of *The Pentagon Papers*. US troop withdrawals continue; the total present is now 157,000.

1972 North Vietnamese 'Eastertide Offensive'. North Vietnamese ports are mined from the air. Bombing by B-52s ('Linebacker I' and 'II'), north of the 20th Parallel is halted after Hanoi agrees to a peace settlement. US troops total 24,000.

1973 Truce and end of American involvement in South Vietnam are formalised during 23 January agreement signed in Paris. Last US troops leave Vietnam on 29 March 1973. US troops total is 50 (the Embassy guard detail).

1974 Saigon claims that the war has re-started on 4 January. Communists move in on the Cambodian capital, Phnom Penh. President Nixon resigns and is succeeded by his Vice-President, Gerald Ford.

1975 Renewed North Vietnamese offensive begins in March. Cambodia falls to the communists. Operation 'Frequent Wind' evacuates remaining US personnel and selected Vietnamese from Saigon. North Vietnamese troops enter Saigon and seize power on 30 April. The Vietnam War ends in defeat for South Vietnam and its American ally.

Chapter 1

PRELUDE

The blinding flash and devastating blast wave of the atomic explosion over the Japanese city of Hiroshima on 6 August 1945 initiated the end of hostilities against Japan and ushered in a new era in warfare. Rather than dissipate immediately, the deadly shock wave gathered pace and reverberated through the nations of the world. It sounded the birth of the world's first superpower.

The atomic fist of the American nation in the immediate post-war years was the stately strategic bomber fleet. Composed initially of huge propeller-driven Boeing B-29s and B-36s,* the deadly nuclear-equipped air armada gave the United States Air Force immense prestige. In particular, Strategic Air Command, that arm of the Air Force tasked to wage the first nuclear war, was seen by both the American public and the military as the new face of warfare. Gone were the trench battles, tank skirmishes and the use of massed divisions of infantrymen to storm enemy towns: strategic air power would be able to win or lose wars without the need for ground troops ever to become involved. By the 1950s the popular image of the next war was of the new silver jet bombers streaking toward Russia at high altitude and dropping their deadly cargo before returning to America. The war against communist Russia would be fast, efficient and decisive.

It would not be so simple in practice, as the Pentagon soon discovered when communist North Korea began its invasion of the democratic South. It was as if those first two atomic flashes had blinded the military planners to the practicalities of entering and fighting a war overseas. The US Army seemed totally unprepared to defend South Korea. One year after Hiroshima, it had cut its troop numbers from 7 million down to 1.8 million. By 1948 this had fallen to just over half a million men, and there were many things being asked of it, including the occupation of Japan, the defence of Western Europe and the protection of various American assets around the globe. It was spread too thinly adequately to provide a deterrent against feared communist aggression. In Korea, the cosmopolitan United Nations army was prepared to stop the communist take-over of

---

*US aircraft designations appear more complex than they actually are. Numbers indicate specific designs, while letters indicate roles allocated to them —A for ground attack, B for bomber, C for cargo carrier, E for electronic warfare, F for fighter, H for helicopter, R for reconnaissance, U for utility and so on. A letter after the number designator indicates a sub-model of a specific design.

the South, and in doing so, it illustrated the level to which America had shifted the majority of its military muscle into SAC. 'The Bomb' would cripple the Army in Korea, just as it threatened to cripple the Army in Vietnam fifteen years later.

Almost immediately, on the opening of hostilities in Korea in June 1950, the American forces were humiliatingly pushed back in what almost became a rout. Most of the Second World War veterans had left the service and they had been replaced with young and relatively inexperienced recruits. Training and leadership could have been better, and the available equipment was mostly Second World War surplus. There had been relatively few American advances in military technology in the intervening five years. Just as telling were the undermanned units, and the poor organisation of these units, which failed to take the low troop levels into account. The results should have been predictable.

Much of the blame for this state of affairs lay at the door of President Truman. The Army had become a symbol of the wars of the past, not the future, and it was thought to have little part to play in any nuclear war. But Truman had quickly ruled out the use of the atomic bomb to stop aggression in Korea, leaving him no option but to deploy the neglected US Army to bolster the defences of the South. Immediately a revision of the service was undertaken, even as the United Nations grimly held the very tip of the Korean peninsular against the communists. The draft was reinstituted, the Army's divisions were brought to full strength and new commanders amenable to a revision of established tactics were introduced. The changes soon had an effect, and the United Nations forces were able to win back much of the peninsula. Only when Chinese troops entered the conflict were the Allies pushed back to the pre-war north–south boundary. The border crystallised there in 1953 when the military stalemate came to an end after a cease-fire agreement.

Following the Korean War, nuclear weapons again eclipsed the Army's role on the world stage, although it was now recognised that it had to be kept as well trained and technologically sophisticated as possible. It seems barely credible today, but the threat of a Stalinist invasion of Western Europe was widely feared at the time. There was no practical way that either the US or the other members of the fledgeling North Atlantic Treaty Organisation (NATO) could seriously counter this conventional Soviet threat to Europe: only nuclear weapons were thought to be able to equalise the great disparity in numbers between the Soviet and NATO forces. The 1950s saw the emergence of a military policy linking both troop deployment and the projected use of nuclear weapons. At the time it was decided that a small ground force in Europe would be necessary to trigger a Soviet response, and that this response could be countered by the use of battlefield (tactical) nuclear weapons to drive back the enemy forces. In the aftermath, the Army would move in to secure territory.

President Eisenhower, now in office, termed this his 'new look' policy, and it concentrated on stopping Soviet aggression by promising total nuclear annihilation if that nation did not back down. This strategy was called 'massive retaliation' and gave the Soviets only two options—surrender or atomic destruction. Jarring somewhat with Eisenhower's military pedigree, it also focused on cutting down the conventional forces to a bare minimum and investing in highly cost-effective nuclear weaponry with which to fight all of America's future conflicts. The lessons of Korea were quickly forgotten as sweeping new changes were made to the Army in an attempt to prepare it for combat on the nuclear battlefield. What emerged was the Pentomic division, a military unit composed of five battle groups that had a total strength of 13,700 men. This was 2,000 men short of the traditional Army division. The battle groups were smaller than the brigades that they replaced, but somewhat larger than the battalions that usually made up the brigades. Each battle group was designed to operate and survive in a nuclear environment, being able to manoeuvre and disperse in an attempt to avoid a tactical nuclear strike. But the Pentomic division had little ability to fight a conventional war. Without delay, nuclear arms for the projected conflict began to appear amongst the divisions: atomic artillery shells, atomic recoilless rifle shells and tactical missiles joined an armoury that included the atomic demolition charge used for closing ravines, creating impassable radioactive zones and destroying huge numbers of advancing enemy soldiers. On top of these were the growing stockpiles of atomic bombs and nuclear-tipped intercontinental ballistic missiles.

It was President Kennedy, Eisenhower's successor, who realised how unworkable the system would be in practice, even if it did look attractive in the annual budget lists. Would Washington really threaten the Soviet Union with total nuclear destruction if it did not remove its troops from some backwater nation on the other side of the planet? The answer was not a resounding 'yes', and so Kennedy's Secretary of Defense, Robert McNamara, began to formulate plans to unshackle the American Army from the atomic bomb and return to it its conventional capability. The discredited 'massive retaliation' policy was replaced with the more sophisticated and intelligent 'flexible response'. The Vietnam War was a conflict fought primarily as part of this flexible response.

Robert S. McNamara was the American Secretary of Defense from 1961 to 1968 and was the main architect of the Vietnam War during both the Kennedy and Johnson presidencies. He was an authoritative figure who had won his administrative spurs as President of the Ford Motor Company. McNamara brought his analytical mind and obsession with statistics to the White House and was able to gain a very firm civilian hold over the stubbornly independent US military. The most important changes he made to the Army were to give equal emphasis to nuclear and conventional warfare and to return to it the ability to fight overseas. But with the Cold War at is height, and the Cuban Missile Crisis and the Berlin Wall making front-page news, 'overseas' meant somewhere in Central Europe. An aggressive Warsaw Pact was the enemy with which the US armed forces were preparing to do battle.

The McNamara doctrine endorsed a strategy of fighting a war in Europe conventionally for as long as possible, and recommended against the immediate employment of tactical nuclear weapons. The reorganised Army divisions replaced the battle groups with three conventional brigades. These were given far more capability to wage war on the ground according to conventional tactics. But 'the next war' would defy the planners altogether, proving to be neither a conventional nor a nuclear conflict. The war in Vietnam was a military paradox, a war without front lines and without territory to win. In 1965 large-scale American troop units were deployed to South Vietnam in an attempt to prevent the expected invasion of the South by the communist North. However, they had been given the training, equipment and organisation to fight a conventional/nuclear war on the plains of Europe and would be inadequately prepared to wage a multi-faceted guerrilla war against the elusive Viet Cong. Central to the defence of Germany (considered the crucial battleground of a war with the Warsaw Pact) was the employment of armoured tank formations in concert with mechanised infantry (troops carried within armoured personnel carriers). These would allow rapid manoeuvres that were designed to isolate or outflank enemy units.

As discussed later in Chapter 3, these strategies and expectations would come under great strain in Vietnam, a land that was universally acknowledged as anything but suitable terrain for tank operations. But this land was not uppermost in the minds of the planners when the theory of flexible response had been hatched. Kennedy and McNamara *were* aware of Vietnam: Eisenhower had considered intervening in the war for liberation there in 1954 and had briefed the two about his concerns before leaving the White House. But no one could have foreseen that one of the most significant wars of America's history would be fought in that country, and that US forces would be forced by domestic and international pressure to abandon their stated war aims, leaving the South Vietnamese people to their fate. The American government was not the first Western power to become enmeshed in the confusing conflict. France had maintained a presence in Vietnam for almost a century, and after the Second World War was faced with a savage war of liberation in the colony, masterminded by a politically adept leader—the famous Ho Chi Minh.

The Seeds of War

The American involvement in the continuing conflicts of Vietnam began during the war with Japan, and few in Washington at the time could have predicted the chaos and destruction that was to follow in the years to come. Japanese forces had invaded and occupied the nation of Indo-China, of which Vietnam was then a part. The nation had not been independent and free, but a colony of the French, and it was ruled by the local Indo-Chinese élite, who had been introduced to the French language and culture as well as to the Catholic faith. When France fell to the German *Blitzkrieg* in 1940, French resistance to the Japanese in Indo-China

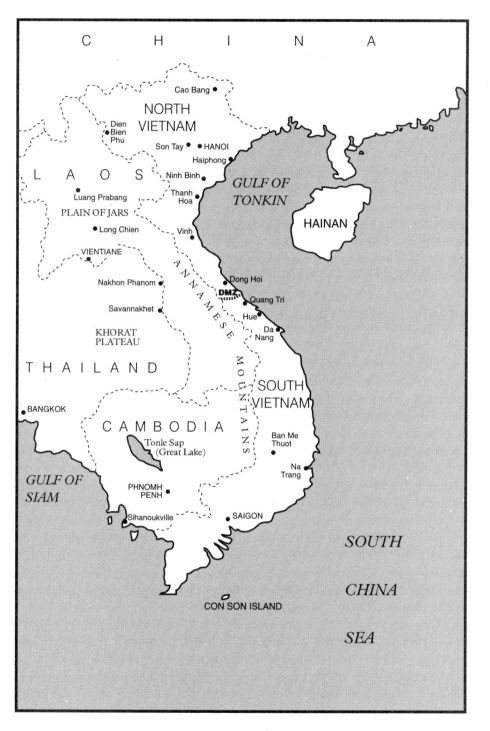

South-East Asia. DMZ = Demilitarised Zone.

also wavered and the colony fell to the armies of Hirohito. It was the brutal occupation of the Japanese that triggered off the native resistance movement that desired not only the removal of the Japanese from Vietnam but also the removal of the French. Ho Chi Minh, a shrewd student of Marxism, led an underground, communist-led resistance movement called the Viet Minh (the League for Vietnamese Independence) against the Japanese invaders.

Well-organised but under-funded, under-manned and under-supplied, the Viet Minh carried out a campaign of terrorism and intelligence-gathering. From mid-1943 Ho Chi Minh was able to muster tentative support for his independence struggle both from China further north (a nation also crippled by a rapacious Japanese invasion) and from the American Secret Service (then called the Office of Strategic Studies), which was willing to foster any resistance to the Japanese. With this recognition and backing, the Viet Minh organised a guerrilla force with which to sabotage the Japanese invasion army, collect intelligence and even rescue Allied airmen flying missions over Vietnam.

As 1944 drew to a close, Ho's close friend and military leader, Vo Nguyen Giap, began attacks on French outposts in the north of Vietnam, setting a trend that was to be followed until the end of the Second World War. Japanese troops surrendered to the Allies the following summer, handing over the rule of Vietnam to the Viet Minh, which had emerged triumphant from the shadows to form the new post-war government. By the start of September Ho Chi Minh and his followers had swept into Hanoi to proclaim a fully independent Republic of Vietnam. The United States had considerable reservations about recognising this new government, torn as it was between open support for colonies wishing to achieve independence and its vehement post-war opposition to all things communist. Even so, OSS officers were at Ho's side as he set-about organising his new nation.

But Ho Chi Minh would not live to see his independent Vietnam: thirty years of trouble lay ahead that would stall every attempt to create a stable and free nation. The troubles began in earnest in September of 1945. British forces occupied the southern city of Saigon to accept the Japanese surrender and then declared martial law as turmoil erupted in the streets. Various Vietnamese groups opposed to the Viet Minh were expressing their frustrations, and the British commander, General Douglas Gracey, in an effort to maintain order, armed over a thousand French prisoners-of-war, many of whom were veteran soldiers of the Foreign Legion. The fighting turned bloody and these French troops removed the Viet Minh from Saigon's city hall, effectively re-establishing French supremacy in the city. The battle lines had been redrawn, and throughout 1946, as the French returned to power in Hanoi, haphazard talks were punctuated by periods of violence between French reoccupation forces and an elusive Viet Minh. By the end of 1946 open warfare between the two sides was becoming the norm, and in the following April Ho Chi Minh led his army into the densely forested Viet Bac mountains in northern Vietnam. From here his troops began a protracted guerrilla war against the French—a struggle known as the Indo-China War.

The war would be savage and unrelenting, with the French occupiers determined to retain a hold on their colony, despite the symbolic granting of independence to Vietnam under the emperorship of the French-backed aristocrat Bao Dai. Fighting with American weapons supplied through its wartime association with the OSS, the Viet Minh outmanoeuvred the French forces and struck from hidden bases, only to fade back into the rural population or the jungles. France found it difficult to meet this threat, having been devastated economically by the Nazi occupation, and it had to rely heavily on American funding and equipment to stay in the field. Following the end of the Second World War, Washington had swiftly switched support in Vietnam from the communist Viet Minh to the French, for reasons of global security. Although the US ostensibly supported the dismantling of the old colonial regimes, France was allowed to carry on with its reoccupation of Vietnam and the rest of Indo-China. The postwar enemy had become the communist Soviet Union with its monolithic control of Eastern Europe. Following the fall of 'free' China in 1949, the West suspected a 'domino effect' of Asian states all falling prey to communism in rapid succession. In 1950 the communist invasion of South Korea had only just been repulsed by a United Nations force, led by the United States. It was greatly feared that China was now exerting influence on Vietnam, and that it too would topple to the communist insurgents, the Viet Minh. France was also part of the newly created NATO, a military organisation created solely to counter the vast communist bloc and deter Stalin from invading Europe. France was an important linchpin in Europe's defence, and she could not be snubbed without affecting this crucial military alliance.

So, as the inevitable showdown with Ho Chi Minh and his guerrilla forces grew ever nearer, American support for French actions steadily increased. In 1953 the new US President, Dwight D. Eisenhower, mindful of the Korean War that had just ended, clearly saw the war in Vietnam as an anti-communist crusade, not a nationalist war of liberation. Backed by his Secretary of State John Foster Dulles, Eisenhower allocated almost one-third of America's 1954 foreign aid budget to the French defence of Vietnam. Although this figure amounted to well over one billion dollars, it was a cash transfusion into a terminally ill patient and would do the French military mission in Vietnam no good.

Dien Bien Phu, a sprawling French garrison out in the north Vietnamese wilds, would be the test of Eisenhower's true commitment to the halt of communism in Asia. In an attempt to cut off Viet Minh supply and retreat routes into Laos, and to act as a forward base from which to launch attacks against them, the French military commander, General Henri Navarre, built up a strong troop concentration at Dien Bien Phu. The outpost also served a secondary purpose—a vast trap into which Ho Chi Minh's guerrillas would be enticed and in which they would be eradicated by superior French firepower. In 1953 Navarre had predicted, with the immortal phrase 'Now we can see clearly, like light at the end of a tunnel', an imminent end to the Indo-China War. But it was the Viet Minh who would bask in that light, not the French. For almost two months throughout the spring of 1954 General Vo Nguyen Giap's guerrillas lay siege to the 'deadly trap' of Dien Bien Phu, and with unexpected firepower totally isolated the beleaguered garrison. Constant bombardment from newly procured Chinese artillery pieces, and a withering anti-aircraft fire directed against French attack and supply planes, soon proved decisive. Without proper resupply, and cut off from friendly ground forces, the outpost was doomed. Eisenhower was extremely reticent to come to France's aid, and so with the fall of the garrison at Dien Bien Phu that nation's rule in Vietnam also toppled. In July all the interested parties were signatories to the Geneva cease-fire agreements which also made arrangements to partition Vietnam temporarily into a communist-controlled North and an unaligned South until proper elections could be held. For a period of 300 days, freedom of movement was allowed for those in either region to move across the demarcation line (later known as the Demilitarised Zone, or DMZ). Thousands of Viet Minh lay low in the South for the rest of the decade, waiting for the day they would be re-activated as Viet Cong (Vietnamese communist) guerrilla fighters. The Indo-China War was over and the Vietnam War was about to begin.

Chapter 2

THE EARLY YEARS OF INVOLVEMENT

Secretary of Defense Robert S. McNamara came to personify the war, and, as he took responsibility for and control of it, the Vietnam conflict came to be known as 'McNamara's War'. In these early years, the emerging conflict was a fog-shrouded and impenetrable affair, and indeed it always remained such. McNamara admits, in his book *In Retrospect*, that the United States worked on two contradictory premises: first, the fall of South Vietnam to the communists would be detrimental to Western security; secondly, only the South Vietnamese *themselves* could prevent that from happening. Concluding that no good could come from active US intervention, Kennedy had planned phased withdrawals of advisers from the region in late 1963. His death prevented these from occurring.

There were further misconceptions that became set in concrete at this juncture, and, enacted as policy, they proved disastrous. Again and again McNamara regrets the blinkered advice offered by both himself and others in the administration, and points to the seeming monolithic nature of communism as one example. Ho Chi Minh was seen as a communist first and a nationalist second. And communism itself was understood, even by the Cold War experts, to be a single, multi-national conspiracy aiming to destabilise Third World countries. To McNamara, Hanoi represented Peking; yet the truth was that, although China was eager to supply North Vietnam with arms and equipment, she was hated and feared by all Vietnamese. Within five years of the victory for North Vietnam in the 1970s, the two nations were at war! In the early 1960s little information was sought and few experts consulted as to the nature of Far Eastern affairs at the time. Thus the conflict and the forces that drove it were misunderstood from the start. Crucial questions were not answered because they were never asked.

The Special Forces War

Whilst the French had on occasion employed small, highly trained combat units in Indo-China with which to carry the fight to the Viet Minh, it was the newly arriving American advisers who would eventually be the great advocates of this type of warfare. Perhaps the central reason for France's military failure adequately to deal with the communists was her inability to locate and fix the guerrillas. In their native land, and using Mao Tse-tung's tried and tested revolutionary method of becoming invisible 'fish' swimming in a 'sea' of sympathetic peasants, the communists were an ever-elusive and rarely identifiable enemy. With the Geneva Accords and their strict supervision of border integrity between the old Indo-Chinese regions (now independent states) of Cambodia, Laos, and North and South Vietnam, the need for secret armies for infiltration and counter-infiltration had suddenly expanded.

From supplying primarily economic and material aid to the fledgeling South Vietnamese government (the GVN), the United States troops began to provide advice and training. The vehicle for this assistance was at first the Military Assistance Advisory Group (MAAG), a multi-force training and advisory unit for the newly created South Vietnamese Armed Forces. It had been present in the country since 1950 and was based in Saigon, the capital of South Vietnam. By the end of the decade there were 900 MAAG personnel operating across South Vietnam. Under President Kennedy, who entered the White House in January 1961, the advisory force rapidly increased in size, and by December of that year MAAG numbers had rocketed to 3,205. Kennedy, in his inaugural address, pledged to support any nation in its defence of freedom, whatever the cost to the United States, and South Vietnam was to be his test case. It would be a proving ground, too, for the Soviet Union, which was eager to see if 'wars of national liberation' were the way forward in the Cold War against capitalism.

President Kennedy was a proponent of special forces warfare and of the concept of giving small units of highly trained élites the opportunity and equipment to fight war in their own unique way. The participation of various élite units in the Vietnam War would mark a major change from wars of the past, and in Vietnam that participation could have proved to be crucial. As it was, the use of élite forces by the US was encouraged, but not actively so, by the military establishment, which seems to have feared them. They were there at the beginning of the war, and they were there at its end, and some commentators on the war have dared to suggest that if there had been more of them, then the later communist invasion of South Vietnam may never have occurred. The exploits of these élite force units, and in particular those of the Green Berets, were controversial at the time, and in retrospect may have been the overlooked key to success in halting the growing Viet Cong domination of villages and towns. Also linked with the Special Forces war were the top-secret Special Operations Group teams, and these too would suffer from misuse—in a way that can truly be said to have sparked off the Vietnam War.

During the 1950s a small cadre of American intelligence experts led by Colonel Edward G. Lansdale had arrived in South Vietnam to do battle against the communists. As the French prepared to pull out of the colony for good, Lansdale's Saigon Military Mission (SMM) moved in to provide the emerging South Vietnamese government with some expertise in counter-insurgency warfare and 'psyops' (psychological operations). SMM was, in fact, backed by the Central Intelligence Agency, a group already familiar with Vietnam in the 1940s under the guise of the OSS. Now, however, the tables were turned, and the CIA was about to direct a covert war against Ho Chi Minh rather than on his behalf. US-backed special operations in the region can said to have begun with the training of two SMM infiltration teams, 'Binh' and 'Hao', that travelled north with thousands of other refugees sympathetic to the communists when the country was partitioned. Agents of 'Binh' sabotaged the Hanoi transport system as the French began their evacuation, but could not attempt the crippling of more important targets due to the wording of the Geneva Accords which forbade such terrorism. Reconnaissance work was also carried out for future operations if the chance for them should ever arise. The 'Binh and 'Hoa' teams were not long-lived, however, and were soon eradicated by the efficient North Vietnamese security forces. But Lansdale continued his secret fight against communism, employing a 'dirty tricks' campaign of psychological warfare. In one operation the SMM distributed leaflets that attempted to trick those Vietnamese wanting to move to the communist North into staying in the South, and northern peasants into fleeing to South Vietnam.

From 1954 to 1956 Colonel Lansdale proved an invaluable ally for South Vietnam's new premier Ngo Dinh Diem, and became both an aide and a confidante of the quiet and reclusive Catholic. With an all-out invasion by North Vietnam of the South out of the question for the time being, and with the obstacle of the Geneva Accords preventing Diem's South Vietnamese government from carrying a war northwards, this period was characterised by pre-war manoeuvrings and 'black' operations of all kinds. Eventually Lansdale put his unit's talents towards the stabilising of the GVN and its newly formed army of the South, the ARVN. Rivals of the southern government, such as the leaders of an overthrow plot in 1954 and the Binh Xuyen secret society a year later, were dealt with sharply by the Diem–Lansdale partnership, and the two became colleagues and friends. But there were still serious threats to the integrity of the South, including the Cao Dai and Hoa Hao religious sects as well as any of the newly appointed military chiefs who contested Diem's rule. And then of course there were the communists.

However, SMM had proved that special operations had a unique role to play in Vietnam, and it was Lansdale's personal report to President Kennedy in 1961 that was totally to transform the level of both interest and commitment that the United States would show in this part of the world. In particular, Lansdale recommended covert actions in support of Diem, and he was instrumental in affecting Kennedy's attitudes and reactions to the growing conflict in the region. It was a conflict that was low-intensity in nature: it was, in the language of the times, an 'insurgency'. Fought by members of the Viet Cong, which was essentially a disaffected indigenous movement, the war received impetus through the arming and training of local forces by communist cadres from the North. Villages and sometimes entire districts would be terrorised and forced into providing food, shelter and recruits for the revolutionaries as they planned and executed ever more daring attacks on the Saigon government and the ARVN. This was a type of Cold War conflict for which the United States had no appropriate response, although several nations (in particular Britain, with experience in Palestine, Malaya, and Kenya) had already encountered and dealt with such insurgency. 'Counter-insurgency' was the vogue label applied to military techniques that were designed to protect the people from such guerrilla activity, and by 1960 the American military had acknowledged that it was this kind of warfare that would dominate the arena. This was a reversal of thinking. Since the fall of Dien Bien Phu, the Pentagon had expected a conventional invasion of South Vietnam by the North—a virtual replay of the Korean War. All aspects of the advisory effort, including the foundation of conventional armed forces in the South, had revolved around this misconception.

Vietnam was to be the proving ground for a whole series of Special Forces units, some of which will still be active in the twenty-first century. In introducing Special Forces to the conflict during the early 1960s, Washington was able to participate in South-East Asia without the fanfare of a full-scale invasion, and was then able to influence the various factions with a minimum of outlay. President Kennedy dispatched one of his chief advisers, Walt Rostow, and a trusted Army General, Maxwell Taylor, to Vietnam for a frank assessment of what was needed to win the war against communist subversion, and to prevent a possible invasion by North Vietnam. Their recommendations, that regular troop units, in large numbers, should be sent to South Vietnam for its defence, were not met with welcome ears. But, fearful of the great threat to the integrity of that new nation, Kennedy did increase his commitment to the MAAG mission there.

Simultaneously, the President gave his full backing to the enlargement of the United States Army Special Forces, the élite group established in the 1950s to operate behind Russian lines in the event of an all-out war. A new task was given to them: fighting the Cold War in out-of-the-way places, and out of the headlines. Kennedy presided over the formation of the 5th Special Forces Group in 1961, which sent teams of soldiers to Vietnam in a training role, joining an earlier Special Forces unit, the 1st Special Forces Group (based in Okinawa). Initially based at Fort Bragg, North Carolina, members of the 5th Special Forces Group were authorised to wear the famous green beret with all uniforms as a mark of distinction and *esprit de corps*. With much of its expertise desperately needed in South-East Asia, the unit (unofficially known as the 'Green Berets') later transferred to Nha Trang in South Vietnam, from where it ran the US Army's covert war against the communists.

In the field, the Special Forces operated in twelve-man 'A-teams' with individual soldiers specialising in subjects as diverse as communications, medicine, intelligence, heavy weapons and demolitions. Other services, too, received their own élite units, and between them they gave the American military a formidable new tool to be used against an aggressor. In Indo-China that aggressor was an increasingly belligerent North Vietnam. On their own, these forces were often impotent, too lightly armed and manned to participate in even moderately sized conventional battles. But they were far more efficient as 'force multipliers', carrying out tasks such as training much larger, self-motivated native units, calling in air strikes within enemy territory, rescuing hostages and POWs and reconnoitring well-used enemy trails and using stealth and deception to ambush enemy units using them. Personnel from the Special Forces were given ample opportunity to carry out these kinds of missions, and did so with little or no credit since most of the operations were classified top secret. All called for rugged, well-trained and highly disciplined and motivated individuals, marking a member of the Special Forces, as an éite soldier, one of the best.

Securing the Highlands

By far the greatest triumph of the Special Forces was the Civilian Irregular Defense Group (CIDG) programme that flourished mainly along the borders with Cambodia and Laos. It lasted a decade, from late 1961 until the Americans pulled out in the early 1970s. It had initially been a CIA-run programme, but Green Berets were used for much of the actual military training. What the programme aimed to do was mobilise the country's indigenous tribespeople, the *montagnards* (who lived within Vietnam's inaccessible interior), as an irregular self-defence force. It proved to be one of the war's greatest successes, and one of its greatest missed opportunities. Unlike the programme involving average Vietnamese peasant youth, dragged into the ARVN to fight with thousands of other displaced Vietnamese in a part of the country he could not really care less about, the 'cidgee' success hinged on the tribe's own community spirit and knowledge of the local terrain. In addition, the CIDG project allowed the population to remain where it was, contrasting sharply with the unpopular village resettlement programme of the Diem government (see Chapter 5). In fact, without the close border locations of most of these indigenous villages, the project could not have worked. It was in the main a defensive move to reduce the strain from the under-manned ARVN, which was busy chasing the Viet Cong around the countryside while also attempting to defend the cities.

The new CIDG strategy was first tested at a site called Buon Enao in the southern highlands. There a tribe of *montagnard* natives was trained by a Green Beret A-team led by Captain Ronald Shackleton and (as was customary) a small contingent of their South Vietnamese equivalents, the élite Luc Luong Duc Biet (LLDB). So primitive were the crossbow-armed *montagnards* that Shackleton once said of Buon Enao, 'It was like a setting from a Tarzan movie.' These people were the indigenous mountain-dwelling natives of Vietnam, and their hatred of the lowland Vietnamese farmers was much akin to that of the native Americans to the first white settlers. Social welfare and medical programmes were directed at the primitive tribespeople in a (successful) attempt to foster friendship and loyalty amongst them. Often the Green Berets would share the lives of the *montagnards*, eating, sleeping and socialising with them. Many, indeed, partook of religious or ceremonial rituals that bound them to the tribe and wore brass wristbands as a mark of acceptance by their pupils.

It has been pointed out that the primary task of the Special Forces in wartime had originally been the organising of native resistance movements *behind* enemy lines, which in the case of Indo-China would be within North Vietnam. But as far as the war in Vietnam was concerned, the front line was in effect somewhere through the Central Highlands, the home of the *montagnards*. If the Green Berets and LLDB had not actively recruited them, then communist cadres from the North certainly would have, providing Hanoi with a valuable strategic gain. The tribespeople were caught up within the Ho Chi Minh Trail network, the forward deployment area for the North Vietnamese Army.

The Trail was the main infiltration route of the NVA into the South, and was christened the Ho Chi Minh Trail by the US military. It was a complex network of interlocking trails and jungle paths that passed through the harsh mountainous terrain of Laos before snaking into the South either through the Central Highlands or further south through Cambodia to emerge in the Mekong Delta on Saigon's doorstep. In this early stage of the war the journey to Saigon via this secret trail network took around three months of travel on foot, bicycle and sometimes truck. Mountain passes, thick jungle, rivers and other nightmarish terrain had to be negotiated by the porters, who were often pressed into service against their will to carry the formidable loads of ammunition and supplies to the VC.

Patrols all across the Central Highlands were begun, to try to prevent North Vietnam infiltrating the South and organising local base areas, and just over a year later communist activity in the area had dropped off significantly. Soon the CIDG programme was being applied to minority populations all over South Vietnam, including the Nung Chinese, the ethnic Khmer Cambodians and the Cao Dai and Hoa Hao sects. Each CIDG camp would share its responsibilities between two main groups. First a 'strike force' would be permanently on standby for daily patrolling, reconnaissance and ambush tasks, while the rest of the male adults would form an unpaid militia, drilled in the use of firearms and in basic tactics. This two-tier combination enabled even these tiny communities to put up a flexible response to local Viet Cong activities.

The American advisers up in the Central Highlands, where the project began and where it flourished, became trusted and well liked by the locals. And in return the Green Berets respected the tough fighting spirit, hard work and honesty of the various tribal minorities. In these people, the Special Forces saw something of themselves, and a deep empathy and camaraderie was created between the two groups. Social and medical programmes designed to help the *montagnards* impressed them, and the little field hospitals became important not just for their physical benefits but also for both morale and intelligence-gathering. The ethnic Vietnamese (of both North and South) had shown the hill-people nothing but cruelty and exploitation, calling them *moi* (savages), and so the

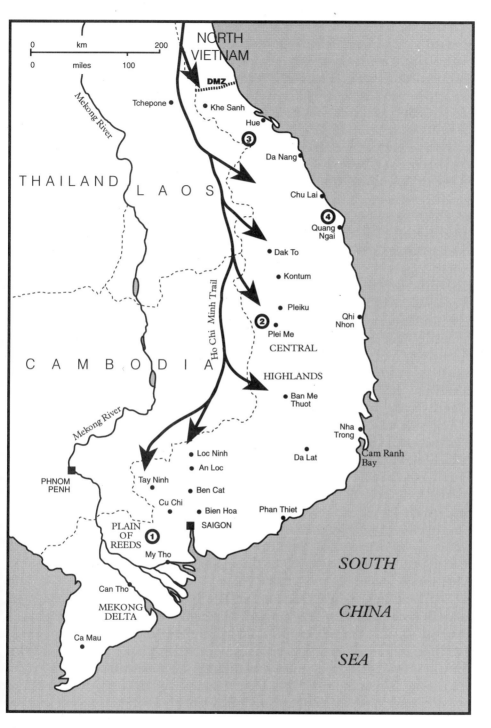

South Vietnam. Locations of note: 1. Ap Bac. 2. Ia Drang Valley. 3. A Shau Valley. 4. My Lai. DMZ = Demilitarised Zone

montagnards responded warmly to the American efforts to help them to help themselves. The programme went very well for the United States—initially. With lonely jungle outposts spread right across the South Vietnamese border and throughout the vulnerable Central Highlands, the 'cidgees' created a loyal patchwork of territories, denying their valuable strategic use to the communist Viet Cong. There were, at the end of 1963, around 11,000 strike force members and over 40,000 militiamen, all under US command and in Special Forces custody.

That year, too, the CIDG programme was handed over officially from CIA control to the US military in Vietnam, and with the transfer came a distinct shift in the attitude of the United States to these irregular forces. Kennedy had expanded and reorganised the American commitment, and MAAG had already been replaced by the Military Assistance Command Vietnam (MACV), which took control of the 'cidgees' and began looking at the role they could play in the overall build-up. The successes of the Green Berets and their 'cidgee' wards would not stand the test of time. One of the saddest misuses of a programme that had seemed to offer so many solutions was the way in which the military hierarchy in Vietnam appropriated these small native outposts for their own planned large-unit conflicts. By 1964 the war was hotting up and communist attacks, backed increasingly by North Vietnam, became larger and more daring. At the year's end entire units of the North Vietnamese Army would cross the border to redeploy in the South. The nature of the war was changing, from a native insurgency conflict to the cross-border invasion of the South by the Army of the North.

Unfortunately John Kennedy did not live long enough to see if his policies in Vietnam would bear fruit. Neither did Ngo Dinh Diem, the GVN premier who had depended on American aid to fight his ineffectual war against the communists: he had been assassinated in a military *coup* at the start of November 1963, twenty days before JFK himself was killed by Lee Harvey Oswald. The following year would see an end to Kennedy's see-saw policy: wanting to build-up the advisory force, but always afraid to commit (or admit to committing) combat troops. Lyndon B. Johnson, Kennedy's Vice-President now installed in the White House, was more easily swayed by the arguments for a strong commitment to Vietnam.

The Viet Cong irregulars had, up until late 1963 and 1964, given the 'cidgee' camps a wide berth when they crossed into South Vietnam. Although beginning to be pressed into service as a border protection force, the hill tribes were spread too thinly to provide an adequate defence against a communist invasion. Their main use lay in local intelligence, local defence and the denial of their talents to the enemy. As part of the change, MACV had started closing down the camps and operating the CIDG strike teams from even more remote outposts to act as raiding forces across the border in an attempt to cut the Trail. The Viet Cong and North Vietnamese Army (NVA) could not ignore these bigger and more aggressive units, and attacks on the camps became more frequent.

If the shift was not popular with the communists, it was just as unpopular amongst the *montagnards*. Cut off from his home territory, and fighting an enemy that seemed to pose no threat to his tribe, the *montagnard* became merely a less well-equipped version of the ARVN peasant soldier. Morale dropped and desertions increased proportionately. Retired Special Forces Colonel Larry Trapp put it bluntly: 'If you took these guys somewhere far away to fight, they wouldn't do it, but bring them back to defend their villages and they'd fight like hell.' Tensions continued to escalate as the LLDB, the ARVN Special Forces unit, also became much more involved in the running of the 'cidgees'. In a rash of camp mutinies in September 1964, 34 Vietnamese were killed by *montagnard* irregulars, and it was only the goodwill that existed between the Green Berets and the hill tribes that prevented far more serious levels of bloodshed.

At Nam Dong Special Forces camp, only 24km from the Laotian border, a violent conflict suddenly flared up on 5 July 1964 between the local Nung 'cidgees' and the Vietnamese LLDB. The short firefight that ensued proved, however, to be the prelude to a much more serious conflict. Unknown to the Nam Dong garrison, there were two Viet Cong battalions massed around the little camp ready to attack. During the defence of Nam Dong an American Green Beret officer, Captain Roger Donlon, won the first Congressional Medal of Honor to be awarded to a soldier serving in Vietnam. His A-team, A-726, had at the time been preparing to establish a border surveillance camp closer to Laos but was unprepared for the huge enemy force that was ranged against it.

The communists initially opened fire on the small forest camp with automatic weapons, mortars and grenades, the classic communist prelude to a ferocious ground assault. Captain Donlon helped the Nungs and Vietnamese and the other Green Berets lay down suppressive fire in an attempt to prevent the waves of Viet Cong infantry from overrunning the perimeter. Spotting VC sappers attempting to blow the main gate, Donlon, although wounded by burns and shrapnel, ran over and shot them dead with his M16 rifle. Wounded again as enemy fire chopped up the defenders and destroyed most of the camp, he was still able to direct the fire of an intact 81mm mortar in an attempt to push the communists back. The majority of the defenders had been wounded, and ammunition was running very low, when government aircraft arrived overhead. The VC began pulling back as flares illuminated the area and supplies were dropped to the A-team. By mid-morning the guerrillas had vanished into the jungle, leaving behind 62 dead; in return they had inflicted a total of 55 fatalities, two of which were Green Berets.

Nam Dong was indicative of how seriously the Viet Cong were now taking the border camps. CIDG strike forces posed a definite threat to the bold communist war strategy, and Hanoi did not hesitate to rise to the challenge. A new phase in the Vietnam War was beginning, and the grim and desperate battle of Nam Dong proved that it was these lonely outposts of the South upon which a growing burden of the war would fall. This phase would draw larger and better-equipped units into the Central Highlands and culminate in the famous battle of Ia Drang in 1965. Close to the porous border with Laos and Cambodia, the Special Forces *montagnard* outposts saw some of the most desperate fighting of the entire war.

The new emphasis on cross-border raiding and intelligence-gathering that had begun to affect the employment of the 'cidgees' mirrored developments in other areas of the US military. McNamara had presided over the establishment in January 1964 of the CIA-backed Special Operations Group (SOG) that was to conduct deep reconnaissance and 'black' operations in Laos, Cambodia and North Vietnam. Even today, SOG activities during the war remain highly classified. A total of 8,000 indigenous troops and 2,000 Americans were assigned to SOG, and individual reconnaissance teams (RTs) conducted a wide range of missions directed mainly against North Vietnam. These included commando raids in the Mekong Delta (Op 31), air insertions into enemy territory (Op 32), propaganda transmissions (Op 33), raids into North Vietnam (Op 34) and a variety of cross-border insertions into enemy territory by small, highly mobile commando teams (Op 35). These latter missions were successfully carried out, for the most part, until the end of the US involvement in Vietnam.

Ground raids across into Laos under the designation 'Shining Brass' began in 1965 and had the objective of reconnoitring the Ho Chi Minh Trail. US Special Forces led twelve-man 'cidgee' RTs into Laos to search out NVA troop concentrations and encampments for targeting by air strikes. Other RTs moved into Cambodia for the 'Daniel Boone' operations in 1966 with similar objectives, and at the same time SOG expanded its Laotian missions under the designation 'Prairie Fire'. On an ultra-secret level, reconnaissance raids into North Vietnam were conducted that went under the name 'Kit Cat'. As a consequence of this successful, triple-front, top-secret war, SOG was reorganised into Command and Control North (CCN), which operated in North Vietnam and Laos, Command and Control Central (CCC), operating in the tri-border region where Cambodia, Laos and South Vietnam met, and Command and Control South (CCS), operating across the border in Cambodia. Rather than wait defensively for the communists to wage their war on South Vietnam, the SOG missions (although they were technically illegal) carried the fight directly to the NVA and Viet Cong strongholds. Important intelligence was gathered that could not be gained in any other way, and the 'safe havens' over the border were no longer truly safe for the enemy. Ammunition dumps, when discovered, were often rigged to explode, and the unique 'roadrunner' agents waged a psychological war across the Trail network. Each agent was a local (often a Nung) who masqueraded as a communist soldier to infiltrate units as they moved south down the Trail. At rice stations, hospitals and truck parks, these brave soldiers gathered first-hand intelligence and carried out deadly sabotage.

The highly secret Special Operations Group took volunteers from the Army Special Forces as well as the Navy's own élite unit, the SEALs, and members of the Marine Force Recon units. Increasingly, the tribal minorities that had formerly been part of the CIDG programme were recruited for these cross-border special operations as virtual mercenaries, whilst the remaining 'cidgees' were reorganised as Mobile Strike (MIKE) forces that carried out swift, airmobile attacks and raids independently or in support of other Special Forces operations. The concept of community defence and mobilisation that had proved so successful had been diluted by MACV in the late 1960s, and by 1971 the remaining CIDG camps were handed over to the ARVN as regional and border ranger troop units.

In I Corps, close to the DMZ, where the Marines were responsible for the defence of the northern part of South Vietnam, 'clear and hold' operations became very important. The coastal enclaves around which the Marines were based were heavily populated, and the Corps could not ignore the pacification campaign as the Army had done in more sparsely settled areas. Called Combined Action Platoons (CAPs), the Marine units were assigned a Navy medic and operated much like the Green Berets, being assigned to work in conjunction with a Vietnamese village defence unit. The deployment of a CAP focused the pacification effort and helped the local defence force to hold an area that had been cleared of enemy influence. Unfortunately, it was conventional military operations that found favour with the big Army divisions. These cleared areas of guerrilla activity but failed to establish any sort of permanent presence there as the CIDG and CAP programmes were attempting to do.

MACV had missed a great opportunity to coordinate its military strategy with civil action to secure the pacification of the population. Yet this was something that General Westmoreland had pledged do. His later Mobile Advisory Teams (MATs) were composed of six special warfare soldiers, working at the village level, but they concentrated almost exclusively on matters of defence. Village and district militias, the Regional and Popular Forces (RFs and PFs), were trained and advised by these MATs. Although successful, the MATs were part of a CIA pacification drive in the late 1960s that had been formulated more through necessity than a pre-planned strategy. Although 'clear and hold' techniques had been used by the Army Special Forces in the CIDG programme, the US Army had decided not to carry them any further. In late 1964 MACV had other, more pressing, worries. An all-out invasion of the South, a strategy that had seemed barely possible during the Kennedy administration, now seemed imminent. The local Viet Cong soon became highly active in tying up large portions of the US military in local defence, while the latter responded with 'search-and-destroy' missions to locate and eliminate guerrilla units and NVA regiments. This two-way war dangerously divided the troop levels: MACV was attempting everything itself, and failing across the board. Valuable personnel, resources and energy were expended hunting down the elusive Viet Cong while the NVA prepared its divisions for major operations.

The CIDG programme had provided one answer to this strategic problem: local communities could, with expert help and motivation, provide for their own defence against the guerrillas. With a more positive application of the CIDG and CAP projects to the rest of South Vietnam, the United States could have concentrated its immense firepower on the invading North Vietnamese regulars. When the ARVN was tasked with 'pacifying' an area, it badly flouted the most basic rules of counter-insurgency, sometimes employing force and terror in an effort to coerce the local population. The rural population sometimes feared and hated the ARVN as much as the Viet Cong, and its loyalty and trust were not easily gained. Wracked by corruption and inefficiency, the Saigon leadership feared communism because it promised to liberate the poor. But, paradoxically, the Green Beret pacification drive aimed to give the *montagnards*, the poorest of all, a measure of self-determination. Saigon found this hard to stomach. The CIDG programme had shown that local mobilisation in both civil and military areas was intrinsic to community defence in the face of guerrilla activity.

In the final analysis, MACV and Westmoreland paid lip service to the concept of counter-insurgency and attempted to divorce the political aspects of the insurgency from the military. The CIDG and CAP operations were the exceptions, not the rule, and other highly promising programmes, such as the 'Strategic Hamlets', discussed in Chapter 5, were poorly implemented and eventually proved disastrous. Little attempt was made during the early and crucial years of the US involvement to wed military defence with active community development. This was despite the much lauded targeting of 'hearts and minds' that had seen real successes amongst the *montagnards*.

The CIDG project in the Central Highlands had become just another factor in the grand military strategy for South Vietnam's defence. For the CIA, the primary concern was that this vital strategic heartland should not be subverted and controlled by the Viet Cong, while MACV saw the region as a militarily important jumping-off point for raids against the Trail—political versus military, CIA versus MACV. In military terminology, the whole operation eventually became one of aggressive defence in an area that could not successfully be garrisoned by regular forces. And the pressing need somehow to seal the border saw the brave 'cidgees' ultimately wasted in the futile attempt.

Covert War in the Tonkin Gulf

Meanwhile, a darker and more sinister war was being carried to the North Vietnamese. Although most of the SOG missions began in earnest in 1965, the little-known operation entitled 'OPLAN 34A' had got underway the previous year. The operation was a clandestine programme of secret strikes and commando raids against military installations on the North Vietnamese coast. Highly classified at the time, the actions of OPLAN 34A were greatly overshadowed in August of that year by what is regarded by most historians to be the spark that lit the Vietnam War—the Tonkin Gulf incident. Although this brief military encounter received much publicity at the time, and is always referred to in narratives of the war, much less is said of the OPLAN 34A missions that were part and parcel of it. The events of August 1964 in the Tonkin Gulf led directly to full combat commitment by the United States a year later, and, ironically, it was the use of the covert SOG units against North Vietnam that triggered the whole incident.

SOG advisers had assembled and trained Vietnamese and indigenous personnel to man a force of armed patrol boats, actually Norwegian-built *Nasty* class attack craft, fitted with 40mm cannon and a variety of light machine guns. The teams were drilled in night manoeuvres, coastal raiding, the landing of commando teams on North Vietnamese beaches and sabotage. Each boat could make 50kt and could easily outpace its enemy equivalents, which were Chinese gun and torpedo boats based around the Gulf. The first series of raids was planned for 31 July, with the *Nasty*s putting out from Da Nang and travelling northwards, far out to sea. Heavy civilian traffic meant that the raiders were forced to approach the enemy coast from the open sea to avoid detection. With full surprise the OPLAN 34A boats opened fire on a North Vietnamese radar station on the island of Hon Me, and later on a radio transmitter on another island off the coast, Hon Ngu. Both were deep within enemy territory, the latter island being over 180km north of the DMZ. Commandos were unable to put ashore and after the raid the successful *Nasty*s turned south for Da Nang.

In the morning light, sailors on the deck of the USS *Maddox*, an American destroyer in the Gulf, spotted the fast-moving craft speeding southwards. When the ship's captain radioed his superiors to report the sighting, he was informed that they were the OPLAN 34A raiders returning home. This meeting was far from coincidental: the mission assigned to *Maddox* that day was to eavesdrop on the enemy defences as the coastal raid began. The location and frequencies of the various communist radar and radio installations would then be plotted as they burst into life. This electronic spying mission, Operation 'Desoto', had been a continuing one and would provide the United States with a great deal of valuable information about the North Vietnamese military. On 1 and 2 August the *Maddox* found that its own pennant number, D731, was figuring more and more prominently in the excited Hanoi radio traffic. It was clear that North Vietnam was well aware of the raid and also of the *Maddox* steaming just a few kilometres off the coast. Captain John Herrick, aboard the *Maddox*, was suddenly informed of a communist transmission that indicated they were preparing for 'military operations'. Herrick could only assume these must be some kind of attack on his ship, and he relayed his concerns to his superiors. Orders received back from the commander of the Seventh Fleet, however, insisted that the *Maddox* remain in the area and continue the 'Desoto' patrol. Captain Herrick complied, and within a few hours his crew spotted three North Vietnamese motor torpedo boats speeding towards them. Fearing a confrontation, the *Maddox* turned and headed out to sea at full speed, while the MTBs gave chase. At around 3 o'clock the *Maddox* opened fire on its pursuers as they approached to within 10,000m. For a full twenty minutes the battle raged, the plucky communist sailors running in close to the *Maddox* with each boat firing a single torpedo at the destroyer. The warship twisted and turned in the water to evade the torpedoes, and was successfully able to dodge two of them. The third hit, but failed to explode. The *Maddox*, guns blazing, was joined in the fight by US Navy Crusader jets that began strafing the torpedo boats (now attacking with machine guns). Between them they destroyed one of the boats and crippled the remaining two. There had been no American casualties, and only one enemy bullet had struck the destroyer. Wanting to finish the job, Herrick was told to disengage from the fight and withdraw from the area.

President Johnson, although wanting to prosecute the war in a more heavy-handed way, declined to leap into full retaliatory action. He was in the midst of a presidential campaign and could not afford to be seen to be reacting hastily. Barry Goldwater, the Republican nominee, was being portrayed by the Democrats as a warmongering Cold War hawk, willing to commit US forces to war without thought. Part of Johnson's campaign hinged on appearing firm on communism but also more restrained than Goldwater. This meant that the *Maddox* was not to react in any way to the communist attack.

Much to his concern, Captain Herrick was ordered to resume the 'Desoto' patrols in the Tonkin Gulf. *Maddox* was joined by a second destroyer, the USS *C. Turner Joy*, while further low-key military precautions were taken. American combat troops were put on standby, and at American air bases in South Vietnam and Thailand additional jet fighter-bombers arrived. They would soon be needed.

Not only was the 'Desoto' electronic espionage patrol continued, but further OPLAN 34A raids were carried out almost immediately. Whether Washington knew this is uncertain, but the MACV Generals in Saigon and the commanders of the Pacific Fleet certainly did. In fact, although the US military later denied any involvement with the SOG raiding missions (manned wholly by Vietnamese), a leak from the Pentagon connected the 'Desoto' spying mission with the OPLAN 34A attacks. This forced Robert McNamara to declare that 'Our navy played absolutely no part in, was not associated with, was not aware of any South Vietnamese actions, if there were any . . .'

Maddox and *C. Turner Joy* had now become bait for the communists. Both had been ordered to make close, eight-mile (12.8km), approaches to the North Vietnamese coastline in the hope that electromagnetic (radio and radar) impulses would be triggered for the two vessels to monitor. The three-mile (4.8km) international limit was not to be crossed, but Washington must have realised that Hanoi, like other communist countries, had probably claimed a twelve-mile (19.2km) territorial limit. And with two more attacks by the OPLAN 34A patrol boats planned for 3 August, the scene was set for a further incident in the Tonkin Gulf.

Again, the OPLAN 34A boats made a covert raid on a North Vietnamese radar installation, this time at Cape Vinh Son, and they also opened fire on an NVA barracks at the Cua Ron estuary base. Again the USS *Maddox* picked up radio and radar transmissions from the communist defenders, and the commanders of both the *C. Turner Joy* and the *Maddox* were concerned that they would again be associated with these coastal raids. Their superiors at Pacific Fleet ordered the two vessels to remain in the area, and even expressed the hope that they might act as decoys for the raiders! As darkness closed in over the warships, the weather, too, closed in, bringing high winds, rain and flashes of tropical lightning. Radio transmissions from North Vietnam picked up by Captain Herrick suggested, just as before, that communist torpedo boats were planning an attack. Jets scrambled from the carrier USS *Ticonderoga* were unable to detect the presence of enemy vessels, but, with nerves strained to the limit, the crew of the *Maddox* were convinced of an imminent and deadly threat.

Suddenly sonar operators claimed to be tracking numerous torpedoes, and both destroyers began manoeuvring wildly to avoid them. Gunners opened up on unseen torpedo boats, without actually coming under fire themselves. Chaos reigned in the darkness. After two hours of confusion, the gunners had claimed to have sunk two or three communist boats, but none of the crewmen on either destroyer could be sure that they had actually seen an enemy.

As the guns fell silent, Captain Herrick almost immediately had his doubts about what had happened. More experienced operators were allowed to listen to the sonar recordings in an attempt to verify the torpedo attacks. Had the multiple torpedo tracks been simply rain, or the swell of the sea? Even more likely, bearing in mind the fact that the torpedoes seemed to disappear when the destroyers ended their defensive manoeuvres, was the possibility that each vessel was listening to the thrashing propellers of its partner. Members of the Joint Chiefs of Staff, as well as the President, learned quickly of the second Tonkin Gulf incident, and Herrick was bombarded with questions concerning the veracity of the 'attack'. Immediately President Johnson moved to brief the leaders of Congress and drafted a Congressional resolution that would allow him to widen the war in Vietnam. Part of this resolution sanctioned a series of retaliatory strikes, code-named 'Pierce Arrow', against North Vietnamese port installations the following day. These air strikes had already been worked out in advance and were ready for immediate implementation, suggesting that the President and his advisers were only too aware of the threat to the 'Desoto' vessels.

'Pierce Arrow' was an American triumph of air power that destroyed over half of North Vietnam's torpedo boat fleet and up to 90 per cent of the city of Vinh's fuel installations. At last Johnson had extended the war against the communists into North Vietnam and, in contrast to the subterfuge of the Special Operations Group, he had done it overtly, in the public gaze, and with full Congressional approval. The war was about to become a serious commitment, and, pre-empting this, the President had been able to consolidate both public and Congressional opinion. But there were still lingering doubts over the nature of the Tonkin Gulf reports. What had really happened? Had North Vietnam really attacked the 'Desoto' warships a second time? Although 'LBJ' used this second incident as a mechanism for immediate retaliation, he did not personally believe it had taken place; few in Washington did. Two or three days later Johnson said, in a conversation with George Ball, 'Hell, those dumb, stupid sailors were just shooting at flying fish!'

Both the first and second Tonkin Gulf incidents had been carefully engineered to produce a fitting excuse for an American show of force. The first provocation, by SOG patrol boat raiders, had initiated an enemy response against which President Johnson had seen fit not to retaliate. He had no real wish to deepen the Vietnam crisis, since he was occupied with the 'Great Society' legislation that he feared would be in jeopardy if forced to compete with the war for Congressional funds. But the large conservative right upon which he relied for support demanded some kind of show of force against the communists. Thus, when muddled reports of a second attack came in, Johnson saw in them a way to silence his detractors. He found himself playing a game of acquiescence with the 'Cold Warriors' in Congress, and of token commitment to propping up the South Vietnamese government. If Saigon fell to Hanoi, Johnson knew that he would also fall. And so began the slow slide into Vietnam, not because such a build-up made strategic sense, but because Johnson was loath to let communism make yet another gain in the struggle for world domination. Once begun, the ground war spiralled further and further out of his control, killing his 'Great Society' reforms as well as his presidency.

Some historians have seized upon President Johnson's submission of the South-East Asia Resolution (the so-called Tonkin Gulf Resolution), shortly after the crisis, as his main aim in the fabrication of the 4 August incident. The resolution gave him the wide-ranging powers of a declaration of war, without the international political ramifications of such a declaration. It promised that 'there will continue to be regular consultations' between the President and the Congress on American conduct of the war in Vietnam, and would allow 'the President . . . to take all necessary measures to repel any armed attack against the forces of the United States and to prevent aggression'. This view of the 4 August 'attack' rests on the assumption that President Johnson sought to widen the war but lacked the mechanism with which to do this. In fact, harried by Congressional hawks, as well as his own advisers, demanding ever tougher action against an intractable North Vietnam, Johnson was fearful that the war would be used by the Republican conservatives as a weapon against both him and his 'Great Society'. The pretence of a second Tonkin Gulf attack gave him an opportunity to display a measured response, thus proving his firmness to resist aggression without appearing to be locked in a mutually assured cycle of escalating retaliation.

Proof of Johnson's reticence to wage all-out war against the communists was his low-key response to further Viet Cong attacks in South Vietnam. On 1 November a successful guerrilla attack on the American Bien Hoa air base resulted in the deaths of five US servicemen and the destruction of six recently arrived B-57 bombers. Johnson did nothing. On Christmas Eve a devastating terrorist bomb blew apart Saigon's Brink Hotel, used by American officers as a billet. Two were killed and over fifty were wounded, yet the President still refused to retaliate against North Vietnam. Bombing operations against the North had been on the drawing boards for some time already, yet it was a firm belief in the White House that if such operations were initiated, a Viet Cong offensive would in all probability erupt across the whole of South Vietnam. Therefore, until a stable Saigon government had been installed, the bombing of North Vietnam could not occur. But pressure to act against the communists for the continuing atrocities was steadily increasing.

At Camp Holloway, the US base near Pleiku in the Central Highlands of South Vietnam, a Viet Cong attack on 7 February 1965 would provide the Johnson administration with the excuse it needed to carry out another token retaliatory strike on the North. Communist sappers destroyed five helicopters in a surprise raid, and a mortar barrage damaged eleven more while wrecking eight warplanes. There were, again, more American dead and wounded, and, for Johnson, the time had come to act. The American ambassador to Vietnam, Maxwell Taylor, told McGeorge Bundy, one of Johnson's special advisers, 'This is the time we must strike back', and Bundy, at the time on a fact-finding mission in Saigon, recommended as much to the President. Other voices, however, recommended further negotiations with Hanoi, but Johnson finally exploded with frustration: 'We have kept our guns over the mantle . . . for a long time now. And what was the result? They are killing our men while they sleep. I can't ask American boys to go on fighting with one hand tied behind their backs.' A series of hard bombing strikes against the unsophisticated nation of North Vietnam would follow, strikes that would eventually stretch to three long years of concerted bombing under the designation Operation 'Rolling Thunder'.

Thunder in the North

Barely four hours after the Viet Cong had retreated from the burning remains of the Camp Holloway airfield, US jets were in the air over the Gulf of Tonkin, on their way to pre-selected targets. This was Operation 'Flaming Dart', not just a retaliatory strike, but the opportunity to begin a concerted bombing campaign against the North, starting with military targets at the port of Dong Hoi. South Vietnamese pilots and their American 'advisers' also carried out air strikes at Chap Le and Vinh Linh. Although the American aircraft were to have hit three other targets, all were weathered in and the raids did not take place. President Johnson decided to abandon these targets, thinking that the North Vietnamese would consider later strikes against them as part of a systematic bombing campaign. Johnson was still apprehensive about launching such a full-scale attack, but the mood in Washington was swinging away from unifying the Saigon government as a precursor to the bombing towards using air strikes against Hanoi to consolidate popular support in South Vietnam. The 'Rolling Thunder' bombings that followed were at the time controversial and divisive, and few today agree that anything positive came from them. Air power, harnessed and shackled by civilian and political concerns, was asked to win the war without the need for troops on the ground. It failed to do this, but it succeeded in teaching America that air power, from Iraq to Bosnia-Hercegovina, cannot win a war on its own. Pilots, military commanders, journalists and politicians (later including McNamara, who instituted it) were all critical of the operation, bringing attention to the ineptitude and irony of the strategy employed.

Although Johnson initially fought the trend, there were many supporters of bombing in the White House and the Pentagon. Perhaps the most vocal of these was General Curtis LeMay, the Air Force Chief of Staff, who said of the American effort to date, 'We are swatting at flies, when we should be going after the manure pile'. His bold and unsubtle language mirrored his blunt military recommendations. 'We should bomb them back to the Stone Age,' LeMay had suggested, arguing that the destruction of North Vietnam by air would strangle the lifeline of the Viet Cong guerrillas in the South, ensuring a bloodless victory for US forces. As a strategic option, LeMay's massive aerial bombardment was termed the 'full/fast squeeze' by Johnson's Working Group on Vietnam, and it entailed a Second World War-style bombing campaign against targets in the populated areas of North Vietnam. But there were obvious drawbacks to the 'full/fast squeeze', one of which was the relative inefficiency of carpet bombing. George Ball, the Under-Secretary of State, had served as a director of the US Strategic Bombing Survey after the war and noted that the Allied bombers had not inflicted the serious damage to Germany's wartime production that had been predicted. Like some other members of Johnson's close group of advisers, Ball favoured the 'slow squeeze' of controlled escalation, not least because it allowed a constant assessment of the war and its progress.

Feared by all was the spectre of direct Chinese intervention on to the Vietnam battlefield, with Chinese and North Vietnamese units pushing ever southwards in a re-fight of the Korean War. Since the 1953 armistice, however, China had gained possession of the atomic bomb, and the loss of South Vietnam was nothing to the nightmare scenario of nuclear devastation. Provocation of China and the Soviet Union was to be avoided at all costs. The Joint Chiefs of Staff (JCS) have recently been depicted by McNamara as more cavalier in their attitude. They recognised that their programme involved the possible use of nuclear weaponry, yet 'they nonetheless urged that it be adopted'.

But President Johnson had to do *something*. His resistance to the lure of Vietnam crumbled week by week as he was pushed and prodded into action. It was clear that, by the start of 1965, Hanoi was preparing to move in on a weakened and disorientated Saigon. McNamara, caught between Johnson's determination to 'Win the war!' and the JCS's willingness to contemplate atomic escalation, seemed to walk a tightrope. He advised that Johnson adopt the strategy of a slow and graduated response, allowing careful monitoring of results, while avoiding a direct affront to the communist bloc. Operation 'Rolling Thunder' began on 2

March, extending the 'Flaming Dart' air strikes across much of the North in a devastating attack on communist military installations. A new plan had been formulated: Hanoi's military machine would be crippled by repeated air strikes as a punishment for supporting the VC insurgency in South Vietnam. Meanwhile troop units and installations that contributed to the infiltration in the South would also become legitimate targets of the American bombers. The strategy was not all-out war, but it hinged on preventing the fall of the South, not on the destruction of the North. North Vietnam was encouraged to break off the war via a policy of 'strategic persuasion'; it was hoped that Hanoi could be bombed to its senses and would see the folly in continuing to support insurgency activity. As one member of the Working Group, John McNaughton, put it: 'We want to keep before Hanoi the carrot of our desisting, as well as the stick of continued pressure.'

'Rolling Thunder' became a huge undertaking that went on almost every day from March 1965 to November 1968. Over a million tons of ordnance, including conventional 'iron' bombs, 'smart' bombs, napalm, rockets, missiles and cluster bombs, were dropped on North Vietnam and Laos during the operation, an amount that equalled over seven hundred tons per day for over three and a half years. The majority of missions were flown by F-4 Phantom and F-105 Thunderchief fighter-bombers, and later by the awesome B-52 strategic bombers. Most seriously hit was that part of North Vietnam above the 17th Parallel, used as a mass staging and launching area of men and *matériel* down the Ho Chi Minh Trail into South Vietnam. To prevent a liberal backlash, Johnson, who closely and personally supervised much of the 'Rolling Thunder' operation, targeted only military and communication sites for the bombing strikes. And since North Vietnam was essentially only a conduit for Chinese and Soviet war supplies, the transport network came high on the list of targeting priorities. In one year alone, seven thousand air strikes hit roads, five thousand hit individual vehicles, while over one thousand hit railway lines and marshalling yards. The strikes were soon divided between fixed sites and mobile targets of opportunity, with the latter located and destroyed by armed reconnaissance jets. Such was the scale of bombing on the North that from the beginning of 1966 the number of remaining fixed targets had dwindled significantly in number, making the search for mobile targets along roads and railways the primary task of 'Rolling Thunder' missions.

Pilots were not allowed to roam across the North at will, however, but were forced to follow a complex set of rules for engagement. With international politics and not military tactics in mind, air strikes were 'restricted' within 30 miles (48km) of Hanoi and within 10 miles (16km) of Haiphong, North Vietnam's major seaport. In practice this meant that an aircraft within the zone was not authorised to conduct ground attacks unless it was retaliating against an anti-aircraft artillery (AAA) or surface-to-air missile (SAM) site that had fired at it. Further delineating the US area of operations were two 'prohibited' zones around Hanoi (10 miles or 16km in radius) and Haiphong (4 miles or 6.4km in radius)

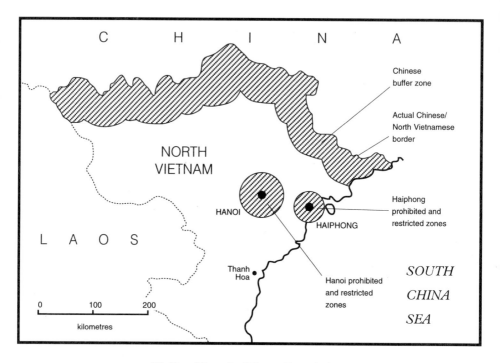

'Rolling Thunder' Target Restrictions

in which bombing was forbidden unless specifically authorised. Along with various populated areas and other sensitive regions, including the 30-mile (48km) wide 'buffer' zone along the Chinese border, these zones protected the majority of the nation's population and industry from US air strikes. The creation of these 'sanctuary' areas virtually neutralised any positive effect the bombing might have had on the conduct of the war. Further hampering its effectiveness was the method of target selection, since for much of the time it was carried out by President Johnson himself, who chose targets in Washington from a list forwarded to him by staff in Vietnam. Assisting him in his selection were his civilian advisers, who met every Tuesday to discuss the progress of the war. As long ago as January 1964 McNamara had received a memo from the JCS that expressed frustration at the 'self-imposed restrictions'. Despite the wider and more aggressive commitment of 'Rolling Thunder', the JCS were still unhappy with the way the White House continued to hamper military operations.

With so much air power flying north, an organised scheme for the distribution of targets was developed for the armed reconnaissance flights. This was the 'Route Package' system that divided up the map of North Vietnam into seven areas, shared out for combat operations between the Air Force and Navy. The exception to this was Route Package 1, just north of the DMZ, which came under the jurisdiction of General Westmoreland because the region was treated as an extension of the South Vietnam battlefield. Of all the Route Packages, 6A and 6B were the most notorious, and between them they became known as 'The Barrel' or 'The Corner'. The two areas included both Hanoi and Haiphong and were very heavily defended. Use of the Route Packages, combined with the 're-stricted', 'prohibited' and 'buffer' zones, made 'Rolling Thunder' a highly complex and at times bewildering operation. That such a huge military operation could be controlled down to the smallest tactical detail by civilians rankled with the military hierarchy, who were resentful that 'armchair generals' like McNamara had post-strike photographs in one hand and a cheque book in the other. Like the notorious 'body count' that became the basic measuring block of success in the ground forces, McNamara used the number of combat sorties as his yard-stick with which to measure the success of Operation 'Rolling Thunder'. Whether the targets had previously been destroyed or not, or whether mist or low cloud prevented a visual sighting of the target, missions would often be initiated just to increase the sortie rate of a particular unit. In one issue of *Aviation Week*, a Phan-tom pilot decried sorties he had flown where his plane had taken off with only a single pair of bombs under its wings. This was but a fraction of the Phantom's potential bomb load.

'Rolling Thunder' was not, it should be remembered, a single-service opera-tion but was shared between the United States Air Force and Navy. Traditional rivalries persisted, with a constant jockeying for available targets. The number of mission allocations, too, had to be equal to satisfy the upper-echelon officers in both services. Such competition, inter-service rivalry and autonomy created dangerous overlaps in combat. Occasionally Navy jets would arrive over a target after being launched from a carrier in the Tonkin Gulf, only to find that Air Force fighter-bombers from Saigon had already dropped their bombs on it. Such redundancies were not only wasteful of material and money, but dangerous in the extreme. While the world rightly considered North Vietnam a Third World power, the American pilots who flew bombing missions over it quickly devel-oped a healthy respect for its air defences.

As 'Rolling Thunder' began to pound its piecemeal targets from March on-wards, aerial reconnaissance of the local defences indicated that surface-to-air missile (SAM) sites were being installed around potential targets. The missiles at these sites (actually SA-2 'Guidelines') were Soviet-supplied, radar-directed anti-aircraft missiles that were able to cripple an attacking plane just by explod-ing near to it. They represented a serious escalation in the air war, but, rather than destroy the SAM sites from the air as soon as they were discovered and before they became operational, the United States decided to resist the tempta-tion. Instead, it waited until proof could be obtained that the missiles were tech-nically operational. This made little military sense, but the 'Rolling Thunder' campaign as a whole was not directed by military sense; it was motivated and operated by a civilian administration concerned with international and domes-tic politics. Fear of blundering into a potentially nuclear conflict with the Soviet Union gripped President Johnson, since Russian workers would be likely to come under fire from American planes if the sites were attacked. His preoccupation meant that the 'Guideline' missiles were photographed and monitored by electronic warfare planes but remained unmolested until 24 July 1965, when an F-4 Phantom fighter became their first victim.

Avoiding the SAMs did not prove too difficult for American pilots. Flying very low and very fast meant that the missiles had a hard time manoeuvring into an attack trajectory. Instead, the bomber pilots subjected themselves to a constant barrage of low-level anti-aircraft artillery in the form of Russian-designed 37mm and 57mm guns. The latter weapon was especially effective since it was radar-directed and fired 12kg shells up to altitudes of over 4km, day or night, whatever the weather. By the end of 1965 there were an estimated 2,000 of these guns sited either near vulnerable installations or on the approaches to them. As pilots rolled in to their bombing runs they were forced to fly through virtual curtains of fire. At a target like a bridge the defenders ringing the structure would simply fire straight up into the air, knowing that to bomb the bridge the American pilot would be forced to fly directly over it, and through the deadly barrage.

SAM sites were highly vulnerable to low-level attack, and were always defended with anti-aircraft guns. In fact, knowing that the SAM sites were such choice targets for the Americans, the North Vietnamese were known to fabricate dummy SA-2 sites and ring them with camouflaged guns. As the war progressed, the air defences were strengthened, and near the end of the conflict, in 1972, there were an estimated 300 SAM sites in North Vietnam. The Air Force possessed various technological alternatives to flying at suicidal altitudes to avoid the surface-to-air-missiles, and these somewhat mitigated the deadly threat. Firstly, the SA-2 'Guidelines' were not, by any means, the most sophisticated air defence missiles in production, and though 180 SAMs were launched at US aircraft during the first year of 'Rolling Thunder', only eleven planes were hit by them. With the help of radar detection instruments aboard a sophisticated electronic warfare plane, the first bombing of a SAM site took place on 17 October 1965 by a flight of five Navy jets. Although successful, it was thought preferable to try to use technology to disrupt the targeting radar rather than just detect it. Dedicated electronic warfare planes (such as the Air Force EB-66B, Navy EA-3 and Marine EF-10B) accompanied bombing raids and jammed the signals of the SAM radar, preventing them from firing at the bombers. Later, the bombers themselves were each able to carry their own countermeasures pods on underwing pylons.

One of the most sophisticated weapons in the electronic war was the anti-radar Shrike missile, fired by aircraft loitering around the target area on 'Wild Weasel' missions. Following the detection of a SAM radar by the plane, it would turn towards it and fire the Shrike. The missile homed in on the enemy radar impulses and would destroy the targeting radar of the SAM site, preventing its 'Guidelines' from firing at US aircraft. Often the mere presence of a 'Wild Weasel' aircraft in the neighbourhood would have the effect of forcing all the local SAM radar to switch off in the interests of self-preservation. But the cat-and-mouse tricks of the electronic air war were such that the communist radar would sometimes switch on briefly to goad the 'Wild Weasel' into firing its Shrike prematurely, and when the plane moved on to an attack run it forced the radar to shut off again. All this took place as the bombers flew into the area, and ended with a deadly 'quick draw'. The Shrike was launched at the SAM radar as the latter directed missiles for a few desperate seconds at the bombers overhead. It would then either switch off or be permanently destroyed by the incoming Shrike. With such a modern form of air defence, the US military machine could successfully match it with ultra-modern countermeasures. For much of the Vietnam War, this would be a rarity.

It was not only SA-2 'Guidelines' that the Soviet Union supplied to North Vietnam, but also less sophisticated jet interceptors. The North Vietnamese Air Force was a purely defensive organisation, devoted to shooting down US aircraft with MiG-17s and a number of MiG-19s and MiG-21s. When coming up against the ageing MiG-17s, American pilots were at first sceptical of the old Russian plane's ability to put up much of a fight. But, despite crash training and an ill-equipped force, the communist pilots showed tenacity, courage and some skill in their aerial engagements. Dogfights in the skies over North Vietnam took place, often with the more manoeuvrable MiGs out-flying the fast jets of the US Navy and Air Force. Peculiarly, the American military had overestimated its opposition, and in designing warplanes for the Cold War era the planners had come to the conclusion that, in the fast-jet age of radar and missiles, dogfights in the tradition of the Second World War and Korea were now obsolete. Thus the early F-4 Phantoms, as already discussed, had been designed without a gun of any kind. As a further consequence, pilots new to air combat were unprepared for the MiGs and at first the losses inflicted by the North Vietnamese fighters were considered unacceptable. Retraining and the use of mock air combats quickly turned this situation around. Blessed with the early warning of approaching MiGs by friendly radar on the ground, at sea and in EC-121D aircraft, the American fighter-escort pilots were also forearmed and were often able to intercept the incoming MiGs before they could attack the bombers.

President Johnson had not given the armed services the authority to attack MiG fighters on the ground, again fearing the political repercussions that such raids might entail. The spectre of Chinese or Russian involvement loomed over every decision, and Johnson later admitted, 'I spent ten hours a day worrying about all this, picking the targets one by one, making sure we didn't go over the limits.' Just like the policy of hitting individual truck convoys rather than the cargo ships in Haiphong harbour that supplied them, shooting down individual MiGs rather than bombing them in their shelters cost money and lives. Operation 'Bolo' was conceived by an Air Force Colonel, Robin Olds, as a way to overcome this obstacle. Carried out on 2 January 1967, the operation entailed the use of F-4 Phantom jet fighters as a substitute for the more usual F-105 Thunderchief bombers. The Phantom pilots cleverly imitated the bombers' flight plan. This lure attracted a flight of MiG defenders, whose pilots were not expecting the more manoeuvrable and well-armed F-4s. The ruse worked and seven MiGs were shot down that day.

Bombing restrictions caused rancour and resentment within the Air Force and Navy, both of which felt that, if prosecuted more effectively, 'Rolling Thunder' could achieve some of the aims that had been set out for it. As it was, the emphasis that had been placed on certain military targets, and the occasional pauses in the bombing to allow Hanoi to back down, proved counter-productive. The pauses only gave the communists time to rebuild, rearm and reorganise, while at home the right harangued the President for softening his stand on communism and the left urged him to continue the pauses indefinitely.

The gradual escalation envisaged by McNamara continued, with a firmer response following in 1966. Manufacturing plants were bombed, as were oil and petroleum storage depots: an estimated 90 per cent of North Vietnam's measurable oil supply went up in smoke by the end of the year. However, many of the remaining stocks of oil had been relocated amongst numerous smaller sites throughout 1965, making the long-awaited air strikes against them difficult. McNamara's 'bean-counting' analysis had severely overestimated the effects of a superpower's air force on a mainly agrarian Third World nation. Fledgeling industrial centres were relatively recent innovations that the Vietnamese had been used to living without, and serious manufacturing targets just did not exist. Unlike Nazi Germany's, Hanoi's war effort in the South did not depend on tank, plane, ammunition and petroleum production. This did not prevent the bombing campaign from being widened still further. Throughout 1967 targets included industrial plants in the Hanoi area as well as MiG airfields and a plethora of opportunistic 'moving targets' attacked within the Route Package plan.

One of the key targets early in the war was the Thanh Hoa bridge that carried a railway and road across the Song Ma River. Over this bridge trundled rail freight bound for Vinh and the various dispersal areas in the south of the country for later staging down the Ho Chi Minh Trail. Other bridges, too, received the unwanted attention of American bombers, but a certain mythology sprang up around the bridge at Thanh Hoa, inspired by its sheer resilience. 'Rolling Thunder' pilots, searching for some way to explain its apparent indestructibility, mused that the world must be composed of two spring-loaded hemispheres that were hinged under the Atlantic Ocean and were held together on the opposite side by the Thanh Hoa bridge. Destroying the bridge would mean that the world would fly apart! Over 700 sorties failed to sever the bridge and eight aircraft were lost in the attempt.

From conventional 'iron' bombs the Navy turned to 'ultra-high-tech' Walleye TV-guided bombs that enabled the pilots to steer the bombs in to their targets via a television camera mounted in the warheads' nose. Unfortunately the Walleyes were about as successful as iron bombs when launched against the Thanh Hoa bridge. Finally, in 1972, the Air Force was able to bring even more sophisticated weaponry to bear on the bridge. Laser-guided 'smart' bombs, which, twenty years later, received massive media attention in the 1991 Gulf War, made their début in Vietnam. One of their great successes was the eventual destruction of the Thanh Hoa bridge, cutting the railway line to the South and simultaneously dispelling a legend.

The later bombing campaign in 1972 was not connected with President Johnson's 'Rolling Thunder' operation but was part of his successor's attempt to cripple North Vietnam in another concerted bombing effort. By 31 March 1968 Johnson's hopes about the success of his bombing operation had been dashed. Hanoi had been given repeated opportunities to back down from its position as patron of the war in the South and had failed to do so. The nation's ability to wage war had not appeared to have decreased, and its morale seemed unshaken. The President announced an end to air attacks north of the 20th Parallel (400km north of the DMZ) and shocked America with his announcement that he would not be seeking re-election as President. His dreams of the 'Great Society', enacted through his legislation and funded by the US Congress, had been ended by this costly Asian war. He had tried, valiantly, to juggle the war with his reforms, but the latter had become overshadowed and then entirely eclipsed by the former.

Exactly six months after his announcement, President Johnson brought an end to Operation 'Rolling Thunder'. The escalating air war, the 'slow squeeze' and the systematic bombing campaign that it entailed had ended. Military analysts, led by the air campaign's foremost coordinator, Robert McNamara, could not see that their efforts had made a difference to the eventual outcome of the Vietnam War. With few vulnerable targets to destroy, the North Vietnamese had weathered the attacks successfully and much of their society remained intact. Power stations, oil dumps, railway networks and the communists' pride and joy, the Thai Nguyen steel mill, were not the industrial crutches that they might have been in the United States and Europe. Their loss became a sacrifice that the North Vietnamese government and its citizens were willing to pay. Only an all-out assault on all potential targets could have bombed the communists to the peace table, but such a move had been unacceptable to President Johnson. His policy had balanced right-wing pressure to resist communism with international calls for an end to the American involvement in the region. Likewise, in the attempt to sever the flow of supplies from the Soviet Union and China, the bombing had had little effect. It was hampered by endless restrictions on target type and location, and complicated by a fear of the possibilities of escalation to involve the communist superpowers further north. When President Nixon began his air war against North Vietnam four years later, it was not to be another handicapped 'Rolling Thunder' but a campaign that would be prosecuted with full awareness of the former's many failures.

Time and again Lyndon Johnson had been advised to follow a policy of graduated escalation and a deepening commitment. McNamara's 'Rolling Thunder' was preceded by reprisal strikes and became a limited campaign of bombing. This escalated in 1967 to a wider bombing operation. Each step escalated the conflict, not according to a Washington timetable but as a reaction to military stalemate and a failure of strategy. Although the policy of total and unrestrained conventional warfare proved unpalatable to both the President and his advisers, it would certainly have been a policy of control. Such a use of force gives the initiative to the deploying force: it knows where, when and how. Instead, Johnson's strategy of the 'slow squeeze', and of piecemeal advisory and air base troop commitments, was one of defence and reaction, handing over the initiative to both the Viet Cong and the North Vietnamese. He had, through this 'slow squeeze', invisibly committed himself to the widening of the ground war in the South and to the active participation of combat troops—something he had vowed never to do.

The first combat unit in Vietnam was to be the 9th Marine Expeditionary Brigade, called for by General Westmoreland almost as soon as 'Rolling Thunder' got under way. This request was totally unexpected, yet it should have been foreseen as a natural consequence of the bombing campaign. The Marines had been requested as air base security troops for Da Nang airfield in South Vietnam, and Johnson could hardly have demurred, since communist reprisals in the South for the bombing campaign in the North had been expected. Ambassador Taylor cautioned against the wisdom of deploying combat troops: 'Once you put that first soldier ashore,' he had said, 'you never know how many others are going to follow him.' Many more soldiers *would* follow these first few, and they would bring with them a method of waging war that would be tested to the limit by both the communist guerrillas and the landscape that they inhabited.

Chapter 3

MILITARY MOBILITY

For five months the Marines at Da Nang patrolled and conducted reconnaissance while other enclaves along the coast at Phu Bai and Chu Lai became home for further troop build-ups. Initially they provided air base security for the expected retributive attacks by the Viet Cong. But, despite the strong reinforcements, it seemed as if the enemy were declining to meet the challenge, and so more aggressive patrols were initiated by General Westmoreland. Gradually the area over which the American troops were able to move and establish a presence expanded out from the coastal enclaves. Inevitably there were clashes with local VC patrols, and, as incidents of combat increased and the fear for the safety of the enclaves grew, Westmoreland was given the go-ahead in June to employ the Marine forces in any way he saw fit. A conference on 20 April concurred that bombing alone could not deter Hanoi; rather it simply increased the cost of communist victory. A decisive show of force that could seriously hamper the VC effort in the South was considered the only way halt the aggression. This meant offensive operations against the communist guerrillas, and MACV wasted no time in the creation of a battle plan for the eradication of the gathering enemy forces south of Chu Lai.

The first military operation of the ground war was to be Operation 'Starlite'. Like campaigns later in 1965, it proved a huge success and seemed to bode well for future military actions. The operation was a perfect encircling manoeuvre on the Van Tuong peninsula that caught the 1st Viet Cong Regiment between five separate Marine forces. The success of 'Starlite' was attributed to the speed and surprise of the manoeuvre that trapped the 1,500-strong enemy force with its back against the South China Sea. As a Marine company dug in after travelling overland from the north to cut off that direction as an escape route, a battalion surged on to the beach south of the peninsula in amtrac amphibious vehicles. Simultaneously at three landing zones (LZs) further inland, Marine HH-34 helicopters disgorged troops almost directly on top of the defending Viet Cong. The fighting was at times desperate, but with supporting air strikes and Marine reinforcements, including tanks and further amtracs, the VC were defeated, losing a total of 614 men. American casualties amounted to only 45.

'Starlite' had depended for its success on the speedy encirclement of the enemy to achieve total surprise, and on rapidly moving reinforcements to hold the

Viet Cong as air strikes pounded them into the ground. A portion of these reinforcements had been an amtrac force that intended to support the more southerly Marines, but it had got lost in the confusing maze of trails on the peninsula and had been ambushed. Three tank escorts proved to be of little help as the column came under devastating fire, and, unable to advance or retreat, the armoured vehicles became trapped. Fierce fighting continued to rage but the Marines successfully held out against the guerrillas. But a flaw in military thinking had been exposed. Heavily armoured tanks and lighter armoured amphibious vehicles, bristling with an assortment of heavy weapons, had been beaten to a standstill by peasant foot-soldiers. These were soldiers who lacked vehicles of their own, who lacked anti-tank weapons and who lacked even any decent hard cover. This seemed to validate the uncertainties of several minds in the Pentagon that had questioned the deployment of armoured vehicles to Vietnam.

Armoured Warfare in Vietnam

Although the amphibious vehicles and tanks used during Operation 'Starlite' had come ashore with the Marines in 1965, armoured vehicles had made their début in the country several years before. Like the use of helicopters, the proposed deployment of tanks and armoured personnel carriers (APCs) to Vietnam had been highly controversial. So-called 'wise men' in the Pentagon had insisted in the early 1960s that Vietnam was not 'tank country'. What wasn't mountain was mostly thick tropical jungle, and the only flat terrain was made up of flooded rice paddies. What use would tanks be? Indeed, the French had found that their armoured vehicles spent much of the time trapped on roads, escorting vulnerable convoys.

In April 1962 the M113 APC, a fairly recent innovation on the post-war battlefield, was shipped out to the ARVN for use in the Mekong Delta region of Vietnam. It would prove to be a mixed blessing, giving troops mobility and firepower but at an unexpected price in vulnerability. The M113 was an armoured troop transporter, a 'battle-taxi'—in effect an aluminium armoured box on tracks—that was designed to provide cover for an eleven-man squad until the latter could dismount to fight the enemy on foot. These early M113s were each armed with a single .50-calibre machine gun on the top deck and a heavy M2HB Browning with an effective range of over 1,000m which provided vehicular protection and some measure of support for the infantry squad.

The two ARVN companies receiving the vehicles should have been fully trained infantry companies whose members would further cross-train in APC operations. However, the troops proved badly trained, and their new commanders were familiar not with infantry tactics but with tank operations. Unsurprisingly, the deployment of this force did not match the expectations of those planners who had recommended the use of APCs in-country. In one engagement late in 1962, the force closed in on a Viet Cong formation on the Plain of Reeds, in the Mekong Delta. With typical tactical flair, communist guerrillas ambushed the

APCs and pinned their crews down. Unwilling to dismount the infantry, the ARVN commander presided over an exchange of fire with the enemy until the US adviser insisted that the troops be deployed into the paddy fields. The troops warily splashed into the rice fields, but, unable to find adequate cover, and encumbered by waist-deep water, the South Vietnamese soldiers sustained rising losses, forcing the ARVN commander to recall them. He then tried employing the APCs as light tanks and outmanoeuvred the attackers, forcing them from cover. A victory had been gained over the Viet Cong.

This firefight showed that the tactics for which the APC had been designed would not translate easily into the South-East Asian theatre, and this was a trend that would continue throughout the war, with the role of armour having to adapt to local circumstance. It was obvious that Vietnam in no way resembled the rolling countryside of Western Europe, which had been the terrain dominating the minds of the tank designers when the M113 was built. But it was surely the poor performance of the ARVN soldiers that limited these early successes with the M113. Later experience showed that the vehicle was otherwise quite suited to the rice fields of the country. The APC was adept at fording the numerous rivers and canals of the Delta, and was unhindered by the flooded paddy fields. It had a good cross-country speed and was thus easily able to outflank the Viet Cong foot soldiers. The early ARVN machine-gunners did, however, find themselves very poorly protected, and after the deaths of fourteen gunners in a single ARVN–VC engagement (the Battle of Ap Bac, in January 1963), a great effort was made by crews to scavenge armour plate and customise gun shields for their M113s.

Further successes convinced the Pentagon that the M113 had a future in South-East Asia, and as increasing numbers of M113s travelled westwards to Vietnam they were joined by the M114 armoured reconnaissance vehicle. By the time of the Battle of Ap Bac there were two ARVN armoured regiments, complete with M24 tanks, M8 armoured cars, M114s and M113s. Light armour certainly had a place alongside the more traditional way of fighting in Vietnam, but the US military were still to be convinced. In 1965, while he commanded US forces in Vietnam, General Westmoreland said that 'Vietnam is no place for either tank or mechanised infantry units'.

The impressive M48A3 tanks that had come ashore with the Marines that year were not specifically chosen for combat duty in Vietnam but were an integral part of every Marine battalion. As Operation 'Starlite' was to illustrate, Vietnam definitely *was* 'tank country'. Seven of the M48s were badly damaged during 'Starlite', but they proved their worth, supporting infantry assaults, blasting bunkers and conducting armed reconnaissance. Each machine weighed in at 47 tons (compared with the M113's 11 tons) and carried the devastating 90mm M41 gun, able to fire high-explosive rounds (quite capable of destroying bunkers) as well as highly lethal canister and beehive rounds designed to shred human targets. The sheer size and weight of the M48 meant that it could easily clear a path through heavy jungle and collapse any Viet Cong bunker and tunnel system that it drove over.

Despite some initial successes with tanks, they were still not considered appropriate weaponry for counter-insurgency jungle warfare. Little provision was made to support US infantry with the gamut of armoured vehicles in the US arsenal, although the 1st Infantry Division (the 'Big Red One') was allowed to assess the performance of a single squadron of its M48 tanks. The application of this heavy armour in a combat environment was often mismanaged, with much of the force remaining in storage. Few could foresee an effective role for the lumbering machines in a war which seemed, to Vietnamese and Americans alike, one of stealth and deception, fight and flight. Perhaps the greatest reservation that the US commanders had was that there were no enemy tanks to be countered. Much of the tank warfare during the Second World War had consisted of tanks seeking out and destroying other tanks. This differed drastically from the original concept of the vehicle during the trench battles of the First World War. There the machines had been used to provide mobile fire support for advancing infantry. In Vietnam, where the communists had no armour in the South (at least in 1965), tanks in the South Vietnamese and American forces were able once again to fulfil their original purpose. Despite its power and seeming imperviousness to guerrilla attack, the M48 was too large and too slow for many military duties, and the M113 came increasingly to dominate armoured warfare.

American troops had been introduced to the M113 APC in the late 1950s when it had made its début in the US Army. Practical, as opposed to theoretical, usage of the vehicle was, again, radically different from that envisaged by the Stateside mechanised warfare instructors. What the South Vietnamese Army had begun, by retrofitting armoured shields for the M113 gun mount, the American troops completed. Where it came to be employed, the M113 was recognised for its superior firepower (the lethal .50-calibre machine gun), its mobility and its relative invulnerability (it was able to shrug off rounds up to and including the .50-calibre bullet that formed the mainstay of the Viet Cong's heaviest firepower). Able to act like a light tank, the M113 came to be used in this role more and more often. To supplement the vehicle's firepower, two 7.62mm M60 light machine guns (of the type ordinarily assigned to infantry squads) were fitted on pedestal mounts on either side of the upper deck. These too, were given armoured shields. The customised APCs now had the formidable combat potential of an infantry platoon sheathed in armour! Far removed from the unsophisticated troop transporters first conceived by the APC's manufacturers, the M113 had now been developed by those who used it into the ACAV (Armoured Cavalry Assault Vehicle)—from passive armoured vehicle into aggressive infantry support platform.

A second role was quickly identified by the military as a task that the ACAV could readily perform—that of convoy escort. Contrary to popular opinion, troops in the Vietnam War were not supplied solely by an endless stream of helicopters but more often by road-bound trucks. And the vulnerability of these trucks, travelling in convoy for protection, was soon apparent. The rearmed M113 was able to provide a formidable deterrent to ambushers, and what it could not deter it would destroy. The convoy battles on Route 13, north from Saigon to the regional town of Loc Ninh, proved early on in the war that the ACAV concept was workable. But the anti-armour tactics of the communists were coming into full flow, supported by a host of lethal weaponry, from RPG-2 shoulder-launched anti-tank rockets to 57mm and 75mm recoilless rifles. Deadliest of all for the M113s was the wide assortment of anti-tank mines that the enemy was able to lay. More than anything else, these would overturn the tactics of mechanised warfare in Vietnam.

Mines had been in the armoury of the Viet Cong since the very earliest days of the struggle, and when the ARVN began using armoured APCs the Viet Cong merely intensified the use of mines on roads and trails. There was little that could be done to counter the threat from anti-tank mines. Unlike the sophisticated Russian mines of the period, the Viet Cong constructions were often made from wood and recycled explosive. Mines of this nature were difficult to detect with minesweeping equipment, and it was decided that the prevention of minelaying by regular but erratic patrolling, rather than mine detection *per se*, was the answer to the threat. In convoys, the troops were inclined to let an M48 tank lead at the head of the column, since a mine would barely shake up its crew and, at most, throw one of the tank's tracks. For an M113 the result of mine detonation was far worse: the APC would often be flipped off of the ground and the passengers trapped inside would be sprayed with molten fragments. Such was the intense and immediate fear of a horrible death inside the metal carcass of an M113 that many troopers took to riding on top of their vehicles! Not only that, but the floor of the APC would often be lined with sandbags, flak jackets and sand-filled ration tins—anything which would soak up some of the mine's deadly concussive damage. By riding on the deck of an ACAV, a soldier could expect to be shot at by Viet Cong or be blown off on to the ground as a mine detonated, but both were seen as preferable alternatives to sitting passively inside the M113's aluminium body. Fear gripped the crews so badly that sometimes even the drivers rode on top of the vehicles, manoeuvring the M113 via a system of improvised levers connected to the steering and throttle.

Any use the M113 as an armoured troop carrier had now been negated by the communists' use of mines. Since the fear of mine shrapnel forced the crews out on to the top decks of their vehicles, they were subjected to the same combat risks as unmechanised infantry. The only benefit that these vehicles could provide was their formidable, heavy-weapon firepower, something the communists found hard to match; when they could, it lacked the speed and manoeuvrability of the ACAV.

The ACAV had, essentially, turned the M113 into a light tank, a concept in which the US Army had already invested money and effort in the form of the

M551 Sheridan reconnaissance vehicle. But the Sheridan, a promising concept from the outset, failed to deliver and it was up to the M113 and its crews somehow to make up for the lack of close armoured support. The Sheridan had arrived in-theatre from 1969 onwards and was described as an Amphibious Combat, or Airborne Assault, Vehicle. At 15 tons it was a light, air portable, amphibious armoured vehicle that was both versatile and highly mobile. A bad maintenance record and the fact that its revolutionary anti-tank gun/missile launcher had been designed for combat against more conventional formations quickly gave the Sheridan a bad image. With some foresight as to its impressive turn of speed and amphibious capability, however, the Sheridan eventually found widespread use in most cavalry units.

What the troops on the ground had warmed to about the ACAV was its sheer volume of fire, and in an attempt to take this concept one step further the Army introduced the M42 Duster into the fray. Essentially a set of small-calibre, rapid-firing, anti-aircraft guns mounted on an armoured chassis, the Duster was the ultimate contender in a war that increasingly seemed to rely purely on 'weight of fire'. These vehicles boasted powerful 40mm guns that were able to devastate tree lines and bunkers, as well as the Viet Cong who hid within them.

It was the bizarre nature of the ground war in Vietnam, and the US Army's reaction to it, that led to armour being used as something other than fast-moving, mechanised cavalry in the recognised and traditional manner: rather, the armoured elements of most Vietnam engagements were used as fixing forces, able to withstand considerable punishment whilst 'airmobile' infantry was deployed around the enemy to complete an encirclement. As American intervention deepened in 1966 and 1967, battles in which armoured elements had provoked and enflamed the violence had become routine. In February 1967 MACV was determined to force the Viet Cong to fight in defence of the elusive COSVN communist headquarters. This operation, called 'Junction City', would prove to be a decisive test of the strengths and weaknesses of US armour. Paratroopers made a parachute assault in an attempt to cut off the Viet Cong 9th Division's escape route into Cambodia, while a massed force of armour moved into the cordon to flush out and kill the enemy. At Ap Bau Bang, north of Saigon on Route 13, the 3rd Squadron of the 5th Cavalry (the 'Black Knights') set up an unusual ambush with six M48A3 tanks and a score of M113s and ACAVs. Few other wars could lay claim to have seen armour used in such a static ambush. The Viet Cong were not ambushed, however, but began firing on the 'wagon train' of vehicles, destroying and disabling several with mortars. At one point, as enemy infantry overran the armour, American tanks opened fire on one another with canister anti-personnel rounds. This desperate tactic blew away the attackers, who were swarming over the tanks, whilst leaving the vehicles relatively unharmed. A relief column, supported by artillery fire missions and air strikes, eventually routed the Viet Cong infantry, but COSVN was never found and, as the US troops pulled out of the area, the communists moved straight back in.

'Junction City' proved that armour certainly had a place in the Vietnam conflict, but also that it could not be used according to established theory. At Ap Bau Bang, the Black Knights had remained in position as artillery strikes and bombing runs were repeatedly made on the massed Viet Cong infantry attackers around them. They had been the fixing force, engaging the enemy and soaking up tremendous amounts of damage as other forces had come into play. Vietnam, in both its landscape and its inhabitants, had subverted and upended conventional thinking on the nature of warfare. It would happen again and again.

The classic role of the tank was to kill other tanks, something difficult to achieve when one's enemy does not possess any. In fact, as the war reached a climax at the start of 1968, the NVA did send a small number of Russian-built PT-76 light tanks into South Vietnam. They were used in the siege of the Lang Vei CIDG camp close to the DMZ, during a concerted effort to capture the base. The PT-76s were used to smash a way through the flimsy defences and provide immediate fire support for the supporting NVA troopers. The defending Green Berets were pushed back by the overwhelming firepower of these machines. They were almost forced to flee what remained of the Lang Vei camp as the NVA rolled into the inner perimeter and began an assault on the command bunker. Only tremendous air support from Da Nang was able to save the beleaguered defenders.

It was not until 1969 that US tanks were given the opportunity to hit back at NVA armour, but it would be a unique encounter. M48A3s that had been dispatched to reinforce the defences at the Ben Het CIDG camp returned fire on a PT-76 assault force that was attempting to storm the camp's perimeter. Without losing a single tank, the American M48s knocked out most of the light tanks and forced the remainder to retire. A PT-76 was no match for the M48 main battle tank, since it weighed only 14 tons compared to the M48's 47 tons and was armed with the middle-weight 76mm gun. It was primarily a tracked reconnaissance vehicle with an amphibious capability, and was intended to hold its own in an infantry skirmish, not a full-scale tank war.

As a final rejoinder to all those who had claimed that Vietnam was unsuitable tank country, the final NVA invasion of South Vietnam in 1975 was spearheaded by Soviet T-54 main battle tanks. But by then the conflict had abandoned any vestige of a guerrilla war. It was an invasion of one nation by the heavily armed forces of another and the US military machine, which had pulled out by 1972, could only watch from the sidelines as South Vietnam fell victim to the NVA armoured columns.

Airmobility and the Air Cavalry

Operation 'Starlite' had also depended on the 'airmobility' of the Marine helicopter force to achieve some measure of surprise. This was a tactic that had, until Vietnam, been relatively untried in warfare, since troops had traditionally walked into battle or rode in convoys of trucks. As various units back in the

United States began training with helicopters in the early 1960s, the entire concept generated a great deal of controversy. It was an untested form of warfare. Helicopters were perfectly suited, as Korea had already proved, to casualty evacuation, reconnaissance and cargo drops, but there were those in the military establishment who could not accept that these machines had a more serious combat role to play. They were to be proved wrong, although when helicopter forces *were* deployed to Vietnam, controversy continued to plague their use.

The 1950s were an experimental time for helicopter designers, since the aircraft had only just made their début with the armed forces in the aftermath of the Second World War. Most of the helicopters serving with the newly formed ARVN were of this piston-engine generation, but as US Army and Marine units began deploying in-country in 1965 they brought with them a second generation of machines that could easily outstrip the capabilities of their predecessors. And they brought with them more than just new-fangled turbine-engine helicopters: they introduced a way of utilising them that had never before been tried in combat. Airmobility was a concept that was as radical and controversial as the use of the tank had been in 1916. It began with the first attempts at helicopter operations in Vietnam.

As part of the American advisory programme, troop-carrying helicopters were first sent to Vietnam in late 1961. Lacking experienced pilots, the Vietnamese troops that were assigned to them were flown into battle by American advisers. Immediately the helicopter made a difference to the prosecution of the counter-insurgency war. It proved a highly useful tool, able to lift troops into a battle zone that no truck had a hope of reaching, conduct low-level reconnaissance, provide logistical support for units in the field away from airstrips and evacuate casualties quickly and from inaccessible terrain. In short, the helicopter was the perfect anti-guerrilla weapon, striking, like the Viet Cong, any time, anywhere, and able to take the fight to the communist strongholds deep in wilderness areas.

A test organisation, the 11th Air Assault Division, at Fort Benning in Georgia, had put the concept of helicopter-infantry combat into practice in the early 1960s. But the imminent commitment of combat troops to Vietnam had forced the Army to put the unit into military service as the 1st Cavalry Division (Airmobile), a formation that would go on to be one of the most famous military units of the Vietnam War. What airmobility could provide was full helicopter support in combat operations, a tactical advantage that the French had sorely missed. For example, when French forces were ambushed by the Viet Minh, troop reinforcements were usually dispatched by road convoy to provide support. Often, however, the Viet Minh would orchestrate a second ambush designed to catch the convoy unawares as it sped to the rescue. With helicopter support, American reinforcements could be inserted directly on top of the enemy without fear of ambush. Indeed, the concept lent itself to swift-moving, encircling manoeuvres more reminiscent of traditional cavalry or armour charges.

It was no accident that the first operational airmobile unit was called the 1st *Cavalry* Division.

The 1st Cav, nicknamed the 'First Team', did everything on the blades of a rotor. With five times more helicopters than a standard Army division, the 1st Cavalry transported itself by helicopter, fed and supplied itself, provided its own artillery and aerial reconnaissance, was coordinated by helicopter-borne command and control posts and medevacked out its own troops. It was a self-contained, fully mobile air fleet, but with the troops, heavy weapons and howitzers of a more mundane mud-bound division. Initially deployed to II Corps of the Central Highlands, the 1st Cavalry became almost immediately involved in one of the most decisive battles of the Vietnam War.

At the end of 1964 Ho Chi Minh and General Vo Nguyen Giap had made the decision to send whole North Vietnamese Army divisions down the Ho Chi Minh Trail into South Vietnam. A message of imminent defeat had to be sent to Saigon, and that signal was to be heralded by the severing of South Vietnam in half across the Central Highlands, from Pleiku inland to Qui Nhon on the coast. Giap saw a clear advantage over the Americans, since his chosen terrain was tough and impassable, and he doubted their ability to send reaction forces into the jungle-clad mountains. But General Westmoreland recognised that the 1st Cavalry, with its unprecedented mobility, would be the perfect counter to any communist offensive in the region. On 19 October 1965 the small Special Forces camp at Plei Me became the first target for the massed NVA forces. Once relief forces that were expected by Giap to rush to its aid were ambushed and destroyed, the way would be clear for the drive to the coast. Unfortunately for Hanoi, the airmobile 1st Cavalry was able to overfly the carefully set roadside ambushes and provide support for an ARVN column sent to break the siege. The communist forces, rocked by this defeat, slipped away westwards. From then on, the 1st Cavalry moved into an offensive mode, hunting out the NVA as it regrouped in the Ia Drang valley. The battle that followed depended totally on helicopter air support, field reconnaissance and leapfrogging troop deployments to eradicate the communist troops and force the survivors back into the Cambodian jungles. An estimated 1,200 enemy troops were killed during the battle, while the Americans lost 300. The fiercest fighting had been around the incongruously named LZ 'X-Ray'. Airmobility had proved itself capable of matching the toughest formations and tactics of the North Vietnamese, and would quickly be absorbed into the basic doctrine of both the US Army and Marine Corps.

Another Army division, the 101st, also converted to full airmobile operations, and the tactics tried and tested by both units were disseminated and re-used by others within the armed forces. Most Army brigades now contained organic helicopter assets that were routinely employed in troop transport, heliborne search-and-destroy missions and what became known as 'vertical envelopment' situations. Such became the American dependence on the helicopter that the machine became commonplace, and few operations were conducted without its use. *Newsweek* had, as far back as 1962, called Vietnam 'The Helicopter War', and that phrase proved prophetic. In total, some 4,642 American helicopters were lost over Vietnam in one capacity or another, while the South Vietnamese lost an even greater number. As helicopter missions increased through 1965 and 1966, a greater effort was made to protect vulnerable aircraft from hostile ground fire, for it seemed that one of the machine's greatest assets, being able to fly 'low and slow', and land directly on to hostile terrain, was one of its greatest disadvantages.

Most vulnerable to communist ground fire was the ubiquitous UH-1 Huey, a powerful new general-purpose helicopter that carried eight fully armed troops into battle. It was nicknamed the 'Slick', due to its (relative) lack of defensive armament. Most 'Slicks' mounted a 7.62mm M60 light machine gun on each side door, but these weapons were used purely as a defensive measure to provide dismounting troops with some form of covering fire. As they hovered low over a landing zone, the helicopters remained highly vulnerable, and, despite overwhelming air power (up to and including B-52 Stratofortress strategic jet bombers), the use of exposed helicopter formations proved a serious headache for the military. Jets could dump tons of bombs on an enemy that was engaging a helicopter force, but were unable to remain in the area alongside. Neither could they strike with pinpoint accuracy, and so guarantee the safety of friendly troops climbing into or out of the helicopters. A weapons platform was needed that could fly alongside the vulnerable helicopters and loiter for long periods to make repeated attacks in support of troop landings.

One such aircraft was the A-1 Skyraider, a propeller-driven fighter-bomber affectionately dubbed the 'Spad' because of its antique origins at the end of the Second World War. The A-1 often flew in support of Navy helicopter search-and-rescue missions and was able to remain over the battlefield for some time, its tough airframe soaking up tremendous amounts of small-arms damage. Its hefty bomb load meant that it could hit the enemy numerous times without needing to return to base. But the Skyraider was old and was still unable to deliver ordnance with the precision required. As the Vietnam War approached its inexorable end, a warplane emerged on the drawing boards that would capitalise on the A-1's strengths, while addressing its weaknesses. Known as the A-10 Thunderbolt, the result was a jet-powered equivalent of the venerable Skyraider, a slow, manoeuvrable and very tough aircraft. It combined an impressive bomb load with an awesome onboard gun, the 30mm Avenger Gatling, which was designed purely for deadly accurate ground attack missions in support of friendly troops. Although inspired by the problems facing airmobile operations in Vietnam, the A-10 arrived too late to see service there.

The US Army decided that the best protection for the UH-1s would be more heavily armed UH-1s (nicknamed 'Guns' or 'Hogs'). These gunships were equipped with 2.75in folding-fin rocket pods, door guns and four M60 outrigger machine guns. A variety of other lethal armaments were developed, includng miniguns and 40mm grenade launchers, but, despite this enhanced protection, the troop carriers were still under threat from anti-aircraft fire. To meet the need a dedicated ground-attack helicopter gunship was developed by Bell, based on the engine and rotor system of the UH-1. It entered service during the latter half of 1966. Called the AH-1G Cobra, or more familiarly the 'Snake', this new gunship had the speed and manoeuvrability to keep up with the UH-1s and the capability to provide accurate covering fire for an airborne assault.

The AH-1G Cobra was a helicopter fighter, fast and agile, with pilot and gunner sitting in tandem rather than side-by-side as in the Huey. For firepower the Cobra was unrivalled in helicopter warfare: it boasted a nose-mounted 7.62mm six-barrel minigun and 40mm rapid-fire grenade launcher, and carried either miniguns or rocket pods on its integral stub wings. Unlike the jet bombers of the Air Force, the Cobra could get in close alongside the 'Slicks', providing close and accurate suppressive fire. The gunships were in effect flying artillery that could repeatedly pound an enemy position as the troop-carriers moved in to deploy infantry which could assault it. An efficient system was developed by the 1st Cavalry for the landing of airborne troops into a combat zone: the air assault.

A 'Pink Team' made up of an OH-6A Cayuse and a pair of UH-1 or AH-1 gunships conducted low-level reconnaissance in the area where a troop landing was to take place. The proposed LZ was identified by the Cayuse observation helicopter, and repeated passes by the gunships goaded the enemy into opening fire, allowing the helicopters to respond in kind. A 'hot' LZ meant that the area was a battle zone, with all the risks that that entailed. As the incoming flight of troop-carrying 'Slicks' approached the LZ the gunships continued their covering fire on enemy positions, one machine making its attack run while the other made a racetrack loop, coming back on station as the first broke off its attack to circle around. Over 280 Cobras were lost in South Vietnam, grim proof of the dangerous nature of gunship warfare. A heliborne command post (CP) directed the air assault as the first flight, flying in V-formation, slowed for landing. As many helicopters as possible were landed at once to prevent the Viet Cong concentrating their fire on a single aircraft. Even while they were touching down, the troops were out and running, fanning out to cover their allotted portion of the LZ. The door-gunner on either side of the helicopter provided covering fire for the troops as they sprinted from the machine. Orbiting gunships would often continue to pour fire down onto the enemy even as the vulnerable 'Slicks' lifted off and picked up speed for the ride out of the clearing.

Both pilot and co-pilot were supposed to keep hold of the controls in case either was hit during the assault. Many were, since protection for both passengers and crew was limited. The aluminium skin of a Huey did not stop a rifle bullet, and just one or two well-placed hits from a heavy .50-calibre projectile would bring down a helicopter in flight. Pilots sat in armoured seats, but these provided only partial protection to the rear and the side. Many jammed their pistol sidearms down between their legs and tried to scavenge flak jackets from the infantry. Some pilots with an abundance of this body armour piled it into the nose of their helicopter in an attempt to reduce the risk of being shot from the front during an air assault. Every 'Slick' pilot felt highly vulnerable, and lacked the cold comfort of being able to shoot back at his attackers as the gunship pilots were able to do.

The ease with which helicopters could be shot down was just one shortcoming of airmobility. There would soon emerge another—one that would detract from the otherwise illustrious successes of the air cavalry units. Commanders were realising with relish that they could wage war almost anywhere they desired. Infantry could be airlifted into combat at a moment's notice to attack or defend, reinforce or redeploy. Ammunition, supplies and medical care were just a helicopter ride away, and flying artillery was available to soften up a target beforehand. In addition, as already noted, the classic guerrilla method of striking with 'hit and run' tactics could be foiled by leapfrogging the retreating Viet Cong in order to cut off their escape route. But, once on the ground, the airmobile troops seemed more immobile than ever before. Attacking from the safe area around the LZ, the American infantry had regular ammunition supplies and immediate casualty evacuation. Most units were reluctant to move away from this lifeline, digging in to defend the LZ and all that it represented. Meanwhile the communists manoeuvred, engaged, disengaged and retreated with impunity; on the ground it seemed as if the enemy was all too easily able to regain the initiative. Airmobility increased the tactical mobility of air cavalry units while they remained in the air, but when on the ground infantry mobility suffered accordingly. This dependence on the security of the landing zone was exploited by the guerrillas, who noticed that suitable helicopter landing sites were not that common, especially in wooded terrain.

Showing an acute consideration for the tactics of the helicopter, probable landing sites were sometimes booby-trapped by the VC, either with explosives or with sharpened punji stakes that could pierce the thin bellies of descending helicopters. In some cases enemy soldiers popped coloured marker smoke at their rigged landing zones in an attempt to trick the helicopter pilots into landing there. Coloured smoke was one of the main methods of signalling from the ground, and aircraft commanders soon learned to verify the colour of the signalling smoke by radio before making a landing or an attack run.

At the end of 1965 both the Army and the Marines could point to massive and decisive victories over large communist troop concentrations. However, the Battle of Ia Drang taught the NVA a valuable lesson. At all costs, the American military build-ups must be avoided and the war must be fought on the North's own terms. From the start of 1966, the enemy would be difficult to locate and even harder to engage. The Viet Cong, too, were reflective, and decided to return to the covert form of warfare at which they had, until recently, excelled. There would be few stand-up fights from now on.

The Army had not monopolised the use of the helicopter: every service had recognised the numerous functions that it could perform. Like the Army, the Marines employed helicopters for use as troop-carriers, recon ships, air ambulances and gunships. The differences were mainly in the type of machines used by the service, and the emphasis that the Marines placed on certain kinds of missions. Central to the role of the Marine Corps was the aerial support that helicopters could provide during an amphibious landing. For the movement of troops and supplies, the old UH-34 had served well, but it began to be replaced by the twin-rotor CH-46 Sea Knight, a heavy lift helicopter that was both powerful and capacious, from March 1966. Although the Marines did operate UH-1 Hueys, they were rarely used to carry troops but were employed on command post, recon or gunship duties. It was becoming clear that in Vietnam airmobility had superseded the Second World War amphibious assault, and, like the Army, the Marines were keen to take to the skies. The disastrous Bay of Pigs invasion of Cuba by US-trained dissidents back in 1961 was perhaps indicative of future conflicts. The amphibious landing had been a débâcle primarily because of the absence of the air support that the Cuban rebels had been promised. In more recent times the Marines have continued the tradition of amphibious landings on hostile beaches around the world. But with the advent of the helicopter, and its trial by fire in Vietnam, the Corps would always give as much emphasis to airborne landings as those by sea.

The US Navy did not, for obvious reasons, concentrate its helicopter resources on troop transport and air assault. For a naval fleet, ground combat was (and still is) the province of onboard Marine contingents, not naval ratings. Again, however, the Vietnam War twisted the expected and reversed standard procedures. The Navy would become intimately connected with the ground war being fought in the swamps and rice paddies of South Vietnam. It did this not through the use of its vast aircraft carriers, its destroyers or submarines, but through a small fleet of river boats designed specifically to negotiate the winding waterways of the Mekong Delta west of Saigon. And with ground (or rather river) forces came the need for air mobility.

Operation 'Game Warden' was the official designation for the Navy's interdiction of the Viet Cong supply routes through the dense network of canals and rivers in the Delta. Its boats, mainly fast-moving Swifts and PBRs (Patrol Boat Riverine), plus a variety of more heavily armed and armoured boats, conducted reconnaissance and observation as well as combat operations. Before we look at the riverine war, what it was, what was expected of it, and what it eventually delivered, we should first mention the use of the UH-1 Huey in this theatre. The naval unit responsible for policing the Delta was the River Patrol Force (Task Force 116) which had a floating headquarters in the My Tho river. It soon became clear that patrols could be taken a step further to encompass actual combat assaults on communist bases that lay within the Delta. As a result, a new force was organised in 1967.

The new combat organisation was christened the Mobile Riverine Force (MRF) and gunboats from its naval component, Task Force 117, began successfully working with the Army component, the 9th Infantry Division, in the organisation of amphibious assaults. Crucial to these operations was air support, not only from fast-moving jets launched by the Navy's carriers out at sea but also from UH-1 helicopter gunships. The Navy, like the Army, recognised the potential of these aircraft in low-level precision attacks in support of troops. And of course their minimal landing requirements allowed them to be based on floating air bases in mid-river, alongside other MAF support vessels. The helicopter unit was officially designated Helicopter Support Squadron One but went under the more common name of the 'Seawolves'. It was divided into two fire teams and worked closely with PBRs and Assault Patrol Boats to strike hard at enemy riverbank positions. The Seawolves proved that air power was an integral part of combat operations in every theatre of the war, including the riverine conflict.

The Brown Water Navy

There can have been few fleets in naval history as obscure as the US Navy's riverine force, and few combat arenas as peculiar as the Mekong Delta. Its size was staggering: sixty thousand square kilometres of paddy fields, swamp and water-logged terrain, interlaced with a confusing network of canals, rivers and irrigation ditches—over five and a half thousand kilometres of them! Roads and bridges were inadequate and poorly maintained, and consequently much of the traffic moved by water and was difficult to track. This fact made the Delta a communist hotbed: estimates vary, but in the early stages of the war there may have been well over 80,000 Viet Cong active there. Food, arms and manpower moved invisibly through these waterways. Compounding the seriousness of the Delta insurgency was the fact that it was home to almost one-third of South Vietnam's rural population. Most were rice farmers, feeding not only themselves but the rest of the nation, and the communists continued to take ever larger 'cuts' of the annual rice crop. Their grip over the people and the province increased so much that by 1966 it was feared the entire Delta region might fall.

General Westmoreland was faced with the prospect of somehow policing this volatile and mysterious region. He chose, like the French commanders before him, to employ riverine power rather than land forces or airmobility. The Navy was up to the task, but it lacked the necessary vessels on its inventory and found itself compelled to begin the construction of a riverine force from scratch. The result was a 'brown water navy', an *ad hoc* amalgam of floating fortresses and fast-moving craft that had never been seen outside Vietnam before. The Mobile Riverine Force was unique in warfare, but did it work?

By far the greatest part of this riverine combat force was constituted of light patrol boats, built of fibreglass and able to reach speeds of 45kph. Drawing only 30cm, these PBRs could negotiate the shallowest of waters and with their revolutionary water-jet engines had little chance of becoming entangled in reeds. In a similar vein, the Navy successfully tested hovercraft in the region. Called Patrol Air Cushion Vehicles (PACVs), these machine gun-armed craft were able to skim across water, reeds, mud and rice paddies without problem. Unfortunately, their almost perfect adaptation to the Delta was offset somewhat by the noise their propellers created, which usually alerted the enemy to the PACV's presence well in advance. Transferred directly from the Florida Everglades were the fast, adaptable (and equally noisy) air-boats. These were superbly suited to the Mekong swamps and found some use with Vietnamese Popular and Regional Forces.

With the onset of combat sweeps through the Delta (and the heavily infested Rung Sat mangrove swamp separating Saigon from the sea), slower, tougher and deadlier vessels were introduced. Many of these were old landing craft that had been inherited from the French but had had their bow doors welded shut, armour plating covering every inch of the hull and the most modern American weaponry installed on the deck. The waterborne fighting forces were based on floating barracks ships moored in mid-stream known as Mobile Afloat Forces (MAFs). Both the barracks vessel and its attendant supply barges were protected by some of the river warships, while other components of the force would travel up to 50km up river to conduct offensive operations against the Viet Cong. Crucial to the force was the Assault Support Patrol Boat (ASPB), which had been specially designed for use in Vietnam. It proved highly versatile, often sweeping ahead of combat operations as an escort and counter-ambush craft. Some versions were converted into dedicated minesweepers in an effort to defeat one of the guerrillas' most widespread river tactics of mining sensitive stretches of the river network. Typical armament for an ASPB consisted of 20mm turreted cannon, turret-mounted .50-calibre machine guns and two 40mm grenade launchers. Some boats also mounted a dual .50-calibre machine gun/81mm mortar combination in an open deck-well.

Working in concert with the ASPBs were the 'battleships of the Delta', the monitors. Early versions were old colonial landing craft that had probably seen action in the Mekong Delta against the Viet Minh ten or fifteen years beforehand. The great success of the boats encouraged the Navy to develop its own purpose-built monitors. These would become the anchor points in riverine assaults, pinning down the Viet Cong, destroying bunkers and clearing potentially hostile landing spots. Fully armoured, the vessels also featured metal grille-work covering all parts of the superstructure that was designed to detonate enemy anti-tank rockets and recoilless rounds prematurely, thus, it was hoped, rendering the attacks impotent. Armament varied, but some of the later monitor MkV versions were fitted with a 40mm cannon forward, a 20mm cannon aft and turrets amidships that carried .50-calibre machine guns and M10-8 flame-thrower units. M60 and M1919 medium machine guns were usually mounted on the bridge for the crew's use. Other weaponry could be found on individual vessels, ranging from a standard mortar to a 105mm howitzer mounted on the forward turret. Devastating direct fire support to troops on the bank could be provided by this latter weapon.

Benefiting from the formidable firepower of both the monitors and the ASPBs were the vulnerable armoured troop carriers (ATCs). Each carrying a 40-man platoon, these craft had the same anti-rocket protection as the monitors, bullet-proof awnings over the troop deck and a variety of machine guns for defence. A column of ATCs would be accompanied into the combat zone by a monitor and CCB (Command Control Boat, an adapted monitor used for coordinating the mission), while ASPBs would provide a vanguard, sweeping the bank, the water and civilian sampans with their deadly array of weapons.

Similar to the use of main battle tanks by the Army, the monitors were essentially blocking and holding devices about which other forces (units of the 9th Infantry Division, the Seawolves, or air strikes by Navy fighter-bombers) could revolve. Although the ASPBs were more mobile than the monitors (capable of 25kph compared with the monitors' 15kph), both excelled at engaging and destroying enemy troop formations. Such was the potency of the Mobile Riverine Force that by the end of 1968 the level of insurgency in the Mekong Delta and the Rung Sat had dropped off considerably. The VC had wisely abandoned the Delta as its main infiltration route into the south of the country, and instead the Cambodian border became the new focus of communist attention.

Pressure increased on the US military to proceed with 'Vietnamisation', which aimed to transfer much of its in-country equipment over to the South Vietnamese and allow them to take full responsibility for the prosecution of the war. In 1969 the highly successful MRF was disbanded and handed over to the South Vietnamese Navy under the grandiose designation 'SEALORDS', an acronym for South East Asian Lake Ocean River Delta Strategy. Within months the SEALORDS concept was put into full use during the April 1970 push into Cambodia. This offensive, designed to halt the communist infiltration over the border, met with stiff resistance, and South Vietnamese gunboats battled northwards to keep the Mekong supply route open. When the operation finally ended, the newly established riverine force had to cover the hasty retreat back across the border via the Mekong River.

Despite the inadequacies of the SEALORDS riverine force, the actual concept was sound, as the American Navy had already proved. The transfer of $7.7 million worth of naval vessels to the SEALORDS organisation had been somewhat overwhelming, and American re-training could not keep pace with the equipment now available to the Saigon military. The Delta war had demanded special equipment, special troops and a unique method of operating. With little experience in such an environment, the US Navy had suddenly been faced with a difficult task, but it had managed to put together a force that was able to rise to the challenge. In an era of nuclear-powered aircraft carriers, submarines and guided-missile cruisers, the MRF had been an unconventional navy in an unconventional war.

Perhaps the single doubt over the efficiency of the Mobile Riverine Force surrounded the deployment of elements of the 9th Infantry Division to the MRF. Combat duty in the region involved long hours huddled in sweltering ATCs as well as heaving oneself through chest-high mud and dense swamp. This took its toll on the infantrymen. Soldiers were forever soaked through to the bone and drenched in paddy mud. In addition, the tortuous condition of 'immersion foot' plagued every member of a combat unit, forcing their commanders continually to rotate troops out of the field and on to barracks ships. This at least gave both their kit and their feet an opportunity to dry out. The Army was forced to adapt to the peculiar nature of amphibious combat quickly, which seemed wasteful of the great pool of expertise already in Vietnam—the US Marine Corps. Masters of the amphibious assault, and intimately familiar with the Navy's way of doing business, the Marines would have been a powerful asset had they been deployed in the Delta from the start. Perhaps this had been a missed opportunity for the Corps, which was instead restricted to operations in the dry and dusty I Corps up near the DMZ. General Westmoreland had his reasons for sending the Marines into I Corps, however. In 1965 an overt NVA invasion of South Vietnam was feared, and the Marines, the Pentagon's much lauded 'fire brigade', were rushed to this border region. The total lack of port facilities along the South Vietnamese coast did not hinder the deployment, for the Marine Corps was unique amongst the US armed forces in being able to create and supply its own beach-heads. It was this ability to conduct autonomous resupply that convinced Westmoreland to put the Marines in-theatre first.

The 'blue water navy' that operated out in the Gulf of Tonkin performed well, supporting ground troops with offshore bombardments, air strikes and long-range radar coverage. Critics have pointed out that the US Navy was excessively sophisticated for what was essentially an unconventional insurgency conflict, but such criticism can easily be repudiated by the way in which the service committed itself to (and adapted to) a corner of the war that has remained essentially out of the public gaze but which nevertheless formed a crucial part of the American effort.

Chapter 4

VIETNAM'S HIGH-TECH HARDWARE

Following the successful conclusion of the war against Japan in 1945, America unanimously wanted the troops home. This overwhelming mood suited the Truman administration perfectly, since it could begin drastically cutting military expenditure. Such savage cuts precluded research and investment into new military technology for all but the US Air Force. In the late 1940s this service—and particularly Strategic Air Command, with the capability to deliver the 'ultimate weapon', the A-bomb—flourished. For the Army and the Marines, however, the outlook was bleak. When the Korean crisis erupted on to the international stage, American ground forces were rushed to South Korea with Second World War surplus. As a consequence the Allies were severely mauled by the Chinese troop units that swarmed across the border. On the ground at least, the American military seemed out of date and out-gunned by the communist military machine. It was a mistake that would not to be repeated when the country went to war again in 1965 against the Vietnamese communists.

There has been a deluge of criticism focusing on America's technological excesses in the Vietnam War, and claims that the extravagant and reckless use of the latest military weaponry was an attempt somehow to make up for a paucity of manpower and tactical sense. The term 'overkill' is readily conjured when stories of lone Viet Cong snipers being blasted by the entire bomb load from a B-52 strategic bomber are encountered. Such wasteful expenditures of devastation were often more counter-productive than productive. It was not the intensity of the war that made Vietnam different from any other, however, but the vast technological gulf that separated the two aggressors. The Pentagon had learnt its lesson from the emergency mobilisations during the Korean War: not only would troop numbers have to remain at effective levels during peacetime, but the weaponry and equipment of all the armed services would require constant updating. There would be no time to plan, test and deploy new weaponry once a war had begun—the military needed that technology immediately. Major David Miller, of the British Army, has defined three broad phases of technological expansion following the end of hostilities against Japan: 'Second World War Surplus' (1945–55); 'First Generation, Post-war' (1950–60); and 'Second Generation, Post-war' (1960–70).

Up until the mid-1950s, a great deal of Second World war equipment was still in use by all of the armed forces, but the explosive arena of Korea really provided the United States with a great deal of impetus to begin work on a new generation of combat equipment. This first post-war generation of technology found use during the 1950s from the Korean War onwards and fell out of use as the Vietnam War gained momentum. An example of this is the M14 rifle, entering production in 1957 following the poor showing of the then standard M1 Garand rifle against the communist AK-47. Production of the standard M14 ceased in 1964 as American forces became committed to Vietnam, and the firearm was quickly replaced by the second-generation rifle, the M16.

Virtually all the second-generation equipment was deployed and tested in Vietnam. That war had an immediate and revolutionary effect on military technology, with the second generation practically running its entire course during the conflict. Testing, re-evaluation and re-deployment occurred numerous times as the years of fighting passed. However, although several examples of the second generation of weapons were welcomed by troops in the field, not every system found immediate favour. One weapon in particular, the M16 rifle, became an object of contention between those in the military who clung to outdated Second World War ideology and those who encouraged the evolution of postwar technologies.

The Armalite Affair

Of all the weapon systems employed by the US forces in Vietnam, the M16 rifle proved to be one of the most controversial. Unlike Agent Orange or the use of napalm, the M16 was not a weapon that was considered unethical or cruel. It was not the public nor the press who found a problem with the M16, but the troops themselves. For the soldiers who first began to use the new rifle, the M16 was, quite simply, a liability. Still used (in a modified form) by the US forces of today, the M16 was as infamous then as it is famous now. The incredible unreliability of the M16 was due, however, not to any innate design fault, but almost wholly to bureaucratic inefficiency and intransigence.

The adoption of the M16 marked a radical shift in military firearms technology, a shift that was not at all welcomed by some elements of the US military hierarchy. But the change could hardly be avoided, for the M16 programme was at the forefront of a revolution in modern firearms development that could trace its roots back to the Second World War. Throughout the century, infantrymen the world over had marched into battle with a high-powered rifle that held between five and ten bullets and fired single shots. Such rifles had effective combat ranges in excess of 1,000m and most infantrymen were trained to hit targets at this distance. But, as studies made by the Germans during the war showed, most firefights took place at ranges of less than 400m, rendering much of the rifle's killing potential redundant. At the other end of the scale was a proliferation of short-range sub-machine guns that fired a burst of low-calibre bullets that were normally used in pistols. Perfect for close-in jungle or urban conflicts, the sub-machine gun had severe deficiencies at ranges over 100m.

It was the German Army that first attempted to produce a lightweight rifle that could be effective out to 300–400m yet incorporate the fully automatic feature of the sub-machine gun. The result was an intermediate bullet that had sufficient range and killing power but was light enough to be controllable when fired in the full-automatic mode. In essence, the Germans had created an accurate long-range sub-machine gun. The type proved eminently successful and in 1944 was officially designated the *Maschinenpistole MP44*. The gun was later christened the *Sturm-Gewehr*, or Assault Rifle, by no less a person than Hitler himself.

Following the end of the war extensive studies of infantry engagements were conducted by the Allies and all reached similar conclusions as the Germans had a few years earlier. In the Soviet Union, Britain, Belgium and the USA, rifles soon appeared on drawing boards that would benefit from these studies. In the United States the concept of an automatic rifle proved attractive, and a Lightweight Rifle Program was instituted. But top designers in the Army balked at the idea of a short-range and lightweight bullet for their new design, preferring instead a bullet similar to the one used throughout the Second World War. The Army introduced the 7.62mm x 51mm bullet, slightly shorter than the one it replaced but no less powerful due to technological developments in ballistics. To fire this powerful projectile, the Army came up with a strong, sturdy and heavy rifle—the M14. Whilst other nations had also begun research into lightweight bullets, they were now compelled to adopt the powerful 7.62mm x 51mm round due to the logistical requirements of NATO. In turn they had to develop their own heavy rifles with which to fire the round. The Lightweight Rifle Program had foundered.

Properly responsible for this procurement decision was the Ordnance Corps, a team of top Army officials, weapons designers and manufacturers who were proud of the M14. But the weapon immediately had its critics. Its bullets were so powerful that they would 'over-penetrate' when they hit a target, entering the body and leaving via a large exit wound with much of their energy still unexpended. After all, the bullet needed enough energy to reach the gun's effective range of 1,000m. These 7.62mm x 51mm rounds were heavy, the gun was excessively bulky and the recoil kick of the powerful bullet was so severe that the fully automatic feature of the M14 was soon adjusted to single-shot only, leaving the US military with a weapon that was only marginally better than the M1 Garand that it replaced. Across Europe, by the end of the 1950s weapons similar to the M14, carrying twenty 7.62mm x 51mm bullets in a box magazine and capable of full automatic fire, had also been adopted by most armed forces to fall in line with the NATO standard. The Belgians produced the prolific FN FAL rifle, the Germans the Heckler and Koch G3, the Italians the Beretta BM 59 and the Spanish the CETME series of rifles. With such international consequences and a development budget of $500 million, there was no way that the Ordnance Corps could do anything but stand by its choice of both round and weapon.

In the Soviet Union, however, the story of weapons development was an entirely different one, and would result in the radical shift in American design that was to have such deadly repercussions in Vietnam. Mikhail Kalashnikov is probably the most famous name in weapon design, responsible as he was for the development of the Russian AK-47 'Kalashnikov' rifle. He had studied the Nazi firearms reports and carefully analysed the German MP44 *Sturm-Gewehr*. What emerged from the Soviet State Arsenal as a result in 1951 was the AK-47, lighter than the M14 and firing an intermediate round. It was capable of fully automatic fire out to a range of 300m, and incorporated the devastating firepower of the sub-machine gun with the longer range and penetration of a rifle. A new era in weaponry had begun with this assault rifle, and during the Korean War the gun received its baptism of fire. Several Chinese units carried AK-47s and shocked the US troops they encountered with their impressive firepower. The weapon completely outclassed the old M1 Garand with which the Americans were still equipped. Kalashnikov's design showed the disparity between current Russian and American advances, and the M14 rifle that emerged a few years later failed to compare with the radical and effective AK-47.

But designers had not altogether given up on the United States military, despite the latter's intransigence and stubborn view of the infantryman's role on the battlefield. Tentative rifle programmes continued to experiment with new rounds* and materials, and one that was to lead, eventually, to the highly controversial M16 was run by the Armalite Division of the Fairchild Corporation. During the 1950s the company designed and tested a family of weapons that were made with lightweight alloys and space-age plastics rather than the machined steel and selected hardwoods of previous military designs. Such a revolutionary concept was supported by Eugene Stoner, a brilliant weapons designer who joined the small Californian company early in the decade. Stoner's name ranks alongside those of Winchester and Colt as that of an innovative and prolific weapons designer who would change the landscape of firearms development for ever. Unlike the establishment, for whom he was developing his designs, Stoner immediately grasped the idea of new and advanced materials for use in firearms manufacture and proceeded to unveil several extraordinary rifle designs.

One of the earliest weapons was of little interest to the infantryman but displayed all the hallmarks of Armalite's unique approach to weapon design. The AR-5 was a small rifle of old-fashioned bolt-action operation (the bolt had to be cycled between shots, bringing a fresh round into the firing chamber) that was

---

*The term 'round' encompasses the actual bullet projectile and the brass cartridge along with its chemical propellant. The bullet is the lead tip that actually leaves the end of the barrel and strikes the target. Spent cartridges are ejected from the gun once the bullet has been fired.

intended to be carried disassembled in a plastic butt stock. It fired lightweight .22 ammunition and found a market with the US Air Force as a handy survival rifle for shooting small game. Bigger things were to follow.

The AR-10 was a more substantial rifle design that emerged just as the US military were taking delivery of their first M14s. Unfortunately, such was the immense size of this contract that there was absolutely no hope that a new design would be considered by the armed forces for some time to come. Like the outmoded M14, the new AR-10 fired the NATO 7.62mm x 51mm round, but there the similarities ended. In operation, appearance and handling, Stoner's new rifle totally outclassed the military's chosen firearm. In the first place it looked bizarre, with an all-in-line layout that had the barrel directly in line with the butt, and a novel carrying handle over the receiver that also housed the gun sights and cocking lever. The barrel was surrounded by a plastic shroud and featured a combined muzzle brake and flash hider. Twenty rounds fed into the weapon from a magazine forward of the trigger and the gun's operation was semi-automatic (i.e., one shot was fired for every pull of the trigger). The all-important locking mechanism in the gun was a gas-operated rotary bolt-into-barrel lock that has since revolutionised modern rifle mechanisms with its compactness and ease of operation.

Despite the weapon's obvious advantages in reliability, handling and efficiency, the US military could not take a gun seriously that was not made of hardwood and steel and weighed at least 8½lb (minus ammunition). Tests were conducted with Stoner's AR-10, but the Ordnance Corps had already made its decision and could not be swayed. This did not spell the end of the design. As the 1960s loomed closer, the US military realised that the 7.62mm x 51mm round did have serious deficiencies in that it could not easily be fired on full-automatic and that less ammunition could be carried by the soldier in the field. These two factors combined significantly to restrict the American infantryman's firepower at a time when his Soviet counterpart had greatly increased his. But eager participation in the arms race meant that the US had eventually to catch up, and the recent procurement of the M14 had seriously handicapped the American forces in their race to gain parity with the Soviets.

As a consequence, Armalite was approached by General William Wyman of the US Army with an invitation to design and test a rifle based on the advanced AR-10 but firing a new, lightweight round. Wyman was particularly interested in a fully automatic rifle that would be an equal match for the Russian AK-47. Within a period of only a few months Stoner had a prototype ready for trial. Called the AR-15, the experimental rifle was designed around a 5.56mm x 45mm cartridge that seemed puny in comparison with the 7.62mm round of the M14 and AR-10. In fact the round resembled the very light .22 round often used by sportsmen to take pot-shots at squirrels and birds, and was actually developed from a hunting round. But the ammunition (later entering production as the M193) had a lot to offer for its small size. First, it was backed up by a substantial amount of propellant in the cartridge that forced the bullet out of the gun's barrel at 1,000m/sec. This gave the bullet a kill potential almost as great as that of the heavier NATO 7.62mm round. Secondly, its recoil was light enough to allow automatic fire, machine-gun style, without throwing the firer off-balance. Thirdly, the individual soldier could carry more than twice as many rounds for the same weight allowance. It was the perfect match for the AK-47 and marked an entirely new era in American weapons design.

Unfortunately for Armalite, the US armed forces had already settled on the M14 as their weapon of choice, and it would be some time before the AR-15 was to see service in regular infantry units. As the 1950s came to a close, Stoner and his colleagues travelled to the Far East in search of orders for the rifle. They found that its light weight and ease of use made it popular with the slightly built Orientals, and firing demonstrations greatly impressed the various military representatives. Back in the United States, the Army had begun putting the AR-15 through its paces, and the exuberant reports from soldiers conducting the tests clashed head-on with the stolid mind-set of the Army brass. Enthusiastic reports were shrugged off by the Ordnance Corps, who still claimed that the 5.56mm round was far too light to be effective. The weapon's positive points—its reliability, accuracy, light weight and high rate of fire—were stubbornly dismissed. But someone, somewhere was taking note, because the Air Force decided to order the AR-15 for its numerous ground troops stationed around the world. The Air Force, a fairly recent addition to the American armed services, had little concept of 'traditional' weaponry—and it had become known as one of the most innovative organisations in the post-war world.

When President Kennedy was presented with divergent assessments of the new gun, he ordered Secretary of Defense McNamara to determine which camp was actually telling the truth: the Department of Defense or the Army brass. The investigation revealed that the Ordnance Corps had actually rigged selected tests of the AR-15 to produce reports showing the rifle in a particularly bad light. When this became known, little justification remained for *not* purchasing large quantities of the rifle from Armalite. By 1963 the rifle had won the argument. On the day of the President's assassination in November 1963, an AR-15 was in fact carried by a member of his Secret Service bodyguard in the follow-up car. It would soon become a common sight amongst the military, but the Ordnance Corps had not yet finished dabbling in the development of the rifle.

As the design for the AR-15 (now with the more familiar designation M16), was finalised by the upper echelon of the Army, three important modifications were made to its intrinsic design. These changes were effectively acts of sabotage, cunning attempts to cripple the rifle at the last minute, even as it was being handed out to troops in the field. The precision rifling on the inside of the M16's barrel was altered, and the selected gunpowder chosen by Armalite for all of its tests, and recommended for regular use, was also altered. Finally, a manual bolt-closure handle was fitted to the M16, something unnecessary to its operation but recommended for no other reason than that all previous Army rifles had had them.

Stoner was obviously taken aback by these changes. He argued strongly against all three, and against the change in the cartridge powder most strongly of all. The Ordnance Corps had switched the production of the gunpowder from DuPont, who supplied the original test cartridges, to Olin-Mathieson, who were to begin supplying a cheaper, dirtier and less reliable type of gunpowder. The results were to be disastrous. Colt, who were actually to manufacture the M16, were equally worried by the change in the powder and after conducting tests with the Olin-Mathieson cartridges informed the Army that it could not guarantee the performance of the rifles that it was supplying.

Firepower in the Field

Combat troops in Vietnam began to receive the new rifle in large numbers, and along with the weapon came the erroneous message that it required little if any cleaning. It is hard to pinpoint the source of this message, but it must have been generated in part by the M16's futuristic aura. Very quickly the rifle developed a bad reputation: it would jam after firing only a few rounds, or it would refuse to eject the spent cartridges. One Army soldier complained: 'Our M16s aren't worth much. If there's dust in them, they will jam. Half of us don't have cleaning rods to unjam them. Out of forty rounds I've fired, my rifle jammed about ten times. I pack as many grenades as I can plus bayonet and K-Bar [Navy combat knife] so I'll have something to fight with.'

At the battle for Hill 881 in May 1967, the M16 failed to perform satisfactorily, and in combat conditions this meant that needless deaths occurred. The survivors of the battle (160 were killed, and over 700 wounded) complained bitterly about their rifles. One Marine wrote a damning letter to Congress that brought to public attention the inadequacies of the M16, and blamed the rifle for the disaster in Quang Tri province: 'Believe it or not, do you know what killed most of us? Our own rifles . . . the M16. Practically every one of our dead was found with his rifle torn open next to him where he had been trying to fix it.' The same story was told over and over. Some soldiers, including a handful of officers, reported that up to fifty per cent of a unit's rifles had failed to work in combat. The inefficiency of the weapon gradually filtered up the chain of command, but unit commanders were reluctant either to give these reports much credence or to pass on their reservations to Washington. Some high-ranking officers, such as Marine General Lewis Walt, flatly denied that there were any problems with the M16 itself. Again, the conflicting reports being received by Congress galvanised that body to carry out further investigations. Senator Richard Ichord chaired an Armed Services Sub-Committee that was charged with uncovering the real truth behind the spate of recent accusations. Troops from Fort Benning in the US were interviewed, hearings on the development of the M16 were conducted, and representatives of the sub-committee even visited the combat zone. Gradually, through 1967 and 1968, the duplicity and connivance of the Army brass and the Ordnance Corps was brought to light.

The Ichord Committee heard that the rifling in the M16 barrel had been changed to make the bullet spin faster and that this reduced its energy. A drop-off in performance was one thing, however, but the wilful sabotage of the weapon's cartridge powder was something far deadlier. In late 1967 officers of the Ordnance Corps could not give a satisfactory reason for the crucial change in powder. In tests, the new propellant increased the rate of fire from 700 to 1,000 rounds per minute. This resulted in harmful chemical deposits being left inside the rifle chamber and increased the risk of malfunctions. Combined with the incomprehensible advice given to troops that the gun need not be cleaned, the result had been predictable and fatal. The sub-committee was scathing in its attack on the Ordnance Corps, and on both the Army's method of procurement and its conscious and persistent negligence.

With this condemnation came plans for the modification programme that would correct the jamming problems of the M16. It would not, however, immediately replace the gunpowder of the 5.56mm ammunition, nor alter the unsatisfactory barrel rifling. Other details, such as a forward assist lever to aid in freeing a jammed round and a ring around the barrel end to stop the flash suppresser snagging in foliage were, however, added. A great effort was made to re-educate soldiers about the maintenance of their M16s, and the early myth that the weapon would never need cleaning was quickly dispelled. This was due in part to a radically presented preventative maintenance manual issued to the majority of GIs. Designed almost as a comic, the manual featured a sexily drawn blonde girl telling the recruit exactly how to 'strip your baby'. It assumed that a low level of education existed amongst the infantrymen, and hoped to capitalise on the popularity of comics amongst the young draftees. Obviously it worked, despite (or because of) the manual's colloquial language. For example, its advice for troops wading out of streams and rice paddies was: 'Soon as you come out of the drink—if Charlie's not interfering, natch—take the mags out and shake 'em good a couple of times to get rid of most of the water.' This irreverent style was a refreshing change from the dry and tedious format of the official 'TM' technical manuals.

The focus on preventative maintenance reduced malfunctions to acceptable levels. By 1968 modified M16A1s had entered service and reports of combat malfunctions had declined significantly. From then on the combat record of the weapon was outstanding, and its black plastic and metal shape became an enduring image of the Vietnam War. Practically every military unit in Vietnam adopted the M16A1 wholeheartedly, from military police and regular infantry units to Air Force guards and Navy crews on board patrol boats. It was—and still is—handy, versatile and deadly, a suitable opponent for the communist AK-47 which had at that time become the mainstay of the Viet Cong and NVA arsenals.

The performance of the M16 gave each infantryman the potential firepower of a platoon of riflemen and equalised the technological disparity between the communists and the Americans. Usually, when contact with the enemy was made, a tremendous fusillade of bullets was exchanged with the ambushers in an effort to pin them down long enough for artillery and air strikes to come into play. With the novel 'full automatic' feature on the M16, panicked troops were tempted to 'spray' the undergrowth that concealed the attackers with bullets. Ammunition was rapidly expended, and at 700 rounds per minute the 20-round box magazines of the weapon would be used in under two seconds. Obviously unit leaders stressed a less extravagant expenditure of ammunition, but in the heat of combat, and particularly amongst inexperienced soldiers, it was difficult to fire short, controlled bursts while simultaneously keeping a check on ammunition use. A thumb-operated selector lever was positioned on the left of the gun, above the pistol grip. Pointing forward, it would engage the safety, and when pointing upwards the rifle would fire one shot per pull of the trigger. Full automatic fire was selected by pushing the lever to the rear.

To compensate for the unrestrained use of ammunition, most infantrymen weighed themselves down with fabric bandoleers containing numerous M16 magazines. Rucksacks, pouches, pockets and bags were usually stuffed with these precious items. Thirty-round magazines were available for use with the M16, but they were scarce and highly prized by troops in the field. Also sought after, because of the fear of a weapon jamming in combat, were spare cleaning rods, and these were sometimes tied to the gun to prevent them from bending or getting lost. Constant weapon cleaning was a routine that was now drilled into troops, and this, combined with a new chromed chamber and a slightly revised gunpowder mixture, had reduced the malfunction rate. But problems still occasionally occurred. Troops would often load only seventeen or eighteen rounds into a 20-round magazine in an effort to spare the spring and reduce the chance of a misfeed.

As a killing machine, the soldiers had seen nothing like it. When Stoner had taken M16s and M14s to the Far East for comparative demonstrations, several impromptu test-firings had been directed at coconuts. The 7.62mm bullets of the M14 drilled neat holes right the way through them. When the 5.56mm bullets from the M16 struck the nuts, they exploded violently. The rifle had a similarly disagreeable effect on living creatures. An Army Sergeant, John Black, remembered opening fire on an enemy with the rifle for the first time: 'As the bullet slammed into him, it ripped the whole arm and shoulder from his body, spun him around, and rammed him into the ground so hard that he bounced. He was dead from shock even before I covered the twenty yards to him.'

Like most soldiers, Sergeant Black had at first been sceptical about the effectiveness of the tiny 5.56mm round, but it quickly earned the respect of the average infantryman. The M16 was a qualified success in Vietnam—qualified because its birth cost the American military time, energy and lives. Once accepted, however, it proved versatile and deadly, and the perfect sidearm for the revolutionary type of ultra-mobile war being waged. There are two indicators of the weapon's superior qualities. First, a modified M16 still serves each of the United States armed services today, more than thirty years later; secondly, highlighting its great adaptability, there were relatively few variants of the weapon. The M14, for example, saw numerous variations, including a finely tuned sniper version, heavy-barrelled and light machine gun versions and a folding stock variant for use by paratroopers. In comparison, the M16A1 came in only two types, the standard M16A1 and the CAR-15 Colt Commando, a cut-down carbine version with an extending stock for use by Special Forces. The carbine had less than half the range of the full-size M16, but it was excellent at these short ranges and popular with field commanders and Special Forces personnel. Unfortunately, the Colt Commando's muzzle flash was made more pronounced by the shortening of the M16 barrel. To compensate, a screw-on flash-hider was added that had the effect of lengthening the weapon, somewhat mitigating the benefits of its compactness.

Critics of the little CAR-15 have pointed out that its shorter barrel length cut down the gun's range, worsened the muzzle flash and reduced the ballistic capabilities of the 5.56mm bullet to an unacceptable level. But they have failed to see the rifle in its true light. As a close-quarter weapon, the Colt Commando was an undoubted success, and in this respect it resembled a sub-machine gun more than a high-velocity rifle. With its stock fully extended, the CAR-15 was still shorter than the Thompson M1A1, the standard sub-machine gun of the Second World War. Like the Thompson, its short length was perfect for jungle warfare and patrolling, conditions where the enemy could appear without warning at close range and from any direction.

The Art of Ambush

Close-range combat was the prevalent type of contact with the enemy in the Vietnam War. The communists preferred to use cover for maximum concealability at all times, making detection difficult right up until the last minute. This made the ambush the most common method of coming into contact, and the term 'ambush' came to be used to describe almost any short-range encounter, whether a prepared and concealed attack had been made or not. As patrols stumbled into firefight after firefight, it soon became obvious that accuracy was not an issue. When the bullets started flying, an infantry platoon would hit the ground and get into cover, then begin returning fire into the enemy positions with automatic bursts. The accurate acquisition of individual Viet Cong was impossible, and so area fire became the norm. Weight of fire displaced accuracy, and new weapons entered the field to maximise the infantry's killing potential at short ranges.

Men 'walking point' (scouting ahead in the lead position) were often allowed to experiment with a variety of small arms until they decided on a suitable weapon.

M16s were routinely discarded by the pointman for a Thompson, an M3A1 sub-machine gun or a pump-action shotgun. The Marines were the first to issue shotguns to field personnel, and had done so previously during the Pacific fighting against the Japanese. Few weapons are as effective at close range as a 12-gauge shotgun. In Vietnam each 'OO' buckshot shell contained nine lead balls, each 9mm in diameter. As the shot left the barrel it spread out, increasing the chance of hit, but after about 30m or so the balls were so far apart that this chance was reduced dramatically. The short-range firepower of the shotgun, usually an Ithaca 37, Remington 870 or Winchester, made the weapon popular amongst jungle fighters and near the end of the war an extra 100,000 were delivered to Saigon for use by local forces. Most of these were lost to the communists as the nation fell in 1975.

Experiments were carried out to increase the shotgun's only shortcoming— its poor range. Compare the shotgun's 30m to the M16's 300m! One of these projects substituted the steel balls within the shotgun shells for numerous finned steel darts or 'flechettes'. Each 25mm-long flechette had superior aerodynamics to the steel shot, and had a much greater lethal range. Killing power was not lost, since the little flechettes tumbled end-over-end when they hit a target, causing nasty wounds. And because they were so light, the projectiles reached a speed of over 600m/sec, giving them the capability to penetrate helmets and armoured vests. Only one drawback prevented the flechette concept from revolutionising jungle combat: the projectiles were thrown wildly off aim by just a metre or two of vegetation. Flechette loadings for shotguns (and also for artillery pieces) were nicknamed 'beehives' after the ominous humming noise they made as the left the barrel. Used as filling inside 105mm howitzer shells, the flechettes were very successful, spraying out over a wide area when the shell burst (usually at a pre-set point). The deadly cloud of 90,000 finned darts proved one of the war's more effective anti-personnel weapons, especially since the heavier howitzer flechettes were little bothered by thick layers of foliage. In fact, the darts were able to cut down tall grass around the perimeter of camps and bases, denying enemy sapper teams valuable cover as they made occasional night-time forays. Any sabotage teams caught out in the open would be easily cut down by machine-gun teams from behind the defences.

Playing a crucial part in Vietnam's jungle firefights were the M60 machine guns, the 'Pigs'. Ugly, large and with an overtly aggressive look about it, the M60 became the pivot around which members of an infantry platoon were supposed to manoeuvre. It used belt-fed 7.62mm ammunition, identical to that used by the M14, and this gave the weapon greater range and power than the M16. And, like the M16, the M60 was a relatively recent innovation for the Army, replacing the tried and tested (but unwieldy) M1919 machine gun that saw service during the Second World War and Korea. The M60 was never a perfect design: although it had improved on weight and handling ability, it was still heavier and more awkward than other general-purpose machine guns

(GPMGs). In addition, the weapon was found to be slightly more complex than other machine guns. Such disadvantages were unfortunate, since it copied much of its layout and method of operation from the superb Nazi MG42.

Another of the weapon's drawbacks was its lack of a gas regulator, a mechanism on some machine guns that allows the firing cycle to be adjusted. On occasion this resulted in dirt or dust fouling the system and either slowing the gun down or jamming the weapon completely. Then there was the freak malfunction of the M60 when a problem with the gas system caused it to 'run away'. Essentially the gun continued to fire even after the gunner had released the trigger. During a panicked firefight, this must have been a particularly unnerving event, and grabbing a firm hold on the ammunition belt in an attempt to stop it from feeding into the runaway gun was almost the only way to stop it. The assistant gunner was responsible for the proper feeding of the ammunition belt into the M60, a job that required care since snagged or twisted belts could also cause the gun to jam. An impromptu aid to feeding sometimes came in the form of a cylindrical C-ration can spot-welded by the gunner just below the ammunition feed. This field expedient modification enabled the ammunition belt to feed smoothly over the can and into the weapon. It corrected yet another deficiency of the M60.

On a similarly mundane but practical level, continuous firing of the M60 in combat caused the barrel to reach very high temperatures and, like other GPMGs, the weapon featured a quick-change facility. This reduced the chance of a stoppage or other malfunction caused by the expanding barrel. Unfortunately the hefty bipod used by the M60 was attached to each of the spare barrels carried by the gunner and his assistant, increasing the weight each had to bear. Making life even harder for the gunners, the designers neglected to include a handle on the barrel (a standard feature of other GPMGs), making the changeover of a red-hot barrel hazardous! Instead, the M60 crews were issued with asbestos gloves that were used to protect the hands when the barrel required changing. With up to 20kg of other equipment to heave through the jungle, it is not surprising that the all-important glove often went missing. Despite these teething problems, the long (1,000m) range and telling firepower of the M60 made it almost as ubiquitous as the M16. Helicopters, APCs, trucks, jeeps and patrol boats all began sprouting M60s, each trailing golden ribbons of ammunition.

The disparity in parts and ammunition between the M60 machine gun and the M16 rifle was an issue addressed by Eugene Stoner. In an attempt to provide a uniform modular weapon system for the troops in Vietnam, he developed the Stoner 63 System. At that time unique in firearms manufacture, the system used seventeen basic units that could be rearranged and interchanged, allowing the creation of a whole new weapon in the field. The only required parts were the receiver, trigger group, return spring, bolt and piston. The interchangeability was provided by a variety of barrels, feed mechanisms mounts and buttstocks. Like the M16, the Stoner 63 used the 5.56mm round, taking advantage of the millions of these rounds being churned out by Stateside factories. From short-barrelled carbine, the M63A1 (as the US military designated it) could be modified to become either an assault rifle or a light or heavy machine gun. The gun was adaptable and revolutionary, and the concept was taken up in the late 1970s by the Austrian firm Steyr with its very similar AUG system. But the traditional forces were not especially interested in the Stoner, and the only service with which the weapon found acceptance was the Navy's élite SEAL teams. Impressed with the gun's flexibility and its tremendous ammunition options, including 30-round magazines, 90-round drums and 150-round boxes, it became the weapon of choice for individual SEALs.

The Stoner 63 System was not adopted in large numbers, and production ceased soon after the War, yet it had proved itself an efficient combat weapon. Why? It did require more maintenance than the average infantryman was used to, a fact that little troubled the highly trained Special Forces SEALs. The system also placed itself in direct competition with the M16, and the Department of Defense would not have tolerated yet another rifle change after the recent M16 débâcle. On a more technical note, it has been suggested that the Stoner, while able to fulfil many roles, was unable to match the performance of other purpose-built designs. It is an old story, that may, in part, be responsible for the Stoner's short-lived career.

While the M16s and M60s played their part in the close-range skirmishes in Vietnam, the need for more firepower intensified. Unable to discern an individual enemy soldier in the forests, grasslands or swamps, the American infantryman desired to soak the enemy area in flying bullets, shrapnel and fragments in the hope of at least hitting something. For this task hand grenades were always popular: their indiscriminate shower of lethal fragments would easily penetrate foliage. And while no gun in the US armoury could yet fire around corners, the grenade could be thrown over hard cover. But the grenade had the limited range of an overarm throw (30 to 40m) and was difficult to toss at an enemy while remaining under cover. The high-speed technological revolution soon came up with a solution to the soldier's quandary.

This was to enhance the explosive potential of the grenade. A grenade launcher was developed that could fire specially designed grenades out to a distance of 400m. The weapon was somewhat strange in appearance. One veteran has remarked that 'It looks like a rifle that has been in a bad accident.' Similar to a fat and stubby break-open shotgun, the M79 grenade launcher proved to be a useful asset to troops in Vietnam. Two members of an infantry squad, the 'grenadiers', were assigned the M79, and they wore ammunition vests filled with various types of 40mm grenade. Since the weapon weighed 3kg and required the use of both hands, many grenadiers could not carry an M16 as well and instead carried a handgun for personal protection. The 40mm grenades were not as powerful as their hand-thrown equivalents, but there existed a proliferation of useful versions, including a standard high-explosive fragmentation round and an airburst round. Others included marker smoke, illumination flare, CS ('tear') gas and multiple projectile 'buckshot' rounds. This last was extremely popular with troops setting up ambushes. Its 27 'OO' buckshot steel balls turned the M79 into a giant shotgun, with no better range but with vastly improved killing power and area effect. There were some irregular groups that even sawed off the barrel ends of their M79s to widen the lethal 'cone' of shot from the weapon.

Out to 150m, the M79 could be aimed and fired directly at a target with some degree of accuracy. Further than that, out to 400m, the explosive grenades could be lobbed in a curving arc to attack an indirect target behind cover. Essentially, the weapon became a hand-held mortar available to every infantry squad, and its more general-purpose loadings provided a useful capability. A potential danger for the grenadier was the detonation of a grenade before it reached a safe distance. To counter this, the projectiles (all except the buckshot round) had to travel at least 30m before they armed themselves. For one grenadier in the 1st Cavalry Division this proved a blessing. As he clambered aboard a Huey about to lift off on a mission, his M79 went off, firing a grenade through the thin aluminium roof of the helicopter. It passed safely between the spinning rotor blades and landed in the mud next to the pilot's door! Luckily for all aboard, the metal roof of the helicopter had slowed the grenade significantly enough so that it had travelled just less than 30m.

The only real drawback with the M79 was its all-or-nothing deployment: those using it were unable to carry an effective sidearm. Springfield Arsenal, the weapon's manufacturers, tested a highly modified variant in an attempt to counter this disadvantage. The package was called the XM148 and featured a customised M16A1 with a 40mm grenade launcher mounted beneath the gun barrel. Produced on a larger scale as the revised M203, the short-barrelled launcher enabled almost any rifleman, not just a dedicated grenadier, to bring the 40mm grenades to bear in a firefight. Owing to the shorter barrel length, range was reduced to about 350m, but this was a small price to pay for such a handy package. Again, field firepower had undergone a sudden acceleration. The new weapon system weighed around 5.7kg, somewhat heavier than a standard M16A1, but quite acceptable compared to previous rifle weights. Today, with the Vietnam experience as a benchmark, the US Army is seeking a combined weapon system that blurs the distinction between rifle and grenade launcher. This is the Objective Individual Combat Weapon programme, and calls for a 5.56mm rifle with integral 20mm capability. Weighing less than 5.45kg, the rifle component must be effective out to 500m, and the 20mm round (which will resemble a low-powered grenade) must be effective out to 1,000m. Clearly, the military are seeking to extend the M79 concept to new levels in the twenty-first century.

McNamara's Wall
The electronic revolution made an important impact on the conduct of the Vietnam War—important not because it altered the course of the war in any signifi-

cant way, or might have done so, but because it heralded a new kind of modern war. The 'computer war', with digital information and electronics playing key roles at the strategic and tactical levels, had arrived.

It had been obvious from the earliest years of US intervention that the cutting of the Ho Chi Minh Trail that acted as a communist supply route was next to impossible. The intensive use of manpower was not an option available to Secretary of Defense McNamara, and the continuous bombing operations had barely dented the North Vietnamese' ability to send supplies south. In their stead, McNamara decided to capitalise on an American asset that the communists sorely lacked—technology. The application of 'high-tech' solutions to the infiltration problem seemed to offer a method of avoiding both casualties and allegations of war crimes. The climax came at the end of 1967 when construction began on the McNamara Line, a physical barrier designed to prevent infiltration by communist forces south across the DMZ. Controversial even before it was begun, the project was suitably titled 'The Electronic Fence', 'McNamara's Wall', 'McNamara's Fairway' or just 'The Strip'. It was a monumental design that would incorporate several features of surveillance innovation. Much of this had already been tested earlier along the Ho Chi Minh Trail as it wound through the thick jungles of Laos and Cambodia.

Laos, in particular, became a testing ground for items and techniques that were at best questionable and at worst recognised as illegal by the international community. The country was officially neutral, but, as it was a sanctuary and a main highway for communist reinforcements moving south, Laos had become a major target for US bombers. These bombing raids had to remain assiduously secret since they contravened international law; but the need to strike at the heart of this vast staging post was great. As Air Force and Navy fighter-bombers streaked over Laotian jungles to unload bombs on to suspected depots, truck parks and troop units, their pilots knew that their was little chance of hitting the designated target. There were no friendly troops in the area to direct the planes, and the thick jungle canopy obscured the narrow paths and tracks that made up much of the Trail.

To combat the problem of locating and accurately hitting these targets, the Americans introduced a concept tried elsewhere in South Vietnam—Agent Orange. This was a chemical defoliant designed specifically to strip away the multi-layered jungle canopy of South-East Asia. The lush vegetation of the region was the guerrilla's main asset, or so the Pentagon had reasoned, screening both his movements and his tactical deployments. NVA units made preparations to enter the combat arena of South Vietnam while in Laos, and every effort was made to stop them from progressing any further down the Trail. Pilots from Operation 'Ranch Hand' sprayed thousands of tons of of defoliant over Laos, but the Trail's intricate network only shifted and re-formed to cut instead through virgin forest away from the barren moonscapes of defoliated land. And even defoliated forest, bare and ugly, could be crossed at night with little fear of attack from above. One answer was to dispatch ultra-secret and highly trained reconnaissance teams into Laos. These SOG Command and Control North units used indigenous tribespeople to conduct deep recon missions well behind enemy lines. Sometimes operating in tiny four- or five-man units, SOG teams provided MACV with a wealth of target opportunities and post-strike assessments. But SOG was small: the entire project may have had only 2,000 American personnel on its payroll at any one time. It was time to think big.

A shadowy Pentagon think tank, the Institute of Defense Planning, decided to maximise every technological resource in order to foil the NVA infiltration. A particularly bizarre and highly secret scheme to engineer the weather patterns over Laos was attempted. It involved 'seeding' the clouds over the region with chemicals to induce them to release their rain on to the Trail and on to the guerrillas traversing it. The forlorn hope was that the entire network could be made impassable by a year-long monsoon. A more promising project called 'Igloo White' proved more fruitful. It centred on the 'Dutch Mill' Infiltration Surveillance Center at Nakhon Phanom in Thailand and aimed to locate, and prepare, strikes and post-strike assessments on Trail targets. The range and sophistication of the high-technology equipment that was being introduced to solve the infiltration problem proved truly astonishing.

Skimming the trees, a CH-3 Jolly Green Giant helicopter would slow while a crewman in the rear cabin slid back the side door. At the right moment he would lob a two-metre-long, rocket-shaped sensor from the helicopter and watch it plunge through the tree canopy. As it hit the ground, the Spikebuoy was partially buried with just its antenna exposed. The instrument would then begin monitoring particular sound frequencies, one of which was the revving of truck engines. Potential enemy activity was picked up by communication planes circling in the area, and transmitted back to the ISC station in Thailand. A number of the relay planes were in fact Beeech QU-22B Bonanza light aircraft, specially adapted for this hazardous duty and controlled remotely (on occasion) by a pilot on the ground. Back at the ISC the data would be processed by two IBM 360-65 computers. Swift and deadly action would then be taken by fighter-bombers scrambled from one of the American air bases in the region.

Other sensors, too, were used, including the Acuobuoy, landed by parachute up in the forest canopy to monitor sounds from on high, and the ADSID (Air Delivered Seismic Intruder Detector), which became by far the most widely used of the high-tech sensor devices. Like the Spikebuoy, the ADSID was thrown manually from an aircraft and upon hitting the ground partially buried itself. But rather than listen out for certain sounds, this sensor detected seismic vibrations and was less likely to be fooled by the sounds of jungle creatures. One of the most highly advanced sensors developed later in the war specifically homed in on the ignition systems of communist trucks. In practice, the bizarre gadgets did not perform as well as expected. The entire concept, in fact, may well have been promulgated by the Institute of Defense Analysis while it was under the influence of a heady mix of optimism and blind faith in the ability of US technology to overcome any obstacle. If America could send its men into orbit, and around the moon, why could it not even *detect* (never mind destroy) a peasant army in a Third World country?

Just dropping the Trail sensors proved a serious business. Flying 'low and slow', the aircraft had a good chance of being downed by hostile ground fire, and as a result, at the end of 1967, the Navy flew in a number of its OP-2E Neptune propeller-driven planes. Both crews and aircraft had ample experience dropping maritime sensors into the ocean to detect the presence of Soviet submarines, but submarines in 1967 did not return fire on US aircraft. The NVA frequently did open up on the Neptunes with anti-aircraft cannon, and eventually the military settled on the multi-purpose F-4 Phantom to do the job. Fast, accurate and armed, the Phantom was able to launch its sensor and make a speedy evasive flight out of the area. Modified Phantom jets also conducted photo-reconnaissance which supplemented the sensor drops.

A variety of other planes carried out photo missions, and one of the war's most remarkable reconnaissance aircraft was the Teledyne-Ryan AQM-34. An unmanned drone, or remotely piloted vehicle (RPV), the AQM-34 either flew a pre-arranged course over enemy territory or was controlled directly by a remote pilot from an airborne or ground command post. Each drone carried high-specification cameras as well as a real-time TV system, and was capable of being directed from up to 240km away. At the time highly secret, only recently has the remarkable role played by the RPVs been publicised. They were carried to the combat zone under the wings of modified C-130 Hercules cargo planes and released in mid-air. After reaching their allotted sector by ramjet they were able to overfly targets as low as a few metres and return to friendly airspace at safe altitudes of up to 20,000m. On one reported mission a drone was low enough to fly beneath North Vietnamese power lines! A CH-3E Jolly Green Giant helicopter would intercept the returning RPV and snatch it out of the air as the its engine cut out and it began descending by parachute. The dangerous missions did not put a human pilot in danger, and the project was so successful that postwar development of the concept flourished. What if a warhead could be placed on board a drone? What about a nuclear warhead? This, in fact, is exactly what happened, and the direct descendants of the Vietnam drones are the Tomahawk nuclear cruise missiles used, with conventional warheads, against Iraq in 1991.

The strategy of electronic interdiction required that the entire South Vietnamese border should be made secure against communist infiltration. With almost every tree and bush in Laos now sprouting ADSID and Spikebuoy aerials, McNamara turned to the vulnerable Demilitarised Zone separating North and South Vietnam. Robert Fisher, of Harvard Law School, had suggested the idea of a physical barrier across this narrow neck of land to McNamara, and the Secretary of Defense seized upon the idea with some interest. On 7 September 1967 he announced that the audacious plan was already under way, but leading military experts, including General Westmoreland and Admiral Sharp, considered the concept wasteful, irrelevant and tactically unsound. The McNamara Line, as it was termed in the press, would utilise some of the most advanced technology available to the US military. Some of the designs were so radical that they were still on the drawing board. In essence, it was hoped that such a wall would free large formations of men who could be used to prevent NVA penetration further west, or carry out search-and-destroy missions in South Vietnam.

Walls built for the purposes of frontier defence have a long and venerable history, from the Great Wall of China and Hadrian's Wall to the Maginot Line. There have been more recent and more relevant successes, such as the little known Morice Line built by the French during the Algerian War. Designed, like the McNamara Line, to prevent guerrilla infiltration, the defences were quite successful. But the war in Vietnam was different. Its very name was misleading: properly titled the Second *Indo-China* War, it involved Cambodia, Laos and Vietnam. And as Laos remained stubbornly neutral, the electronic wall had suddenly and bizarrely to end 90km from the coast. Communist units and supplies were able to continue pouring south down the Ho Chi Minh Trail by shifting the route further to the west.

The Line was actually designed as a layered zone of defences 18km deep with watch-towers, searchlights, barbed wire fences, minefields and defoliated free-fire artillery zones. Proposals on the table for the construction of the minefields alone were mind-boggling. Mines being considered for the Line ranged from the traditional anti-personnel mine to Claymore directional mines, tiny cloth-covered Gravel mines, and even smaller 'button bomblets' that would cause injury but rarely death. It was calculated that over half a billion of these latter two types would be required—a staggering number, and at a staggering cost.

Surveillance across the entire Line was to be dense and comprehensive, and much of the existing sensor technology already developed was to be employed. Further refinements were added that even allowed Viet Cong conversations in the area to be monitored. Any suspicious sounds would initiate an immediate air strike from circling jets and helicopter gunships. Much of this was more hopeful than realistic, with extravagant and ingenious plans that even included fitting pigeons with explosives and teaching them to land on communist trucks. Equally quixotic was the idea of wiring dormant fleas with electrodes and sowing them over the region. As they detected the presence of humans, the fleas would become agitated, transmitting this fact back to US headquarters. Neither plan was anything more than a fantasy, and the McNamara Line, although construction was initiated, always remained such.

The sheer numerical density of seismic and acoustic sensors across the McNamara Line and dropped on likely Trail routes through Laos should really have helped the interdiction effort. But with the massive build-up and influx of communist troops into South Vietnam at the beginning of 1968, the amazing technological 'fixes' had hardly seemed to have made much of a difference. It is probable that more air strikes were conducted against jungle animals crashing through the trees than against actual NVA units. With tens of thousands of communist troops massing for attacks on the Marine base at Khe Sanh and deploying *south* of both the DMZ and the fledgeling McNamara Line, the entire theory of electronic defence was discredited. Construction work on the McNamara Line was abandoned, and the small portion actually in operation was closed down. The Secretary of Defense's grand solution was a tactical cul-de-sac, and a metaphor of the war in general. In theory, technology, in vast amounts and at great expense, could triumph over one of the most backward people on Earth. But McNamara's Wall, like McNamara's War, was fatally flawed, the victim of unrestrained overconfidence and ignorance of the limitations of technology pitted against determination.

Fighting the Future War

But the science fiction war still continued apace. At about the same time as the military were giving up on the Line, several infantry units were receiving a small number of a new portable chemical sensors for use in the field. Officially designated the XM2E63 but nicknamed the 'people-sniffer', this backpack-carried device was designed specifically to 'sniff out' the airborne particles given off by humans. In a war where the enemy fought an invisible battle and in which Americans were killed by, and returned fire on, communist forces they could never see, the people-sniffer looked like a brilliant tactical innovation. When carried aboard a patrolling UH-1 helicopter, the needle on the sniffer's dial would jump as it detected the airborne traces of human sweat and urine. In response, the helicopter was supposed to turn into the wind and locate the enemy with the sniffer, visually or by coming under fire. Heavy firepower would then be brought to bear to destroy the communist troops.

However, in practice the concept was imperfect. The test units found themselves on one continuous wild goose chase, with lead after lead proving to be no more than women, children, friendly forces and the ubiquitous water buffalo. The device was unable to discern between friend and foe, or even between animal and human. In the Antarctic wastes, in a war between two military forces, the people-sniffer would perhaps have proved of some use, although without much cover in that environment even that is doubtful: in a lush, tropical environment filled with wild and domesticated creatures, and in a guerrilla war where the fight is for the invisible domination of the populace by a chameleon-like enemy, it was next to useless. The gadget again seemed to sum up the US attitude to the conduct of the war: technology had all the answers, but, unless used with careful discrimination, it could become a dangerous liability.

Ironically, the people-sniffer was intended to replace a method of detecting Viet Cong that had been in use in Vietnam since 1963. Tracker dogs were a low-tech triumph in a high-tech war, and, organised into Combat Tracker Platoons, they made themselves invaluable to the infantrymen they served alongside. The discovery of bunker or tunnel complexes, or the sudden retreat of the enemy into thick undergrowth, was often followed by a call for an individual Combat Tracker Team (five men and a single dog, usually a labrador retriever). Tracker dogs followed the ground scents and blood trails of fleeing Viet Cong. German shepherd dogs were also employed, mainly as scout dogs in dedicated Scout Dog Platoons. These were used to provide flank and point security for a patrolling American unit. Dogs in this role were 'alerted' to sounds and airborne scents, allowing the team members to discover mines, bunkers, arms caches and even enemy ambushes. In good conditions they were able to detect groups of concealed people many hundreds of metres away.

When the people-sniffer was undergoing trials in the United States, it was tested alongside two scout dog teams at Fort Benning, Georgia. The trials were conducted over a period of six to eight weeks, and in almost every case the dogs detected planted decoys first, at ranges in excess of 300m. The people-sniffer operator (a sergeant) was reluctant to verify this. Further tests against 'live' targets were then conducted at Eglin Air Force Base in Florida. Again the scout dogs outstripped the capabilities of the device, on one occasion alerting to human scent at a range of over 1,000m! With doubts, the people-sniffer operator accompanied the dog teams as they checked out the alert. At 300m the dogs visually detected the objective, while the device had only just begun to register a target. It proved to be a group of Rangers waiting in a vehicle, *outside* the specified training area!

There was a feeling amongst combat units that the people-sniffer was in essence an expensive toy that *might* work. However, individual soldiers would much prefer to carry more ammunition, grenades, mines and flares they knew *would* work and would give them a fighting chance when it came to combat. While the device earned the mistrust of troops that encountered it, the scout and tracker dogs were, in comparison, well liked and respected by almost every unit that encountered them. In part this must be put down to the dogs' unrivalled position as 'man's best friend', but primarily to their proven track record out in the field.

Not all the experimental devices introduced into the US inventory proved as unpopular as the people-sniffer. It could be argued from the modern-day perspective that the seemingly endless array of technological gadgets that continually preoccupied the Pentagon's 'top men' were costly in the extreme. The budget for 'Igloo White' alone amounted to $1.7 billion from 1966 to 1971, money that could perhaps have been more fruitfully poured into more traditional methods of making war. As a force enters the arena of combat, however, serious deficiencies are commonly and unexpectedly discovered, requiring sudden and energetic programmes of development to try to make up the shortfall. As in the previous wars of this century, technological experimentation accelerated, fuelled by both the need for a solution and the existence of a proving ground in which to test the weaponry of the *next* war. Occasionally such experimentation produces a weapon that will revolutionise the post-war battlefield but at the time is considered a madcap invention wasting valuable resources. Both the tank in the First World War and the assault rifle in the Second are examples of this kind of unforeseen development.

There were a number of 'high-tech' innovations amongst the bizarre electronic devices tested in Vietnam, and some of these would later bear fruit in America's next major conflict, the Gulf War. Rather than try to replace the fighting man with electronic wizardry as had been attempted along the Ho Chi Minh Trail, these developments were designed to enhance the infantryman's effectiveness in battle. Of great importance was the introduction of the Starlight Scope. It was an aphorism that 'Charlie owned the night', and while US troops conducted grand operations, combat sweeps and patrols by day, the VC lay low. Like nocturnal hunters, the communists moved by night, deployed their forces, disengaged and laid siege to American camps. While the darkness seemed to provide freedom for the enemy, it only inhibited and crippled the Americans. Consequently, an idea originating in the laboratories of Nazi Germany was tested out on night ambushes, on camp perimeters and on interdiction flights over the Trail. The ability to see in the dark became a reality in the Vietnam War.

Radar, around since the late 1930s and more commonly used in the tracking of aircraft, was deployed in a more mobile form that was able to detect vehicles out to 10,000m and personnel out to 5,000m. Unfortunately the AN/PPS-5 was of little use when forced to pick out individual targets from a mass of ground clutter, including trees and rough ground. One sensor able to detect targets in the inky black of night was the tripod-mounted AN/TVS-4, a high-powered light intensification device that amplified available light (from stars or the moon) up to 40,000 times. It had a range of 1,200m and became an excellent asset to the field defences of military encampments, allowing the defenders to spot VC infiltrators as they approached the outer wire. A smaller version sometimes allocated to infantry squads for ambush duty was the AN/PVS-2, more commonly known as the Starlight Scope. Resembling a very large telescopic sight, the device was designed to be mounted on an M14 or M16 and gave the rifleman the ability to detect, aim and fire at a target in almost total darkness. The range of the scope was limited to 400m, roughly the effective range of the M16 it was attached to. Used at night by soldiers on watch, the Starlight Scope was portable enough to be carried and used on its own, allowing the surrounding area to be scanned constantly for signs of enemy activity.

If the acquisition of targets was difficult for American troops on the ground, it was immeasurably more problematic for aircraft flying high above the jungle canopy. While 'Igloo White' had pioneered the use of seismic and acoustic sensors on the Trail, more direct action was being initiated by the Air Force in the form of the AC-130 Spectre gunship. Able to detect and attack lone trucks moving through thick jungle under cover of darkness, the gunships had the advantage of being able to provide an immediate on-the-spot assessment. This was something that the latent sensors lacked. The AC-130 was yet another variant of the Lockheed C-130 Hercules, and a considerable improvement regarding the speed and range of its doughty predecessor, the Second World War-era AC-47 Spooky gunship. The Spectre was finished in an an ominous all-black colour scheme and its armament included 7.62mm and 20mm six-barrelled Gatling guns, 40mm Bofors guns and even, in some versions, an aerial 105mm howitzer. These weapons were all on side-facing mountings on the port side of the aircraft and were aimed by the pilot. He put the gunship into a left bank and orbited the enemy position as the destructive arsenal poured its deadly fire down on to the target. The 7.62mm miniguns (so-called because they were scaled-down versions of the 20mm Vulcan cannon) were capable of firing 6,000 rounds a minute. The sight of a gunship pouring its torrent of neon-red tracer on to a position, combined with the chainsaw-like groan of the electrically driven miniguns was purported to strike terror into heart of communist troops.

To detect individual trucks on their journey through Laos down the Trail, the Spectre was fitted with a bewildering array of high-tech electronics. These included light intensification devices, forward-looking infra-red (FLIR), AN/ASD-5 direction-finding radar, searchlights and flares. Infra-red was an invaluable tool on these jungle sorties, being able to see through concealing vegetation and camouflage and pinpoint the heat emissions of truck engines. The kill ratios of these gunships and other aircraft fitted with night interdiction equipment (including a squadron of B-57 Canberra light bombers) was very high. Virtually all the enemy vehicles detected by the roving aircraft were also destroyed by them. Only in the Vietnam War could such an improbable weapon as the fixed-wing gunship acquit itself so well. The project took propeller-driven cargo planes and stuffed them with the very latest in rapid-firing electric cannon and night-vision detection systems. It then sent them over hostile jungle at the dead of night to locate and destroy individual trucks by slowly circling above them. It was a weapon system that should not have worked, and the perplexing marriage of overwhelming firepower and precision acquisition devices was one unique in modern warfare.

Some critics point to the utter futility of American high technology in a low-technology war and are adamant that it was a reliance on this hardware that became the military's greatest weakness. Computers for collating information, lasers for designating targets, radios and spy planes, flame-throwers, defoliants, hovercraft and people-sniffers were just a tiny part of the massive industrial effort to isolate the Viet Cong power base. In truth, however, the technology that was made available to the American military was its only real asset, whatever the fearful pitfalls seemed to be. Without a confident, determined and highly aggressive armed force with which to match the VC, without the support and trust of the local peasantry, and without the essential experience in sub-tropical guerrilla warfare, a surfeit of technology was America's greatest hope. Operating such equipment in what was effectively a technological vacuum became a fine balancing act between the competent use of technology and firepower and an unfettered reliance on it to the exclusion of all other forms of warfare. At times the scales were to tip wildly off balance.

Chapter 5

A NEW KIND OF WAR

'**I** never thought it would go on like this. I didn't think these people had the capacity to fight this way . . . to take this punishment.' Robert McNamara was showing his surprise and frustration at the tenacity of an enemy that just refused to stop fighting, despite constant defeat on the battlefield. It is a little disputed fact that the North Vietnamese Army and the Viet Cong irregulars lost virtually every battlefield encounter against American forces. And yet the popular mood in America forced the US military to abandon its efforts there because of the pervasive feeling that the war was being lost. The problem facing both the military in Vietnam and the populace at home was that no real definitions of 'win' or 'lose' had been formulated. Waging war against Nazi Germany, the victory conditions had been obvious and clearly defined: the occupation of Germany, including Berlin, and the abolition of the Nazi hierarchy. The armed forces directed themselves to this aim, and the civilians supporting the war effort were able to measure successes against it. Vietnam was to be different.

The Second World War saw America adopt the strategic offensive, that is, the invasion of the Axis countries, the destruction of their armed forces and the occupation of their capitals. In Vietnam, it was the North Vietnamese Army that was on the strategic offensive, with its eyes on Saigon and South Vietnam. The American and allied forces were on the strategic defensive in Indo-China, just as they had been in Korea. And, like Korea, such an approach could end only in stalemate. The Korean War had ended for the American military in 1953 by virtue of the armistice agreement signed that year. It divided North from South and formalised an end to the invasion. The Vietnam War ended for America with the 1973 Paris Accords in exactly the same way. A policy of strategic defence cannot be won, but it can be lost. Counter-insurgency became the central mechanism by which the American strategic defensive was to be waged, and it had been introduced under the auspices of the Kennedy administration.

'The best form of defence is offence' is a truism, and it was one that applied wholeheartedly to the American situation in Vietnam. Clearly, the answer to South Vietnam's precarious position would have been to strike hard against North Vietnam and reunite Vietnam under the anti-communist Diem government. But how could Washington perpetrate the very act—the violent unification of Vietnam—that it was so staunchly opposed to? In any event, the sudden rise of communist-inspired 'wars of national liberation' had enabled the theory of counter-insurgency to take root in Washington, and eventually, under President Kennedy, to flourish. Hard and merciless aggression against the enemy state supporting the insurgency was seen as a political nightmare and almost out of date in the post-war atomic age. As we have seen in Chapter 2, the option to invade or destroy North Vietnam was just not available to Kennedy, to Johnson or to the latter's successor, Nixon. Everything in Vietnam was being viewed through the distorting lens of the Cold War, and against the fear of atomic holocaust. Counter-insurgency seemed to be a politically friendly strategy designed to win the allegiance of a people without such Cold War implications. According to General Maxwell Taylor, Kennedy's military adviser and later Johnson's ambassador to Vietnam, America was not directing its efforts at trying to 'defeat' North Vietnam, rather it was attempting 'to cause them to mend their ways'. Although an overall plan for victory had not been formulated, and never would be, one thing was certain: South Vietnam could not be allowed not fall. Every President from Truman to Nixon did the barest minimum to prevent the capitulation of South Vietnam. There was little serious talk of 'winning', even in the very earliest days of intervention. And, following McNamara's resignation in 1968, Clark Clifford took up the post of Secretary of Defense and said, 'It was startling to me to find out that we had no military plan to win the war'—and this at the very height of America's commitment to the conflict!

A Many-Sided War

Almost everyone, observers and participants alike, found it difficult to distinguish exactly what *kind* of war was being fought. MAAG had been preparing for a conventional cross-border invasion by communist infantry and tanks, while Westmoreland later considered that 'the communists in Vietnam are waging a classic revolutionary war'. In fact, neither method of warfare was to dominate the conflict: the Americans, along with their allies, found themselves in what General Giap called a 'many-sided war'—a war essentially without the front lines of a conventional invasion, but one lacking the insular and limited power base of an internal revolution. And for the integrity of the South to be guarded, both of these conflicts had to be addressed, fought and won. The destruction of the large NVA units staging through Laos and Cambodia into South Vietnam could not be completed without the pacification and support of the South Vietnamese people. Conversely, the weeding out and defeat of the Viet Cong guerrillas in the South could not be successful until the military might of North Vietnam was somehow removed from the equation. It was this quandary that essentially dislocated the American war effort.

Like the French *Maquis* resistance groups fighting the Nazi occupation forces, the Viet Cong were an adjunct to the central war effort, which was the planned invasion. Ho Chi Minh had never intended the Viet Cong to be the military or political force that would topple the Saigon regime and install its own communist government in the South. From 1954 onwards the overriding aim had been the reunification of South Vietnam with, and by, the North. The Viet Cong were in place to foment instability, to act against the allies behind the lines and to pave a way for the communist blitzkrieg. But such a distinction was difficult to discern at the time.

This dual conflict proved to be the central paradox to the Vietnam War and provided the media with the images that would eventually produce a collapse of support for the entire effort. To save South Vietnam, America had first to destroy it. This statement may sound absurd, but it is based on the grim reality of the situation. On the one hand, the people had to be protected from communist aggression and political domination; on the other, massed concentrations of North Vietnamese had to be confronted and destroyed on the battlefield. Since the stealthy infiltration of enemy units directly into the forests and rice paddies of the South often blended hostile forces with friendly non-combatants, destruction frequently raged around the villages and hamlets of the rural population. For the NVA and the main-force Viet Cong, the villagers were bait, prize and cover in a war that shifted emphasis from insurgency to conventional conflict and back again.

One junior officer, reporting on a completed operation in 1968, declared: 'We had to destroy the village to save it!' American soldiers fighting the Vietnam War had the contradictory mission of aid and protection as well as death and destruction. Civic action and rural pacification programmes went hand in hand with 'search-and-destroy' operations and 'free-fire zones'. Construction, medical aid and agricultural development were carried out in one province whilst, in the next, villages were being razed, people relocated and the vegetation defoliated. Some were uncomfortable with this dark paradox, not least the soldiers themselves. One of the Green Beret medics has since said that while he could rationalise the shooting and the killing, he was never able to feel comfortable with it. But then civic action had been perfected almost to an art form by these irregular troops. Back home, newsreel footage of GIs setting Vietnamese hooches on fire with zippo lighters caused a storm of protest. Defeating a unit of Viet Cong with overwhelming firepower was on occasion a step forwards and (if the enemy had used a friendly village as cover) a simultaneous step backwards in the other war'. Robert McNamara soon became aware of the 'sobering, frustrating, tormenting limitations of military operations in Vietnam'.

Counter-insurgency experts, including Sir Robert Thompson (whose advice McNamara had sought), noted that all successful insurgencies (wars of revolution) had depended on external help. The Ho Chi Minh Trail provided a constant stream of new recruits, ammunition, supplies, training cadres and orders for the Viet Cong, and enabled the North to field fully equipped army divisions south of the DMZ. Meanwhile, safe havens across the border in the jungle-clad mountains of Laos and Cambodia allowed the communists to rest, regroup and rearm with little threat from the US war machine. Training camps, hospitals, command centres and supply dumps dotted the countryside west of the South Vietnamese border. If the flow of men and material from both the Trail and these sanctuaries could somehow be blocked, then the invasion could effectively be hamstrung. It would also hurt the guerrilla war being waged at the village level, but it would not win it. The native insurgency movement could remain active and antagonistic even without help from Hanoi. The flames of insurgency had to be tackled, not just the foreign power that fanned them.

But, as we have seen in Chapter 4, cutting the Trail was to be an insurmountable task. Lyndon Johnson and Robert McNamara had decreed that there be no deployment of ground forces into the Cambodian sanctuaries or across the Ho Chi Minh Trail. Both nations held a tentatively neutral position, and that could not be jeopardised. So the theory went. However, such an understanding did not prevent North Vietnam from deploying troops into these regions. Hanoi took advantage of the neutrality of the two nations and exploited the American fear of widening the war. In truth, the net of the Vietnam War had been cast far across Indo-China, with US forces unable to fight but a portion of that war. The American build-up in South Vietnam seemed, if not wholly ignorant of, then at least short-sighted towards, the vast scale of the conflict to which it had committed itself.

Consider the geography of South-East Asia. South Vietnam lay at the extreme south-east tip of the Indo-Chinese subcontinent. The south and east were washed by the South China Sea; to the north, the communist state of North Vietnam pushed troops doggedly south; to the west and north-west lay Laos and Cambodia. Both these neutral countries acted as communist base areas for attacks across the entire length of South Vietnam. Beyond Cambodia lay Thailand, an ally and a source of friendly air space and air bases. But the neutral 'sandwich' precluded any ground deployments from Thailand into the Trail networks or the sanctuaries. And so, as Lieutenant-General Dave R. Palmer once remarked, the American military waited for the communist onslaught like a boxer in his ring. As a communist offensive approached, the boxer delivered his riposte, sending the enemy reeling back to his sanctuaries. Ever conscious of a lesser enemy (the VC) striking from behind at unexpected moments, the boxer had either to bloody the enemy's nose so hard that he would back off from the fight altogether or to wear him down by sheer endurance. The first had been attempted by 'Rolling Thunder'—and failed. Hanoi would suffer any loss, however great. The Vietnam War was to be a fight to the last round, a war of attrition.

Salt into the Sea

North Vietnam had the stamina to continue the fight indefinitely, but did Lyndon B. Johnson have the political resolution to match it? Although combat losses on the allied side were mounting, the communists' losses were reaching frightening levels (perhaps 50,000 deaths in 1966, roughly equal to the total American casualty figure for the entire decade-long war). But Ho Chi Minh had a firm grip over his country's determination to prosecute the war in the South. The higher the casualty rate, the more troops were infiltrated to make up the loss. This 'strategy', although crude in the extreme, depended on sending more men down the Trail than could be killed by the Americans and the ARVN. A war of attrition favours the combatant with more men to expend, and with a greater willingness to expend them. In addition, it favours the long term and precludes a quick and easy victory. It was unlikely that Washington and the American people would wed themselves to this strategy with the great costs that it involved. And General Giap knew this. He had publicly boasted that America would need to commit 10 million troops to South-East Asia to prevent the fall of South Vietnam. This led him to comment that 'Another fifty thousand American troops is like throwing salt into the sea!' Both sides were fatalistic about the continuing escalation.

Trying to prevent the infiltration of communist forces into South Vietnam down the Ho Chi Minh Trail by attempting to kill each and every soldier would be a difficult task, a contest of firepower versus manpower. But could a war be won like this? It was like trying to soak up the water from a tap with a sponge. In the short term the water can be mopped up, but the tap is still flowing. How big was the American sponge going to get? Desperately required was a mechanism for turning off the tap for good. The geographical shape of Vietnam, resembling an hourglass with its painfully thin waist at the DMZ, did not go unnoticed by some journalists. Like an hourglass, the countless grains of sand in the north filtered remorselessly down into the South. McNamara and Westmoreland concurred on the policy of attrition currently being pursued. The Secretary of Defense had already displayed his frustration at the hopelessness of the bombing campaign against North Vietnam. Diplomacy provided only a way out of the war for Ho Chi Minh, which meant that any attempt at victory rested with Westmoreland. He saw attrition as the unequivocal answer, and vowed to 'go on bleeding them until Hanoi wakes up . . .'

Since the war had no interest in territory as such, the 'body count' became a popular measure of success. One could not measure loss or gain by how close allied forces were to Hanoi, only by some ephemeral measurement of halting 'communist influence'. Counts of enemy corpses on the battlefield were only one of the ways in which this measurement was attempted. Others were equally bizarre, equally vague. How many refugees were being created? How many roads were 'open'? How many communists were being brought over to the allied camp? What number of villages were under communist control? How many enemy weapons had been recovered? The body count stuck as the yardstick by which progress was measured. After firefights in the bush, commanders would send out patrols to locate and count enemy dead. These dead would often be young men, sometimes older men, women, even children. Who were they? Had they been part of the enemy unit, refugees, or just farmers hiding out? Civilian casualties had been inevitable from the very start of offensive operations against the insurgency. But as the body count grew higher, some of the unfortunate civilian casualties were subsumed within this total. For field commanders, this had a two-fold benefit: the civilian deaths could be glossed over as legitimate enemy kills, and the body count could be increased.

The grail being sought was the 'cross-over point', a point in the ground war when communist losses by death, wounding and defection exceeded the deployment of these forces down the Ho Chi Minh Trail. Robert Komer, the President's pacification expert, had concluded by the start of 1967 that this point had been reached, spurring him to reflect that America was at last 'winning' the war in Vietnam.

Body counts appeared on military press conference charts and on nightly news broadcasts. They were juggled and tabulated, sorted and reconstituted in an attempt to analyse the Vietnam War through numerology. And all these figures flowed upwards to one man—Robert McNamara. He had already used the number of aircraft sorties to measure the success of 'Rolling Thunder', and believed that 'things you can count, you ought to count'. Body counts, however, were, like sortie numbers, patently irrelevant to the overall war effort. Yet a huge expenditure of money, manpower and time was made in their name. One action, Operation 'Macon', could boast a body count of only 500 after a combat sweep lasting more than 100 days. Since promotions, decorations, out-of-area leave and preferential treatment for the unit in the supply line all depended on the body count, it was inevitable that they would, at times, become exaggerated. There were no auditors in the field to verify a unit's count. Large counts made up of dead bodies, whatever their alignment, were sought after by Washington. This made the position of VC and NVA prisoners in the field highly precarious. What incentive did company commanders have for trying to pass them back to the rear? One more corpse could sometimes provide valuable kudos for a unit.

Adding to the confusion was the fact that the communists would make serious attempts to remove their casualties from the battlefield as they retreated, sometimes providing the Americans with *no* bodies to count. To help units calculate the number of NVA or Viet Cong casualties, the Pentagon issued guidelines that instructed them to assume 30 more enemy dead (also disabled or severely injured) for every 100 dead counted after the battle. This system made it easy to exaggerate figures and its misuse was almost guaranteed. Westmoreland himself was forced to accept that the body counts 'were somewhat overdone'.

Major-General Julian J. Ewell was one of those commanders who took the body count very seriously, and his units in the 9th Infantry Division were forced to chase the count to the exclusion of almost all other concerns. He even rated his subordinate commanders on their body count tally and regularly set them quotas to meet. The division was to boast an unrivalled number of enemy kills. But just what percentage of this grand body count was actually made up of communist insurgents was hotly disputed, since the 9th's recovery of weapons following combat incidents was far lower than its alleged kills—almost disturbingly so.

Right, top: *Montagnard* tribesmen returning to Bu Prang Special Forces camp following a patrol in 1970. Despite the degeneration of the CIDG project by this time, its troops (led as they were by Green Berets, as here) remained some of the most highly motivated of the War. (IWM)

Right, centre: US Special Forces patrol down-river following an attack on their camp at My Phuc Tay in 1967. Few wars have witnessed such a proliferation of élite units, and the Army's Special Forces Groups were some of the best. Engaged in work ranging from training local Vietnamese irregulars to conducting cross-border raids and long-range reconnaissance missions, Special Forces 'Green Berets' operated successfully throughout the entire combat zone. (IWM)

Right, bottom: The F-105 Thunderchief, or 'Thud', was designed with a nuclear capability but the Vietnam War up-ended the theory. Throughout the conflict F-105s flew extremely dangerous missions into North Vietnam, dropping conventional bombs as part of 'Rolling Thunder'. (Via Andy Evans)

Above: Phantom pilots had clamoured for a version of the F-4 that carried a cannon since at first the aircraft was armed only with air-to-air missiles. In late 1968 the cannon-armed F-4E, seen here in Vietnam disruptive camouflage, made its operational début in South-East Asia. (Via Andy Evans)

Below: This M48A3 tank is stuck firmly in the mud during an operation in mid-1968. Such scenes reinforced the view that Vietnam was not 'tank country', but in fact tanks and APCs proved to be valuable firepower assets, pinning down Viet Cong while airmobile infantry manoeuvred into position. (IWM)

Right, top: A UH-1 Huey helicopter armed with door-mounted M60D machine guns. The UH-1 was widely used by the US Army for troop transport. It would revolutionise the conduct of the Vietnam War and provide the conflict with yet another label—the 'Helicopter War'. (Via Andy Evans)

Right, centre: One of the Army's AH-1 Cobra helicopter gunships armed with folding-fin rocket pods and a chin-mounted Minigun. Flights of vulnerable UH-1 Hueys benefited immensely from the Cobra's speed, agility and firepower, so much so that a version of this ageing 'chopper' is still in production today. (Via Andy Evans)

Right, bottom: Vietnam overturned established military thinking. Here M113 APCs open fire on a tree-line to provoke an enemy response. Rather than disgorge infantry who would advance into battle, the APCs are operating as light tanks. Note the M2HB and M60 machine guns (and improvised shields), as well as the M16s that litter the deck. (IWM)

Above: M16 assault rifles, here being offered for inspection by ARVN troops in 1971. After a long period of testing and fault-finding, the M16 eventually became the favoured sidearm of US soldiers, and later of the South Vietnamese. Despite its troubled beginnings, the rifle has become one of the most successful in history. (IWM)

Right: A US infantryman with his belt-fed M60 machine gun. Although the weapon was derived in part from the excellent Nazi MG 42, the M60 was far from perfect. Here the soldier has spot-welded a C-ration tin below the belt feed to smooth its passage and prevent snagging. (IWM)

Right, top: Providing unprecedented defensive firepower, the M21 Minigun appeared on the door mounts of UH-1 helicopters throughout the combat zone. A six-barrelled, electrically driven rotary machine gun, it could fire up to six thousand 7.62mm bullets per minute!. Variants appeared on APCs, on patrol boats and in aircraft. (Via Andy Evans)

Right, centre: Clashing head-on with the rice-paddy, punji-stick war in Vietnam was sophisticated technology such as this DC-130 Hercules and its underwing Ryan Firebee drones. The drones were remotely controlled from the Hercules director plane and flown over North Vietnam on the most hazardous photo-recon missions. (Via Andy Evans)

Right, bottom: A most unusual war-plane, the AC-130H version of the Hercules was a propeller-driven, fixed-wing gunship that flew hazardous truck-killing missions over the Ho Chi Minh Trail. Each gunship was packed with an array of sophisticated electronics and rapid-fire Miniguns. (Via Andy Evans)

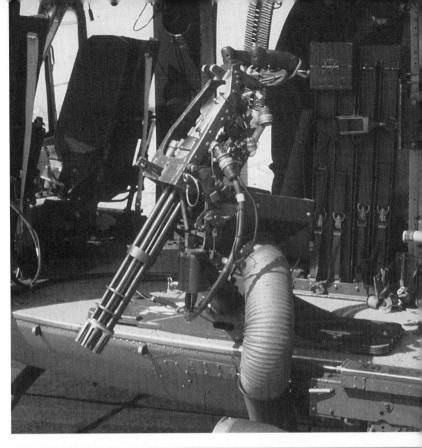

Left, top: The reality of the Vietnam War—despite the later Hollywood gloss—was a painful and exhausting slog through waterlogged paddy fields, through mud, relentless jungle and razor-sharp elephant grass. This ordeal was dedicated to the location of enemy units for destruction by artillery or air strike. It was search . . . (IWM)

Left, centre: . . . and destroy! Vietnam showed the effectiveness of artillery as a 'destructive force' after infantry patrols had first located the elusive enemy. Here a 175mm SP gun blasts communist targets many kilometres distant. (IWM)

Left, bottom: Coming to typify the Americans' use of overwhelming force, the B-52D Stratfortress blasted communist strongholds across South-East Asia during the War. The B-52 carried a staggering 30 tons of bombs, which was enough to obliterate a village, a patch of enemy-held forest or even (as one story related) a lone jungle sniper. (Via Andy Evans)

Right, top: Commun-ist sympathisers or frightened South Vietnamese civilians? If identifying the Viet Cong guerrillas was hard enough, it was an even more difficult task to avoid disrupt-ing, injuring or killing the civilians amongst whom they hid. These children are watching members of the 1st Cavalry search their village, An Khe, in 1965. (IWM)

Right, centre: Not Vietnam but Malaya, 1958: British soldiers pose for the camera after an ambush at the Tengham rubber plantation. Numerous successful strategies employed against the communists in Malaya were tried in Vietnam, but they were unable to overcome the startling differences in population, geography and enemy strategy. (Author's collection)

Right, bottom: In early 1968 the beleaguered Marine base at Khe Sanh depended on its survival for a con-tinuous supply of food and ammunition. Airdrops of both from a steady stream of C-130 Hercules (of the type shown here) kept the firebase open and defeat at arm's length. (Via Andy Evans)

Left, upper: Agent Orange defoliant was sprayed almost exclusively from C-123 Providers. Capacious yet nimble, these aircraft were also used extensively to resupply the beseiged Marine base at Khe Sanh. (Via Andy Evans)

Left, lower: A soldier enjoys the surf at Vung Tau, a popular R&R destination close to Saigon. Other amenities were also on offer, and the sharp contrast between US-style leisure and deadly jungle fighting seriously undermined US troop morale in Vietnam. (IWM)

Below: The HH-53 'Super Jolly' was a powerful combat rescue helicopter that boasted armour protection, up to three door-mounted Mini-guns and an in-flight refuelling probe for long-duration missions. For the US Air Force, it became the principal method of retrieving airmen shot down behind enemy lines. (Via Andy Evans)

The media regularly questioned the veracity of the figures when it became common knowledge that many units were inflating their totals, but General Westmoreland stuck by the figures that he had. In 1982 a CBS documentary accused the General of understating enemy strengths during the war in order more readily to illustrate US progress. During the ensuing libel case, Robert McNamara (then working for the World Bank) testified on Westmoreland's behalf. An out-of-court settlement followed.

The measurement of the war in raw kills further reduced the 'credibility gap' between Washington and the people, a gap that had widened at each intensification of the war. As the war grew ever costlier and larger in scale, MACV planned more and more operations specifically designed to kill communists rather than achieve any tactical victory. And as a Special Forces Captain once remarked: 'Good tactics are evidenced by a large number of enemy dead . . .' These operations would use firepower and mobility in unprecedented manoeuvres that would trap large numbers of communist insurgents in 'killing zones' for destruction. Names like 'Hawthorne', 'Masher' (later termed 'White Wing' to curb the operation's aggressive-sounding title), 'Prairie', 'Hastings', 'Cedar Falls' and 'Junction City' all aimed to find VC and NVA and kill them. Territory only mattered when it had a bearing on where the actual decimation of the communist forces would take place. The high command's seeming contempt for territory that had been fiercely won, often at great a cost to a unit, rankled with troops in the field. Following Operation 'Junction City', for example, it was impossible in practice to sustain a military presence in the infamous War Zone C, and, following the American withdrawal from the region, the communists moved straight back in.

Similarly, Operation 'Apache Snow' began in May 1969 with the intention of clearing the A Shau valley of deeply entrenched enemy forces. The valley was a main conduit for the communists from Laos into South Vietnam, and the source of trouble for many years. As allied forces, made up of the 101st Airborne Division and elements of the 9th Marines and the 3rd ARVN Regiment, swept into the area, the communists prepared to defend their main position. This was to be a mountain riddled with bunkers, tunnels and other fortifications, called by the Vietnamese 'Ap Bia', by the US high command 'Hill 937' and by the troops assigned to assault it 'Hamburger Hill'. That last was a name given with good reason. The enemy were well dug in and prepared to defend every metre of the mountain. American casualties spiralled higher as repeated assaults failed to break the communists. Lack of cover, a stubbornly entrenched enemy, an unfortunate incident of 'friendly fire' and a rainstorm that turned the mountainside into a mudslide tested American morale to the limit. Once on the summit with the final few bunkers taken care of, with 80 US dead and hundreds of seriously wounded to be evacuated, the soldiers of the 101st wondered whether the prize had been worth the fight. After the remaining bunkers had been cleared and demolished the division was lifted out of the area and Hill 937 was abandoned. Few saw the irony of such a redeployment. The cost had been high, the struggle hellish, and—the GIs asked—for what? Senator Edward Kennedy was one of the vociferous critics of 'Apache Snow', calling it 'senseless and irresponsible'. Communists had been killed, bunkers cleared and weapons retrieved but the mountain had been abandoned immediately afterwards, allowing the enemy (if it so chose) to move straight back in.

The same story was told across South Vietnam. In fact the greatest siege of the war, at Khe Sanh in early 1968, the year before Hamburger Hill, would become an outstanding testament to the American disregard for territorial gains. Some 6,000 men, mainly US Marines, were defending the Khe Sanh fire base and its airstrip against a combined North Vietnamese force of perhaps 35,000 men. For the duration of the intense 77-day siege, B-52 bombers and an armada of other assorted aircraft poured a seemingly unending cascade of bombs (Operation 'Niagara') on top of the communist attackers. By the time the siege had been lifted on 6 April, well over 75,000 tons of high explosives and napalm had been dropped on the Khe Sanh perimeter. Within two months, after various mopping-up operations had been conducted in the surrounding valleys, the hill-top base was abandoned. Much of America had followed the siege of Khe Sanh with baited breath, and now that the brave Marines had triumphed in the end, the base was to be evacuated! Like the airborne troopers of the 101st a year later, the Marines at Khe Sanh would ask 'What was it all for?'. The national feeling was critical. If Khe Sanh had been so important to the American war effort, why was it now being abandoned? Although Khe Sanh was seen as an unequivocal victory by General Westmoreland, the mood at home soon saw it as a defeat for the United States.

'Strategic Hamlets'

One of the major problems facing troops in the field was the identification of the enemy. In the guerrilla war that had spread its tendrils of terror into almost every village and town in South Vietnam, the enemy was everywhere. He was dressed like the peasant he dominated, and he used the locals as a convenient cover for his belligerent activities. At night the Viet Cong soldiers would uncover carefully hidden weapons to stage night-time ambushes and perimeter raids on American and allied positions. On many occasions troops returned fire and sent out patrols to recover the bodies of the communist dead. There, caught up in the barbed wire perimeter or sprawled beside a knocked-out machine gun or mortar would sometimes be the body of a local South Vietnamese who had worked each day in the camp, as a cook, cleaner or other domestic. Women and children, too, became willing or unwilling agents of the Viet Cong, and, to the indiscriminate eye of the American soldier, no one could be trusted. It was one of the tasks of counter-insurgency to separate the insurgents from the general populace. Purely military operations tended to treat whole populations as the enemy when they harboured Viet Cong or their supplies. Civilians, however, lacking any alignment in this tenacious struggle for loyalties, unfortunately became common casualties. Major Charles Malloy, defending the shooting of a Viet Cong 'suspect' riding out of a village on his bicycle asked, 'What're you going to do when you spot a guy with black pyjamas [typical peasant garb]? Wait for him to get out his automatic weapon and start shooting? I'll tell you I'm not.'

There were two intertwined attempts to make the war against the secret guerrilla army an easier one. The first centred on relocating villagers to a cleared and 'friendly' region, thus denying the Viet Cong cadres access to this vulnerable section of society. Communist indoctrination, tax collection and assassination teams regularly made the rounds in their effort to consolidate their power base in the countryside. Every village was a potential stockpile of rice, weapons, ammunition and manpower, whether its inhabitants were loyal to Diem and his successors or to the communist cause. Force and appeals to loyalty were exploited by the VC to gain the support of the villages. When President Diem instigated his resettlement policy, known as the 'Strategic Hamlets' programme, in the early 1960s, it seemed to offer the perfect solution to the painful quandary facing patrolling government troops.

'Strategic Hamlets' was a concept that derived from the successes of the 'New Village' strategy employed in the counter-insurgency in Malaya. From 1948, the communist-dominated Malayan Races' Liberation Army (MRLA) had fought an armed struggle against the British colonial government there. Ethnic Chinese made up a significant portion of the MRLA membership and they were able to rely on support from the local village communities. Attacks on plantations, on transport and on the towns were resisted by the police force and units of the British Army. Sir Gerald Templar, High Commissioner and Director of Operations from January 1952, introduced an effective new strategy to the conflict. As intelligence improved and the military inflicted increasing casualties on the communist terrorists (CTs), moves were being made to separate the civilians from the struggle. Social and economic programmes were established, adequate police and self-defence units were organised, and a mood of stability and order was pursued. Advantage was taken of the fact that the Chinese supporters of the movement were mainly settled in illegal squatter villages along the jungle fringes. Templar oversaw the development of 'New Villages' for these squatters, providing serviceable farming or dormitory settlements close to the centres of population. By granting the Chinese rights to the land they were given, and by providing clinics, shops and schools, the discontent of the Chinese was neutralised and the vital logistical crutch they provided to the CTs was removed. In all, half a million people were relocated with meticulous attention to detail. Without the food and succour that the MRLA were reliant upon, the insurgency began to wither. The relocation of the supporting population had been the key to winning the guerrilla war in Malaya. Would it work in Vietnam?

Diem had begun a half-hearted policy of pacification back in the 1950s that had been enlarged within a few years into the concept of 'agrovilles'—defended villages located along the strategically important highways of South Vietnam.

The 'Strategic Hamlets' concept that followed in January 1962 was a more systematised and larger-scale version of the agroville project. When the 'friendly' pro-government population was entirely ensconced in this archipelago of barbed wire and palisade camps, it followed that unregulated peasant activity encountered elsewhere had to be the work of the communists.

Of course the project, although it had been built on the highly workable foundations of the British and French, would not work so well in practice. The British 'New Village' programme tried and tested in Malaya *had* been remarkably successful. Cut off from local support, the CTs were eventually forced to turn to the remote aboriginal tribes of the Malayan jungle for meagre sustenance. Sir Robert Thompson, one of the military advisers who helped to engineer the Malayan 'New Villages' project, helped to convince Diem of its value to the Saigon government.

Diem's rush to complete the total resettlement of South Vietnam proved to be the undoing of 'Strategic Hamlets', for the concept was basically a sound one although it faced problems different from those that the 'New Village' programme had encountered. Numbers were chased in an orgy of hamlet construction, barbed wire encirclement and refugee transportation. It was becoming clear that figures quoted by Saigon, such as the existence of 7,200 'Strategic Hamlets' by mid-1963, were inaccurate and irrelevant. Diem and his brother-in-law Nhu had an eye to political control over these born-again villages rather than an interest in either the villagers' hearts or their minds. Villagers were even more discontented with the government than they had been before, and the flimsy militia guard posted at night did not stop regular infiltration by the Viet Cong: often the Viet Cong were already within the hamlets, and even part of the organised militia guard! A reporter visiting a settlement in 1962 was alarmed when sporadic small-arms fire directed at the hamlet was answered by the young militia guards surrendering forthwith! The gates were flung open and weapons hastily thrown on to the ground. The quality of the camps and of their defences had been forgone in the pursuit of quantity. The eight and a half million resettled Vietnamese were no better off, and many considered themselves to be temporarily located refugees.

As the Special Forces CIDG programme had discovered, the spirited defence of one's ancestral land was easy to inspire with the correct application of training and aid. 'Strategic Hamlets' uprooted families from their ancestral and hereditary farming land—perhaps the only thing the South Vietnamese peasantry would instinctively fight to protect. This marks the difference between Templar's 'New Villages' and Diem's 'Strategic Hamlets'. The Chinese squatters in Malaya had been forced out of the cities by the Japanese occupation forces and were dwelling on government-owned land. By giving them what they wanted (decent village communities of their own), the 'hearts and minds' of this vulnerable minority could be secured. In Vietnam, the hamlets were badly organised, were poorly equipped and gave the villagers nothing new. Rather they took away their freedom, independence and livelihood. While supporters of the MRLA were mainly ethnic Chinese and could easily be separated from the population at large, Vietnamese peasants sympathetic to the Viet Cong were often unidentifiable from loyal pro-government villagers. This formed the crux of the Vietnamese relocation problem. A communist attack on the very first 'Strategic Hamlet', Ben Truong, in August 1963 signalled the beginning of the end. The programme teetered and then collapsed.

'Strategic Hamlets' was part of a whole philosophy that attempted to rally the populace behind the government. It aimed to coordinate economic, political and social programmes in an effort to win the hearts and minds of the rural village folk. The programme was badly implemented and very poorly followed through on all fronts, and it failed to achieve many of its stated aims. Clashing head-on with pacification was the American strategy of search-and-destroy, discussed in more detail later, which would undermine many of pacification's successes. The great effort on the part of MACV's military build-up was always on creating a military shield that protected the vulnerable cities of South Vietnam. General Westmoreland considered the defeat of Viet Cong main force and North Vietnamese Army units to be his major task. But critics have decried his concentration on this shield to the detriment of the 'other war' being waged, and being won, by the Viet Cong cadres and hit-teams in the rural areas. Although it had foundered by the mid-1960s, the 'Strategic Hamlets' programme did not bring an end to pacification in general. A variety of attempts were made to convince the South Vietnamese to switch their support from 'Uncle Ho' to whichever military or civilian potentate currently occupied the Presidential Palace in Saigon.

In 1963 the Chieu Hoi (or 'open arms') programme was initiated. This offered individual Viet Cong complete amnesty if they surrendered to the allies. Many disgruntled communists (or rather anti-government guerrillas) took advantage of this amnesty, for a variety of reasons. A high proportion of the Viet Cong in South Vietnam were not dedicated communist fighters, committed to the cause, but dislocated peasants with a grievance against Saigon or the US military. Others were forced out of their villages and into jungle training camps at gunpoint. Thus the morale of the movement was never uniform and weaknesses could be exploited by the propaganda experts in MACV. From 1963 to 1968 an estimated 27,000 Hoi Chanh ('ralliers') had come over to the government. The message that access to good food, shelter and pay and regular contact with families could be secured blared out from C-47 cargo planes fitted with loudspeaker arrays (the 'Bullshit Bombers'). Printed leaflets were likewise used to try and convert the Viet Cong: they were dropped in their thousands over hostile jungle. For a disheartened guerrilla fighter, cut off from friends and family, needing basic medical attention, proper food and clean water, and weary of his knife-edge existence stalking human prey in the unrelenting jungle, the opportunity to surrender must have at times seemed a blessing.

Not surprisingly, the Chieu Hoi programme came under fire from critics who pointed out that it was virtually impossible to determine which defectors were honest turncoats who had thrown in the towel for good and which were active Viet Cong attempting infiltration of the military effort in the South. Alternatively, some of the communists were taking temporary advantage of the offer to enjoy a respite from the war before returning to their units in the jungle. A high proportion of the defectors were genuine, however, and these were rarely allowed to escape the war entirely. Some even joined American infantry units as scouts. Reminiscent of the Indians spearheading military forays on the American frontier, these men were nicknamed 'Kit Carson Scouts'.

Despised by the men he had abandoned and mistrusted by the American soldiers who followed him on patrol, a Kit Carson Scout was a strange and uncomfortable breed of soldier. As an ex-Viet Cong he would never earn the full trust of the Americans, yet his knowledge of local trail networks, communist tactics and troop deployments, and of jungle warfare in general, made him a valuable asset. In addition, he could prove to be an effective tool to convince other guerrillas to surrender. Chieu Hoi was not the answer to the insurgency, however, only a thermometer that allowed MACV to gauge the commitment of the Viet Cong in the field. While controversial, it did provide clear evidence that the loyalty of the insurgents could be bought.

One year after the 'open arms' had been hopefully flung wide, a new theory of pacification was tried experimentally in the vicinity of Saigon. Again taking the lead from the successful pacification of Malaya by the British, the Hop Tac ('cooperation') programme was introduced into South Vietnam to fill the gap left by the 'Strategic Hamlets'. Hop Tac limited its small achievements to the immediate territories around Saigon. It used the 'oil spot' technique of clearing a zone of communist influence by careful and concentrated targeting of propaganda and intelligence, and then moving on to adjacent enemy-influenced areas. Community spirit and confidence in the pacification process were Hop Tac's main aims in the concentric zones around Vietnam, and, upon an initial success in the inner zone, the programme would move out to the next ring and repeat the process.

As fierce ground combat began with the deployment of American combat units into the country in 1965, the pacification attempts did not stop entirely. The 'battle for hearts and minds' (a contradiction in itself) was seen by MACV mainly as a complementary part of the overall war effort. Pacification was the 'other war', a term calculated to shift the responsibility for its outcome on to someone else. This was to be the South Vietnamese Army, and although the ARVN had been trained by the US Army, it had been trained to fight a conventional war, not a more subtle struggle against VC cadres in marginal villages. Those parts of the native defence force that could have perhaps contributed the most to securing peasant loyalties were the so-called 'Ruff-Puffs'. Actually Regional and Popular Forces, they were local villagers who were trained by MATs and armed and organised to fight in the defence of their homes or their district. Although the entire programme was not as comprehensive as the truly effective CIDG programme of the Green Berets, it did focus local energies and deny manpower to the communists. But the conventional ARVN despised these amateur groups and were content to see them poorly armed and sadly under-used.

The 'Strategic Hamlets' project, which collapsed under its own weight following the demise of Diem, was given a second chance under the inspiring name of the 'New Life Hamlets' programme. Hop Tac meanwhile, although a moderately successful counter-insurgency experiment, was subsumed in 1967 by a new dedicated pacification machine—CORDS, the Civil Operations and Revolutionary Development Support programme. This made significant gains in the late 1960s, and was able to boast more progress than any previous pacification attempt in South Vietnam up to that time. But in 1966 Robert McNamara saw no reason to be optimistic and claimed that the pacification movement was actually going backwards. Indeed, he has since revealed that the death and destruction being wrought on innocent civilians troubled him greatly. One thing that the British presence in Malaya had proved was that pacification took time. A full twelve years of counter-insurgency and 'hearts and minds' was able to win the loyalty of the people and isolate the CTs. In South Vietnam, the emphasis was on a short war—to get in and get out again. Few could realistically envisage (or would publicly admit) that the war would require anything more than two years to win. There were American officers who had some idea, however. Lieutenant-Colonel David Marshall expressed his concern that, to succeed in Vietnam, it would take the Americans fifty years. No one wanted to hear that message.

There was an alternative to pacification. Linked with the programme of peasant relocation, the concept of the 'free-fire zone' (FFZ) was established to enable the military to prejudge the nature of any activity in an area. By forcing 'friendly' villagers out of an area that was experiencing increased enemy activity, the American military could target the entire 'free-fire zone' with indiscriminate fire. There would be little chance of killing or wounding innocent civilians during such an offensive. It was ironic that the term conjured up media images of villages being bombed and of American artillery shelling friendly peasants, when the free-fire zones had been set up to specifically prevent this from happening. MACV understood that the indiscriminate use of firepower could, and did, destroy farms and villages, and that such accidents only forced more Vietnamese over to the side of the Viet Cong. What the system tried to correct was the destructive state of affairs that had existed in Occupied Europe during the Second World War. For practical purposes the entire continent had been a free-fire zone, with few restrictions on the bombing and shelling of targets. By limiting military operations to these new zones, MACV could wage the war free from political and economic pressures and would be able to maximise its ability to fight offensively rather than in the defence of local populations. Only Viet Cong insurgents should have remained in the area when the villages had been evacuated, and any signs of activity, from actual movement to the smoke of cooking fires, could be targeted immediately and effectively. This was the theory. But no war can be fought with such meticulous and surgical precision.

The uprooting of the very people that the armed forces were there to protect caused intense hatred and resentment. Like the establishment of 'Strategic Hamlets', it seemed that the military chiefs had given up on the idea of protecting the population centres of South Vietnam and were therefore trying to eliminate such centres, denying their strategic value to the cadres. In fact, one method of gauging the success of the allied effort was the collection of refugee totals. The increased refugee count was perceived in some twisted way as a direct measurement of distance to victory. There were an estimated 1.2 million refugees rolling like an endless wave across South Vietnam in 1967. Many had been made homeless by the institution of free-fire zones. One macabre joke going around the troops seemed to summarise the FFZ philosophy: to win the war put the Vietnamese in a fleet of sampans in the South China Sea, bomb every living thing in Vietnam—and then sink the sampans.

In practice, the displacement of an entire district was rarely a seamless operation, and many Vietnamese made their way back home to continue farming the family land. Some had refused to leave in the first place. Life in an FFZ was seen by some to be more preferable than the precarious existence as a refugee. Populated or partially populated FFZs were worse than useless, inviting a terrible carnage of innocent farming folk. To try and mellow the violent images conjured by the title of these zones amongst the American public, MACV renamed them 'specified strike zones' (SSZs). But the old name seemed to stick. The free-fire zones had been an attempt to sanitise the war and separate it from political worries. In the long term, the political problems associated with the free-fire zone strategy outweighed any benefits that could be derived from it. It had been promising, but flawed.

The concept was destined to be taken to much greater extremes by the more technical arms of the US military. Once civilian-free zones had been identified, efforts were sometimes made to reduce to a bare minimum almost every advantage that the guerrilla enjoyed from it. First came Operation 'Ranch Hand', the systematic defoliation of whole swaths of jungle carried out by spraying aircraft (usually reconfigured C-123 Providers). Various chemical herbicides were employed, but by far the most prevalent was Agent Orange, and it reduced what was once verdant jungle and mangrove swamp to dry and dusty flatlands—a gruesome parody of the Midwest Dustbowl. Like all herbicides, Agent Orange proved dangerous to *all* living creatures, not just plant life, a fact in which all concerned seemed to show scant interest. The scale of the project was immense. Spraying began during the Diem regime and it was hoped that dense jungle sanctuaries would be (quite literally) laid bare before American reconnaissance and bombing planes. In addition, the lack of vegetation for use as cover would preclude the devastating use of the Viet Cong ambush on allied patrols and bases.

This became part of an entire package of measures that resembled a NASA 'terraforming' project. Terraforming is the (theoretical) modification of an alien landscape to allow the survival of humankind. And for many of the line troops, Vietnam was just as alien and as inhospitable as Mars. In South Vietnam the search for the communist base areas and their attempted destruction carried on apace with few results. Although the Saigon government had known for years exactly from where the VC were deploying and re-grouping, actually penetrating and eradicating these areas was an impossible task. Repeated patrols and large-scale sweeps captured occasional Viet Cong stragglers but otherwise passed by (or over) the hidden bases. But US technical know-how could not ignore this challenge.

Science and engineering had become an established arm of the military well before the Vietnam War, but Vietnam allowed these technicians to take the lead in researching and developing viable applications for use by MACV. In some instances Agent Orange was sprayed to maximise other 'terraforming' techniques. One such remoulding took place north-west of Saigon in the deadly stronghold region nicknamed the 'Iron Triangle', close to Cu Chi. A mass of dense vegetation carpeting a labyrinth of tunnels and bunkers, the Triangle had swallowed numerous ARVN units whole. As the American armed forces geared up for full combat operations in South Vietnam, General Westmoreland devised an engineering plan to melt the 'Iron Triangle'.

Agent Orange was first sprayed across the region, killing the vegetation and reducing cover for the guerrillas to nought. In the hot weather the area soon dried out and to heighten the effect thousands of barrels of petrol and flammable oils were dumped out of overflying planes on to the dusty moonscape. With the killing ground primed, attack planes swept in to drop napalm and phosphorus bombs. The resulting conflagration thundered across the plateau and a vast firestorm seemed destined to truly sanitise the region. But, after a monumental effort in manpower and machinery, a great rainstorm suddenly broke, and the human cataclysm suddenly ended before its full effects could be determined. With welcome rains the plant life began a speedy recovery. It later transpired that the heat of the fires had in themselves sparked off the strange atmospheric anomaly that had drenched the project. Nature seemed to be in league with the communists.

Two years later troops were sent in, and combat sweeps tried and failed to engage the Viet Cong formations still hiding there. Operation 'Cedar Falls', as it was called, took place in January 1967 and ended with combat engineers and specialist soldiers called 'tunnel rats' demolishing some of the 20km of tunnels beneath the 'Iron Triangle'. Caterpillar-tracked 'Rome ploughs' flattened bunkers and cleared long highways into the region, and anything that was considered an advantage to concealment was set alight by Army flame-throwers. Supplies and military installations were uncovered that could have supported a force of perhaps 13,000 guerrillas for a year. Despite the importance of the region, only 775 Viet Cong were killed. What had occurred in the 'Iron Triangle' was taking place on a smaller scale in other parts of South Vietnam too. As the Roman writer Tacitus was to say of the military commanders of his day: 'They made a desert, and called it peace.'

Could this be justified? South Vietnam was an ally, much as Britain had been during the fight against Hitler, yet a vast amount of land was being neutralised in this way, making it not just infertile but uninhabitable. The livelihood of local fishermen and farmers suffered as animals and crops withered or were scraped into oblivion. The devastating combination of defoliants, bomb craters, Rome ploughs and incendiaries wiped out entire farming communities, adding to the influx of refugees into the urban areas and denying (in theory) these areas to the Viet Cong and NVA. They had become awesome tools in the shifting of civilians out of territories being earmarked as future combat arenas. The village of Ben Suc, within the 'Iron Triangle', had been a major centre of resupply and cooperation for the VC. Part of Operation 'Cedar Falls' was dedicated to shifting the local inhabitants out of the area, including the entire population of Ben Suc. Family huts, orchards and rice fields were summarily destroyed—Ben Suc was totally obliterated. Its people were not 'pacified', however: they had every reason to hate and despise the American forces that had ended their old lives and turned them into refugees. After the huge relocation effort had been completed, one of the Army colonels involved admitted his regrets: 'I don't think we can afford any more Ben Sucs.'

A primary tenet of guerrilla warfare, however, is the fact that the insurgents are wherever the people are. Shifting villagers from A to B often did not leave the Viet Cong at A. They moved into B with the refugees, using and abusing them according to the mood of the campaign at the time. An alternative strand of warfare was quietly trying to come to terms with this intrinsic problem. It appreciated and undermined the intensely political motivations inherent in the Viet Cong terror war, and it addressed the all-important 'minds' in the fight for 'hearts and minds'. It was known as the Phoenix Program.

The Phoenix Program

It was telling that CORDS was the province of the CIA, a civilian intelligence agency, not a military unit. The Civil Operations and Rural Development Support programme was pure pacification, attempting to convince by means of propaganda and good works that the Saigon government did indeed have the best interests of the rural South Vietnamese in mind. On its past record, however, this was always going to an uphill struggle. CORDS united most of the pacification efforts extant at the time, and this in itself was seen as a major step forward. That the agency was not a military one also boded well for the project's future: 'hearts and minds' were often seen by the military establishment as the submissive result of civilian interference. From as recently as Colonel Lansdale's adventures in 1950s Saigon, the CIA had always been more subtle than that. Heading CORDS was a former CIA chief, Robert Komer, who was named Deputy to the MACV Commander (General Westmoreland) and given the rank of ambassador. The entire CORDS concept began in 1967—at a crucial moment in the Vietnam War. Within twelve months the country-wide Viet Cong guerrilla army had risen up in a single all-out struggle of defiance. And it had been defeated. Those Viet Cong surviving to re-group after what was called the Tet Offensive were badly mauled, and much of their infrastructure had been exposed. CORDS occupied the vacuum left by the Tet Offensive, coordinating the CIA, the US Information Agency, the Agency for International Development, the State Department and parts of the armed services. Before Tet, Komer himself had recognised that his project would be faced with countering up to 10,000 communist-held villages out of a total of around 16,000. And every move that was made during daylight hours was counteracted at night by Viet Cong forces, moving through the hamlets, stealing the food and blowing up the civic projects. After Tet, the guerrillas were weakened substantially enough to give CORDS a valuable breathing space.

Through the successes made, the VC infrastructure (the seemingly omnipresent VCI) was undermined and the guerrillas weakened. By 1972 the communist war footing had shifted from the indigenous Viet Cong guerrillas within South Vietnam to the North Vietnamese Army on its vulnerable western flanks, Laos and Cambodia. Tet and CORDS had virtually eradicated the Viet Cong as a viable military force.

Komer had the expertise and, with a package of aid that amounted to 1.7 billion dollars, the funding to be able to reach the inaccessible South Vietnamese villages. It came in the form of concrete for building, fresh-water plumbing, cooking oil, medical drugs, soya beans, rice and fertilisers. CORDS differed also in what its creators expected of it. Komer envisaged significant changes, not in two or three years, but after 'a long-term effort'. But Komer was acutely aware of the security aspect of the programme and sought an effective means of weeding out the Viet Cong in the countryside. He had available for this task only the corrupt Vietnamese police force and the poorly supported Regional and Popular Forces. It was Komer who established what has since become for many Americans the worst excess of the Vietnam War—the Phoenix Program.

Established as a scheme for internment and interrogation, the Phoenix Program ran away with its success. When intelligence brought the identity and location of a VC cadre, tax collector or commander, the programme initially sent in indigenous mercenaries—often Nungs under American Special Forces supervision—to apprehend the suspect. Intelligence was collated via informers, ralliers and interrogations and was aided by the nationwide issuing of identity cards. Computers were used to collate and interpret this data, which was received directly from the eighty Phoenix offices spread across South Vietnam. It was an attempt to deconstruct the VCI, discover exactly how far its roots spread and neutralise it. Each individual arrested was interrogated at the local Phoenix office in the hope of picking up more intelligence about Viet Cong activities and networks. These individuals were sometimes targeted directly; at other times they were the victims of random sweeps by the Provincial Reconnaissance Units (PRUs). Officially, the programme was only interested in communist leaders or cadres (instructors and propagandists). The rank and file were supposed to be released.

Komer was succeeded by William Colby, and it was under Colby that Phoenix began its operations—and under him that a great many of the controversial killings took place. The ex-station chief always rigorously denied any management misuse of the project. The intention had been to incarcerate and interrogate the most influential members of the local VCI. But, as the prisons began filling up (alarmingly so), and as the Provincial Reconnaissance Units charged with carrying out these missions became impatient, assassinations and deaths during torture became increasingly common. Colby had officially forbidden any member of the project from murdering a suspect, however reliable the information acted upon, and insisted that deaths occurring were the result of military action, not assassination. Others were not so sure.

One of the Phoenix interrogation centres had a chilling record of deaths under torture. During the Senate hearings convened to investigate the whole affair, a Phoenix employee declared that not one of the suspects had survived: 'There was never any reasonable fact [sic] that any one of those individuals was in fact cooperating with the Viet Cong. But they all died.'

In practical terms Phoenix was a campaign of low-level terrorism (or, more accurately, 'counter-terrorism') aimed at the remaining Viet Cong active in the countryside. At times a useful intelligence gathering machine, it was at others a mechanism for barely restrained slaughter. In one incident a B-52 strike was called in to demolish an entire hamlet in the hope of killing a single, unconfirmed Viet Cong suspect. Partly responsible for the incidents of excess in these final years of American involvement was the speed at which some sort of settlement was expected. Komer would not get his 'long-term effort'. A decisive victory on the battlefield had, by 1970, been forgone, but there were pressures from the incumbent Nixon administration finally to settle the question of pacification in combination with 'Vietnamisation'. This was the handing over of equipment and weapons to the South Vietnamese and with them the sole responsibility for the outcome of the war.

Phoenix actually had a great impact on the Viet Cong infrastructure; Vietnam's Foreign Minister after 1975, Nguyen Co Thach, declared that the Phoenix Programme 'wiped out many of our bases' during the period it operated. Charges that America was employing a systematic campaign of assassination were held up to the world by North Vietnam in an attempt to end the project. This was of course ironic: communist hit-teams had murdered tens of thousands of South Vietnamese village headmen, administrators, schoolteachers and district chiefs during the past two decades.

There were considerable numbers of innocent Vietnamese killed as a result of the PRU 'hits'. At times, teams would enter a village at the dead of night, armed with automatic weapons and 'good intelligence' as to the location of a powerful VC suspect. They would reach his hooch and often kill all of the occupants in the firefight. One senior CIA official involved with Phoenix has estimated that upwards of 30,000 people were the victims of the PRUs, and not all of those were Viet Cong. The level of concern reached by some members of the intelligence community had reached crisis point by 1971, and a Senate hearing was arranged to hear various pieces of testimony concerning Phoenix. Today it still strikes a dark note, not least because it was associated with what was ostensibly the ultra-benevolent CORDS agency. It was a fear that the Viet Cong would destroy the CORDS improvements as soon as they were begun that had spurred Robert Komer to create a deterrent, a shield behind which his 'hearts and minds' could be won. This shield was the Accelerated Pacification Campaign, and it was from the APC that the Phoenix Programme had been hatched.

Search-and-Destroy

As an American infantry patrol left its hill-top firebase and began slowly and quietly to slip through dense rainforest, elephant grass or rough scrubland, the troops involved were well aware of the precarious position that they were in. The majority of infantry actions took place while on patrol, a lonely and vulnerable duty that lacked coordination with major forces and also the momentum of a larger battle plan. Patrols formed the meat of most of the Army and Marine operations in Vietnam. They were vital to keep military intelligence up to date with the current situation, to maintain a presence in the villages and the surrounding countryside and to disrupt communist lines of communication and supply. These are the mission aims of patrols everywhere. But in Vietnam a new role was being carved out for the infantryman on patrol. It was called, in the blunt language of the military establishment, 'search-and-destroy'. To the GIs it was known colloquially as 'a walk in the sun', or 'dangling the bait', with the inference that the troops were the bait for the Viet Cong or NVA fish. More than any previous war, little concerted pressure was put on infantry commanders to commit their units to combat in the field. The onus was on saving American lives in order to maintain the credibility of the war at home. Available firepower from air strikes, artillery fire missions and offshore naval bombardments was utilised to the full.

As a result it was difficult for American units to make full assessments of enemy strengths, intentions and casualties. During Operation 'Junction City', the penetration of War Zone C near the Cambodian border in February 1967, a company from the 25th Infantry Division was making a sweep through dense teak forest. It stumbled upon a Viet Cong encampment and exchanged fire with its defenders at a range of only 15m. Typical of contacts occurring all across South Vietnam during the war, the company pulled back to a more defensible position and radioed in for air support. The Air Force jets made repeated bombing runs against the camp, and after an hour the troops moved back into the camp to take care of any survivors. The camp was completely deserted.

The American forces were relying increasingly on firepower to solve tactical problems, and the traditional role of infantry as a manoeuvre, pursuit and elimination force lapsed. NVA and Viet Cong forces continued to employ classic infantry tactics, even excel at them, while American units became obsessed with minimising casualties. In a war without objectives, where the aim was to 'kill more of them than they kill of us', the explanation for such a reversal becomes clear.

A new tactic had been formulated: infantry units would continually patrol contested ground, goading the Viet Cong or NVA into combat. More often than not, and after the American victories in 1965, the communists declined to give combat. Only when they outnumbered the American troops or held some other advantage did the guerrillas engage infantry patrols. Firepower would then be utilised to destroy the communists once they were located. References to 'artillery support' and 'air support' belittle the important role both played in most of the Vietnam combats, on whatever scale. Rather than provide a measure of support for the ground troops, both of these forces acted as the main destructive powers in battle. Meanwhile the troops who had initiated the slaughter had retreated to a defensible perimeter in order to let the artillery and air strikes do their work. After the bombs and shells had stopped dropping, the ground troops went back into the combat zone, searching for casualties and weapons. This is when the body count would usually be made. This new method of infantry warfare was not officially adopted by the training officers back in the US, but in Vietnam it was fully endorsed. One of the war's most successful big-unit commanders wrote a short field book delineating the new tactics. Terming these operations 'search-and-destroy', he advised commanders to 'look upon infantry as the principal combat reconnaissance force and supporting fire as the principal destructive force'.

General Westmoreland understood that the enemy was now reluctant to face his troops in open warfare and would only do so when forced to, or when the battlefield seemed favourable. Search-and-destroy, then, was a mechanism that forced an encounter with guerrilla units, compelling the communists to fight whether they wanted to or not. In Westmoreland's words, his troops were tasked to 'find, fix and destroy' the enemy. In practice, though, the infantry would rarely 'destroy'.

Much of the troops' time was spent on endless searches, beating the bush, hunting for VC and inspecting local villages. A great many of these patrols proved to be fruitless—just 'humping the boonies' as the GIs themselves called it—with each man heaving a back-breaking weight of kit through thick jungle in the hope of a contact. To many, the enemy became the jungle itself—the mud and the monsoon rain, the leeches, venomous snakes and irritating defoliants. Particularly uncomfortable for patrolling soldiers was the condition called 'immersion foot'. The feet, continually wet and rubbing constantly inside jungle boots, rotted away, making walking agony. The boots supplied to the infantrymen resembled baseball sneakers, with the ankle and upper made of olive green fabric while the toecap, heel and sole were of black leather. Still popular with jungle forces today, this boot had been designed specifically for the treacherous jungles of Vietnam. Leather has a tendency to rot in such climates, and the use of fabric was an attempt to minimise that risk and allow the boot to dry faster. The boots were not waterproof—far from it: the assumption was that the boots would constantly be immersed in mud and water, and two vents on each instep allowed water to drain out.

Making the jungle patrols even more unbearable were the Viet Cong and NVA themselves, concealed in ambush and liable to open up with machine guns, grenades and AK-47s at any minute. Even without an enemy presence, the communists' use of booby traps turned an innocuous patch of undergrowth into a lethal killing field. Staggering through the forest or two-metre-high elephant grass, it took only one man to trip a wire or tread on a mine to get himself killed and his colleagues injured. Less deadly, but no less terrifying, were the more primitive traps. There were dead-fall pits lined with sharpened punji stakes, 'toe poppers'(large .50-calibre cartridges mounted on pins just below the dirt that would go off when a soldier trod on them) and a variety of spike traps, swinging on to trails or hidden within the jungle leafmould. Continually put through the nerve-wracking ordeal of a jungle patrol, the soldiers became increasingly disenchanted with 'search and destroy'.

Grim though it was, the American patrols really *were* bait for the communist forces. Knowing that the enemy would only show himself when he outnumbered the US force, it was hoped that patrolling platoons would be small enough to entice them to attack. The firefight that ensued would usually result in several initial American casualties, but, as both sides dug in, the conflict stalemated with the communists unwilling to move to destroy the Americans, and vice versa. Usually the Viet Cong and NVA tactic consisted of an initial contact and firefight, followed by a speedy withdrawal into the deep jungle. The enemy knew well what would inevitably follow: the air strike or, even more likely, the artillery fire mission. Hit-and-run tactics characterised the communist forces during the war with America: they fully recognised the lack of American resolve to pursue them into the wilds and were themselves wary of lingering in the path of the incoming artillery shells.

Without the ubiquity of American artillery, search-and-destroy would not have been possible. That artillery was made available in the semi-tropical wilderness of South Vietnam was in itself amazing. Effective roads or flat terrain across which howitzers could be rolled into firing positions to support local search-

and-destroy patrols did not exist. To allow the infantry to conduct these sweeps deep in wilderness territory, the concept of the 'firebase' (or, more properly, 'fire support base') was established. Each firebase was an artillery fortress isolated from other military installations, often atop a prominent hill. Most were helicoptered in piece by piece, from sandbags and personnel to the howitzers themselves. Bunkers were built, vegetation cleared, fields of fire determined and the fortifications constructed. Firebases were established in areas of projected military activity for the support of patrols and assaults. Each could fire in any direction required, and multiple firebases employed overlapping fields of fire for redundancy or added firepower.

Although the use of field artillery did have its advantages for the infantry in search-and-destroy missions, it also created its own problems. The non-mobile nature of the firebases meant that the use of artillery support would never be a surprise for communist forces, particularly for the local Viet Cong who knew the area well. In addition, they were often so isolated that they did at times make tempting targets for enemy assaults, increasing the need to tie down more defences at the firebases. The effectiveness of the US howitzer batteries can also be brought into question. Their use undeniably proved telling in countless infantry firefights or pre-assault barrages, but the use of artillery in support of a jungle battle usually failed to eradicate an enemy force: rather, it forced the communists to retreat, taking their casualties with them. A North Vietnamese commander once criticised the American military for 'not taking into account our capacity to resist bombing'.

Perhaps the greatest drawback to the use of artillery as the main destructive force in Vietnam was its indiscriminate nature. The 105mm M101A1 light howitzer, which became the prevalent artillery piece in Vietnam, had a range of 11,500m and fired indirectly. This meant that it could shell targets that were out of sight behind intervening hills and ridges, and be directed via radio by a forward observer close to the action. The potential to bring fire to bear on innocent civilians, especially in the 'many-sided' war of Vietnam, was always present. The institution of free-fire zones had been mainly for the benefit of American artillery operations. They enabled the area effect of each 105mm shell to have a telling impact on dispersed enemy troop units that considered themselves safe in the knowledge that there were no American infantry units in the vicinity. This kind of spontaneous barrage fired at a patch of enemy-dominated jungle or other wilderness terrain became known as H&I—'harassment and interdiction'. It can have done little to blunt the communist fighting machine, but it signalled the Americans' ability to strike at base areas and well-travelled trails in South Vietnam.

Although FFZs were introduced to prevent 'friendly fire' incidents, the shelling of loyal villages was sometimes difficult to prevent, particularly when the VC were operating in or around such a village. The awesome firepower of the interlocking fire support bases did at times prove immensely useful for the allied war effort, but it lacked the subtlety required of a counter-insurgency war. Although search-and-destroy operations depended on these guns, allowing MACV to maintain the armed 'shield' around South Vietnam, their employment at times alienated the civilian population.

With increased media footage being broadcast that focused on American destruction of property by artillery, bombs or soldiers, the phrase 'search-and-destroy' developed unwanted connotations. Like 'free-fire zone', it conjured up images of needless and unrestrained destruction of property, livestock and people. By 1968 MACV had classified these patrols by their drier and more technical titles, such as reconnaissance in force, or heliborne assault. But the dangerous nature of search-and-destroy missions, undertaken in a hostile jungle against an unseen and deadly enemy, did not diminish simply because the name had changed.

Chapter 6

KHE SANH

The greatest battle of the Vietnam War was also its most illustrative. Khe Sanh became at once a military landmark, a turning point in the conflict and a microcosmic version of the war as a whole. And as the battle raged for a seemingly unending 77 days, the American people were held mesmerised. Meanwhile the President watched with horror as the entire war effort seemed to swing in the balance. It was a crucial, climactic year in the prosecution of the war: 1968 would in retrospect be viewed as the year that the United States lost the will to fight.

Border Battles and Hill Fights

Things began badly the year before, in the autumn of 1967. Khe Sanh was located within Quang Tri province, the most northerly in South Vietnam, and a region which was facing a fierce communist onslaught from sanctuaries inside Laos. The province bordered Laos in the west, the South China Sea to the east and the Demilitarised Zone to the north. Many of the Ho Chi Minh Trail's tentacles ended in Quang Tri province to facilitate a fast deployment of North Vietnamese forces into the South. Consequently, Quang Tri was to become a cockpit, and policing it were the United States Marines. One of their bases at Con Thien, close to the DMZ, was put under siege late in the year by a large NVA force. Only after a tremendous pummelling from artillery pieces, gunships, fighter-bombers and B-52 strategic bombers did the encircling troops withdraw. Further south, at the end of October the enemy surged energetically out of his havens in Cambodia to attack the important towns of Song Be and Loc Ninh, close to Saigon. November began with an NVA attack on Dak To in the tri-border region of the Central Highlands. Elements of the American 4th Division, the 1st Cavalry and the entire 173rd Airborne Brigade along with six battalions of the ARVN grimly defended Dak To. Together these seemingly co-ordinated, yet independent and shocking offensives were christened the 'border battles'.

The ferocity of the attacks was coupled with a sinister determination which outstripped the persistence of earlier communist offensives. General Westmoreland had to rush troops from one part of the border to another in an almost desperate attempt to prevent any of the Viet Cong and North Vietnamese at-

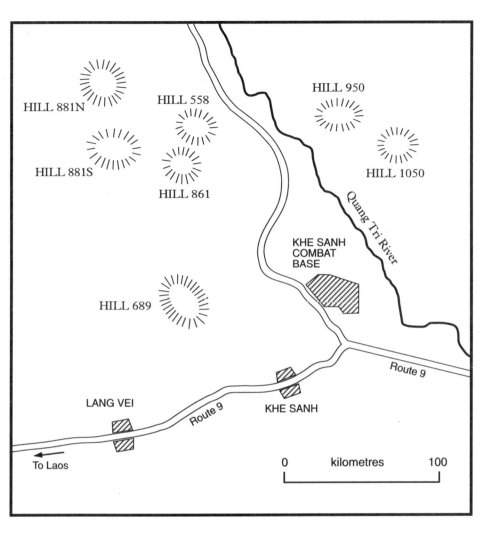

The Khe Sanh Region

tacks from achieving a lasting victory. Although thousands of lives were expended by Hanoi in launching these ill-fated attacks, no serious strategic plan seemed to motivate them. Later, however, Hanoi would admit that these sporadic border battles were merely probing attacks in advance of the unprecedented campaign of 1968. At the heart of this campaign was the siege of Khe Sanh and a coordinated attack on every major town and city in South Vietnam during the Tet holiday. The Politburo in Hanoi had agreed to General Giap's extraordinary campaign. First would come the probing attacks along the border to test communications, equipment and resolve, second the nationwide Tet Offensive, preceded by a diversionary attack on Khe Sanh, and finally a general uprising of the Viet Cong and the people across South Vietnam.

So tenacious were the communists in assaulting the border targets that at Dak To, during a fierce series of battles, more American casualties were incurred than in any other engagement of the Vietnam War, excluding the approaching shadow of the Tet Offensive. Three hundred dead and almost one thousand wounded made Dak To the most costly of the border battles, and of the entire Vietnam War. It witnessed some of the heaviest and hardest fighting since the battle of the Ia Drang Valley. As November gave way to December, and then January, the threat from further border battles seemed to recede. The lull was perhaps intentional on General Giap's part. For the greatest probing attack of all, on Khe Sanh, would trigger an overwhelming American response, up to but not including the use of nuclear weapons, to destroy the encircling formations of North Vietnamese soldiers.

Previously, the Khe Sanh district of Quang Tri province had been relatively quiet, and combat operations on both sides had been low-key. Few considered that the area itself held any special strategic significance. This would change. The French had originally established a presence there: a fort with its own airstrip had been built on a gentle plateau 3km north of the village of Khe Sanh. Most of the local Vietnamese were rice farmers and workers in the French coffee plantations. In and around the remote mountain village lived a tribe of Bru *montagnards*, a race of Vietnamese aboriginals. Some of these Bru dwelt in their own encampments that were located in the lush sub-tropical jungle covering every mountainside. As American Special Forces began to settle into the *montagnard* villages to construct a viable system of local defence, Khe Sanh attracted their attention. With its native Bru population, close proximity (11km) to the Laotian border and the presence of an existing fort, the region seemed a perfect site for operations. A CIDG project was established by the tough Green Berets, and a friendly working relationship developed between the *montagnards* and the troops. The Marines moved into this quiet and secluded section of Quang Tri in 1966 to secure the area and establish some sort of presence there. But immediate friction between the two services forced the Special Forces out of Khe Sanh to a small camp even closer to the Laotian border—Lang Vei. In retrospect the Green Berets had traded the frying pan for the fire, but neither the Marines nor the Green Berets had an inkling of the immense forces that would be massed against them in later years.

Khe Sanh combat base had been titled 'Fort Dix' by the Marines, and in early 1967 it was modernised to suit their methods of making war. Bunkers were rebuilt and their number increased, living standards were improved (from zero to subsistence), artillery was flown in and perimeter defences (trenches and barbed wire) were constructed. As was common across South Vietnam, a military presence invited an enemy retaliation, and the North Vietnamese Army fought a number of close-range battles on the hill-tops overlooking the Khe Sanh base. Called the 1967 'hill fights', the sporadic conflicts proved to be a foretaste of the battles to come. The hilly terrain surrounding the base was crucial for its defence, and the occupation of the hill-tops became a priority for the Marines. To the north lay Hills 950 and 1015 and to the north-west Hills 558, 861, 881 North and 881 South. Hill 689 rose out of the jungle to the west. Dominating the western approach from Laos to Khe Sanh in particular were the Hills 861 and 881 South, both of which were to be the scene of bloody infantry clashes during the 1967 hill fights as well as the 1968 siege of Khe Sanh.

By August 1967 the base at Khe Sanh had received a new commander, Marine Colonel David E. Lownds. A dour, workmanlike man, Lownds strove to improve the defences of the base—there had been infrequent NVA attacks on the hills throughout the summer months. Marine patrols continued to stir up and brush against communist units crossing the border, and it was becoming clear that the region held some strategic value for the war effort. General Westmoreland planned to make the base a jumping-off point for offensive patrols closer to Laos and the NVA sanctuaries there. The American build-up of men and material was accomplished by Air Force transport planes and Marine supply helicopters, since Route 9, the vitally important road to the coast, was not wide enough or secure enough in parts to sustain a viable re-supply. Part of the base's upgrade included the deployment of more armaments that would play a crucial role in any future engagement. Five M48 tanks, ten Ontos (tracked carriers mounting six 106mm recoilless rifles) and plenty more howitzers and mortars were flown or driven in.

The plethora of high-technology sensors dropped across the Ho Chi Minh Trail, just over the border to the west, began transmitting a growing number of signals to the receiving station in Thailand. Communist foot soldiers and fleets of Zil trucks were being detected as they moved southwards towards Quang Tri province. 'Igloo White' had evidence from infra-red, seismic and acoustic sensors that up to 1,000 trucks had moved into the Khe Sanh area in October, 4,000 in November, and 6,500 in December. Enemy activity was hotting up and the strategic stakes had been raised. By January 1968 there were 6,000 Marines at Khe Sanh and incoming artillery rounds infrequently impacted on the dry and dusty base. The troops took to the bunkers, shrugged on cumbersome flak jackets to protect themselves from shrapnel and prepared for trouble. Throughout the month the Marines at the base were aware of the NVA concentration around them. But the savage mountain terrain, the thick jungle cover and the rolling fogs that hindered aerial reconnaissance prevented any sizeable retaliation. Artillery batteries would fire at coordinates deep in the jungle from which sensor readings had been positive, but no one knew how effective these barrages were. They can have been little more than a nuisance to Giap's deploying forces.

General Westmoreland had reached decision time. Should he bolster the defence of Khe Sanh ready for the enemy onslaught that every Marine there knew was about to take place, or should he abandon the base and withdraw from the area? It was not that the commander of all America's land forces in Vietnam doubted the resolve of the Marines to stand and fight the North Vietnamese, or the ability of bomber pilots to provide adequate support from the air. What hung over the Khe Sanh battlefield like the stench of death was the ghost of Dien Bien Phu, the doomed French fortress in the wilds of North Vietnam that had been besieged and overrun by General Giap's communist forces back in 1954. Dien Bien Phu provided over-eager newsmen at the start of 1968 with both a comparison and a metaphor for Khe Sanh. It seemed that no one could mention one without reference to the other. Westmoreland's apparently unreasoning commitment to the base, and his unwillingness to acknowledge a parallel with the French defence of Dien Bien Phu, made the siege of Khe Sanh the most controversial battle of the Vietnam War.

On 20 January 1968 an amazing piece of luck fell into the laps of the Khe Sanh Marines. A deserter from the NVA, *Trung-Uy* (First Lieutenant) La Than Tonc, the commander of an anti-aircraft company, walked up to the wire waving a white flag. He was immediately interrogated and told his captors what they had suspected all along, that an NVA assault was about to take place—that night. Following the speedy destruction of Khe Sanh, the divisions then planned to flood across Quang Tri province, occupying Quang Tri city and the ancient imperial capital of Hue. The border garrisons strung along the Demilitarised Zone would be outflanked in a single move. Colonel Lownds quickly informed his commanding officer at headquarters as well as the Green Berets commander at Lang Vei, Captain Frank Willoughby. Just after midnight on 20 January approximately 35,000 communist troops began the ground offensive that was to immortalise the name of Khe Sanh.

Hell in a Very Small Place

Stanley Karnow, the author of *Vietnam: A History*, has called the comparisons of Khe Sanh with Dien Bien Phu 'preposterous'. This is true only in regard to the scale of the two battles, for otherwise they shared many similarities. The fact that Khe Sanh was a base under siege was hardly unique: from Plei Me to Loc Ninh, concerted communist attacks on allied bases had been a standard tactic since the beginning of the war. It was the peculiar setting for the Khe Sanh conflict that struck an eerie note. Both the French and the American bases were established deep in unpopulated countryside in the far north-west of the country, and close to the porous border with Laos. Just as the French fortress had straddled an important strategic road running into Laos, so Khe Sanh too guarded the vulnerable Route 9, connecting the Laotian border with the coastal cities of South Vietnam to the east. Both bases, French and American, had been envisaged as jumping-off points for further military actions to strike at communist base areas, and were designed to be re-supplied solely by air. Finally, both were surrounded by a ring of hills vitally important for defence and for the domination of the immediate terrain.

The territory that Dien Bien Phu had guarded held little importance in itself, but the huge military presence was seen as justification alone for adopting a rigorous defensive posture. The strategy in 1954 had been a simple and effective one: the Viet Minh had to move through the area to reach the populated areas of North Vietnam, and when they did the French Army would annihilate them. The strategy failed. General Westmoreland saw Khe Sanh as a crucial battlefield of the future, a probable communist highway during any serious invasion of the South by the NVA. The Marines and the media were told at the height of the siege that Khe Sanh was the 'western anchor of our defence' in South Vietnam. As General Vo Nguyen Giap directed more of his troops towards the area, Khe Sanh increased in importance. In fact, its importance could be directly measured by the amount of attention that Hanoi began to pay it.

American newsmen found the likeness of Khe Sanh to Dien Bien Phu irresistible. Walter Cronkite, speaking on a CBS radio broadcast, claimed that 'the parallels are there for all to see'. Almost every journalist who visited the base and spoke to Colonel Lownds made the comparison, which irritated the Colonel no end, just as it irritated his superior, General Westmoreland. The amount of television news coverage dedicated to Khe Sanh grew out of all proportion to the battle's importance. On CBS, at times, fifty per cent of the reports on the nightly news broadcasts were dedicated to assessing the current state of the siege. The French experience was continually discussed, analysed and compared, and phrases such as 'Dien Bien Phu syndrome', 'Dien Bien Phu gambit' and 'historical ghost' were used in connection. President Johnson and his advisers reflected this concern and it was 'LBJ' who summarily demanded that no 'damn Dinbinphoo' would ruin any hope of an honourable end to the war. The military tired of disassociating itself with the French disaster. Westmoreland was at pains to point out that 'there were many similarities but many differences' between the two sieges. In truth he did not want the fourteen-year-old bad press that General Navarre had bequeathed to him. The French disaster suddenly achieved a popular notoriety and paperback histories like Jules Roy's *The Battle of Dien Bien Phu* began appearing wherever journalists wrote copy. Those who could find it referred to Bernard Fall's superior book on the siege of Dien Bien Phu, *Hell in a Very Small Place*. The press corps were educating themselves, and in one way second-guessing the coming battle by studying General Giap's crowning victory of the Indo-China War. What made the comparison even more poignant was the fact that Giap was again the master strategist and that a veteran unit of Dien Bien Phu, the 304th Division of the North Vietnamese Army, was in place to prosecute this siege. But the Command in Saigon could not believe that Hanoi had pushed the American military into a Dien Bien Phu 'all-or-nothing' position, and the very name of that French débâcle became anathema to it. Assertions that MACV was fighting another Dien Bien Phu were insulting, for the very word was equated with waste and death, the pursuit of a hopeless cause ending with a final ignominious defeat.

Westmoreland may actually have been trying to eradicate the ghost of the French war in Vietnam, once and for all. By re-staging the climactic battle of

1954, he could have hoped to silence his critics, who often compared the American experience to the futile strategy of the French, while unequivocally smashing a Dien Bien Phu-style massed array of communist formations. Perhaps he even hoped to end the war. While Westmoreland flatly denied that Khe Sanh was a repeat performance of the French last act, he publicly voiced his opinion that it was in fact General Giap who was vainly attempting to re-create the 1954 siege. Giap's supposed aim at Khe Sanh was to force the Americans out of South Vietnam for good, just as the massive defeat for Navarre had forced Paris to pull out of the region. These arguments are contentious.

What is certain is that General Westmoreland was delighted to have such a vast build-up of North Vietnamese troops in one place and at one time. The great failure of American strategy since 1965 had been the inability to 'find and fix' the communists. Thus the allotted roles of infantry, artillery, armour and air support as envisaged by planners back in Washington could not be carried out. The desperate need for a conventional set-piece battle was great, and had motivated MACV to pursue its grand strategies of search-and-destroy. Operations such as 'Hastings' and 'Junction City' involved pincer manoeuvres carried out by US and ARVN units to force the VC and NVA to fight on allied terms. But, with superior mobility and tactical skill, the communists had flatly refused to give battle, unless it was at a time and a place of their own choosing. Khe Sanh had become such a place.

As it became clear that a large-scale siege, and perhaps the greatest military encounter of the war, was about to get under way, President Johnson glimpsed the danger of defeat. He demanded that the Joint Chiefs of Staff sign a declaration ('in blood' as the President put it) that vowed Khe Sanh would never fall. If the garrison held, Johnson would accept the applause along with General Westmoreland. If it fell, he was determined to force his military advisers to face the fury of public anger, remaining untarnished himself by such a reversal. The President feared that the war lay in the balance with the outcome of the siege, and so he became obsessed with its course. He had a miniature Khe Sanh re-created in the White House basement war room and would pace around it at all hours, immersing himself in a constant stream of tactical minutiae. It was as if his empathy with the trapped Marines up there in a corner of Quang Tri province could somehow help both him and his staff suddenly to glimpse some unforeseen solution to the battle. The brilliant flashes of phosphorous and napalm that exploded over NVA positions outside the wire at Khe Sanh cast a long shadow over South Vietnam and Washington, terminating on the President's sand-table re-enactment—and it was the shadow of Dien Bien Phu.

The Siege of Khe Sanh

Within six hours of a preparatory assault on the Marines holding Hill 861 just after midnight, 20 January, the Khe Sanh combat base came under concerted fire from NVA rocket artillery. Immediately the ammunition dump, with a stockpile of 1,500 tons of rifle rounds, high-explosive howitzer shells, grenades, mortars and rockets was hit and exploded with a destructive shock-wave and a thick cloud of smoke. The recent structures put up by the Marines were flattened, bunkers were damaged and oil tanks caught fire. Ammunition rained down on the base to explode, or sat in the fires slowly cooking off. Black smoke, pools of burning oil and the smashed remains of buildings gave the base an appearance of utter devastation. And hundreds of enemy shells still streaked in to cause havoc and confusion. In dawn's early light, the troops entrenched on the surrounding hills could not believe that Khe Sanh had survived that sickening explosion, until radio messages were received to reassure each unit that the end had not come so soon after the beginning.

Less than 24 hours later, a battalion of NVA took the village of Khe Sanh that sat astride Route 9. That road was the only means of overland contact with Lang Vei, which was now cut off from other allied troops. Khe Sanh base quickly got back to a combat footing and began to weather the almost continuous bombardment from the NVA guns and howitzers. The hill-top Marine positions were also faced with barrages and determined assaults. The massed infantry assault that had been expected, complete with 'human waves' of North Vietnamese soldiers known to charge the wire with bayonets fixed, did not occur. Instead sporadic infantry skirmishes were interspersed with a long-running artillery duel. The nagging fear of a ground assault combined with the very real danger of incoming artillery fire created a grim and depressing atmosphere at Khe Sanh.

Days of bombardment turned into weeks, and the shrill cry of 'Incoming!' became a regular sound that initiated a frenzy of activity as Marines (and sailors—there were over 200 Navy construction engineers trapped on the base) ran for bunkers and foxholes. The use of artillery by the Viet Minh had totally surprised the defenders of Dien Bien Phu. Similarly, the communist guns often out-ranged their American-made equivalents, with many of them firing from secret caves across the Laotian border! The Marines were not without artillery support: a total of 46 guns (varying from 4.2in mortars, 105mm and 155mm, to 175mm howitzers) were on call to return fire on enemy artillery positions (if they could reach them) and provide support for US troops engaged in hill fights with the NVA. At Camp Carroll and the Marine firebase at the Rockpile further east there were also 175mm guns ready and waiting to provide an effective barrage of fire in the defence of the base. Hampering the accurate fire of American guns, however, were the frequent mists and fogs that developed in the deep ravines around the base. The fog and cloud prohibited airborne observation of enemy artillery, and there were few opportunities to send out Marine patrols to spot for the Khe Sanh guns. Obviously, the fact that the long-range guns employed by the NVA were sited in caves made retaliation doubly difficult. These artillery pieces were in the side of Co Roc mountain, 27km from Khe Sanh and just over the South Vietnam–Laos border. The caves proved immune to retaliatory air strikes by Air Force B-52 bombers and the guns were never silenced.

Other guns, closer to the base and its hill-top positions, were not so well entrenched, but by firing short barrages and pulling back into camouflaged cover they remained well hidden from any observers, airborne or otherwise, who might be in the area. The result was a constant rain of shells on the rust-red base, now virtually flat and featureless save for the air traffic tower, an occasional bunker and the tails and wings of cargo planes sticking grotesquely up into the air where they had been blown up by incoming rounds. The dusty plateau was slightly raised from the ground around it, affording the Marines a slight advantage in any infantry engagement, something that the French defenders had not possessed. Neither had they held the outlying hills. In fact, against General Navarre's every expectation, the architect of Dien Bien Phu, General Giap, had managed to occupy the hills surrounding the French base—not with infantry, but with long-range artillery pieces. Navarre had no inkling that Giap even possessed such weaponry, or that his troops had the sheer determination to deploy it by muscle power alone to the crests of steep-sided and heavily forested hills. With impunity, Giap had the guns fire a constant barrage on to the French garrison. Surrendering those hills was Navarre's mistake, and it was a mistake that General Westmoreland vowed not to repeat. Whatever happened, the hills around Khe Sanh would remain in American hands. If they fell, Westmoreland knew that Khe Sanh would be indefensible—despite a continuous deluge of high-explosive bombs from the US Air Force.

'Incoming' became a way of life for the 6,000 trapped Marines on that dusty plateau, cut off from ground reinforcement and re-supply. During daylight hours the rounds would tend to be more infrequent, triggered usually by the movement of vehicles (the base's water truck was a popular target) and cargo planes landing and taking off. But at night the NVA could move freely and its artillery strikes lit up the sky. The nights were 'beautiful', said Michael Herr, a freelance journalist at Khe Sanh, 'beautiful and deeply dreadful'. 'Beautiful' was not an adjective one could use to describe life at Khe Sanh in general. Living conditions were terrible. By the start of February, the base had become a smouldering tip with rubbish and parts of old buildings strewn across the area, along with pieces of aeroplane and helicopter. The stink of burning faeces spewed from large oil drums and shrouded the dust-laden base. Underground, the Marines were relatively safe from incoming rounds, but the alternative, large black rats that bred at an alarming rate, was hardly comforting. The rats and the atrocious conditions caused by the close living conditions made bunker life almost unbearable.

Rats became the Marines' bedfellows as they scuttled in the darkness, across stinking sheets, along floors and on to men's faces. The soldiers wrapped themselves, cocoon-like, into their blankets, fully dressed, but any open piece of flesh became fair game for the fat rodents. Poisons and traps did not kill enough of them, and when someone 'flipped' inside a bunker and opened fire with an M16 or Colt handgun, they were just as likely to hit a Marine as a rat. Those unlucky enough to get bitten on the feet, the hands or the face developed nasty sores that were prone to infection. For comfort, the troops had a least a supply of food, but the C-Rations with which they were issued had to be juggled together in an endless attempt to make them seem appetising. Conditions were bad, but not as bad as those endured by the wretches who survived the ordeal of Dien Bien Phu. And one can only imagine the state of the communist soldiers huddled in the primitive red-mud trenches surrounding Khe Sanh. Water, food, sleep and comfort of any kind must have been highly valued commodities.

The daylight hours were interspersed with enemy 'incoming' (on some days up to 1,000 rounds would hit the base), perimeter forays by communist assault groups and the alarming shots of well-concealed snipers. Snipers faced the wrath of Marine artillery and recoilless rifle teams, some surviving beyond all expectation to harass the Marines again and again. On one occasion a sniper began operating on the Khe Sanh perimeter, but rather than blast his position with artillery as they had his predecessor's, the Marines left him in place. He had failed to hit a single person since he had begun, and the Marines thought it prudent to leave him be rather than kill him. He might easily be replaced with someone who had far greater talent! Snipers were one danger, and, in the dead of night, the digging of enemy trenches closer to the perimeter was another. Marines could hear the digging at night, and called in napalm and high-explosive bombing strikes on the zigzagging trenches during the day. Even so, the trenches crept ever closer, and by 29 February they were within 100m of the wire. The following month they came even nearer, but the danger from these fortifications was far less than from the Viet Minh trenches at Dien Bien Phu. There the complex network of trenches had protected an entire army, and been a well-protected launching point for assaults on the garrison. At Khe Sanh the ground assaults never came, for the attackers were trying desperately to survive the deluge of bombs that poured down on to their positions day after day for over two months. General Westmoreland had christened this bombing campaign Operation 'Niagara', and his choice of title proved apt: it described a seemingly endless cascade of bombs that fell on to the surrounding North Vietnamese forces.

Operation 'Niagara'

The amount of air power available for the support of the beleaguered Marines at Khe Sanh set the siege apart from that at Dien Bien Phu. Effective anti-aircraft guns shot down a great many of the French bombers and cargo planes, isolating that garrison. But at Khe Sanh a constant and unyielding barrage prevented the mustering of an attack force and provided a shield of fire behind which cargo planes such as the C-130 and C-123 could make cargo drops or landings. First considered on 5 January, Operation 'Niagara' began life as a contingency plan to support the Khe Sanh perimeter with a bombing campaign should the NVA mount a concerted assault. The plan became action on 21 January as the enemy began its first offensive. Within the first 24 hours of the operation, over 600 sorties had been flown against targets in the Khe Sanh area, 551 of which were by fighter-bombers (and the rest by B-52s).

An airborne command post, code-named 'Hillsborough', circled constantly to coordinate the incoming bombing sorties with airborne and ground-based target acquisitions. It helped to organise the vast bombing effort, which was divided into two almost distinct halves. One was carried out by low- and medium-level fighter-bombers flying from air bases in South Vietnam, the other by high altitude B-52 strategic bombers based at Thailand, Guam and Okinawa. Between them the combined devastation wrought on the 35,000 North Vietnamese regulars was enough to forestall the expected mass attack, thus saving the combat base from being overrun. For the smaller fighter-bombers of the Marine Corps, Navy and Air Force, the operation was fraught with hazard, not least because of the poor weather. Incessant low-level cloud shrouded the surrounding hills and seeped into the valleys, making accurate bombing runs difficult if not impossible. Visibility at the low levels required by precision bombing runs was reduced to less than 2,000m, and the danger of flying a fast jet into a hillside was very real. As it was, only one A-4 Skyhawk and one F-4 Phantom were lost during the air support operation, amazing figures considering that well over 24,000 aircraft sorties were flown.

Adding to pilots' problems was a fusillade of anti-aircraft fire from troops below the clouds, who fired up at the sound of an incoming jet. Perhaps more of a danger was the prospect of collision with other bombers. The round-the-clock operation involved hundreds of aircraft, with several in the air above Khe Sanh at the same time. A 'daisy chain' system similar to that employed by civil air traffic controllers enabled a stack of jets to circle above enemy concentrations. Each waited, relay-like, for his turn to begin a bombing run. Returning to base, the pilots would catch some sleep while their aircraft were rearmed and refuelled, ready for another sortie against the NVA surrounding the base. The complexity that the operation involved could have ended in disaster had not the command and control in place been so efficient. Stray bombs could have easily wiped out a Marine position atop one of the strategic hills, or devastated part of the Khe Sanh base had it fallen within the perimeter. In addition, had bombers from the three separate services bombed the same piece of terrain, causing unnecessary duplication, then the entire operation may have been blunted considerably. As it was, Westmoreland, who had at last the chance to organise his own bombing campaign free of the 'Rolling Thunder' mentality, ensured that every bombing sortie played a part in the overall air support campaign.

In an important new step, General Westmoreland allowed the chief of the Seventh Air Force, General William Moymer, to take control of the Marine Corps' fixed-wing aircraft. Prior to this point on 18 January, the Marines had hoped that Khe Sanh could be supported purely by their own jet bombers, which was exactly what they were there for. The vast scale of the battle, however, precluded an independent approach. The result would have been chaos, redundancy and collisions. Ranged against the NVA attackers, the US air armada was immense, and it included the full gamut of attack aircraft in the American arsenal. And combined with the bombing were infrequent defoliation missions to rid the surrounding terrain of its lush tropical cover. This, combined with the continual pounding by high-explosive bombs, turned the landscape into a featureless wasteland.

The devastation of the surrounding terrain meant that Giap's troops were unable to form up for attacks. There was little cover available behind the startlines for offensives and few points of reference for units to make for. All the units were under-strength from constant casualties, and attempts to cross the blasted landscape to relay orders or move into attack positions exposed the troops to 'Niagara''s waterfall of death. That operation was so successful that the dug-in troops around Khe Sanh could do little else but try desperately to stay alive. As the bombing tactics were refined, a cell of three B-52s was dropping its huge bomb load over enemy positions every three hours, day or night, bad weather or good. At high altitude, beyond the turbulent and dense cloud formations, and with accurate coordination from 'Combat Skyspot' guidance radar, the B-52s were continually on tap. When these impressive figures are combined with the sortie rates of the fighter-bombers, an air strike took place in the Khe Sanh area on average once every five minutes, for 77 days. In total, the firepower unleashed on the North Vietnamese during the siege exceeded the explosive power of the first atomic bomb dropped on Hiroshima—by five times.

President Johnson, fearful that such awful destruction could escalate to mind-boggling proportions, asked General Westmoreland to assure him that he, the President, 'would not be called upon to use the atomic bomb to save Khe Sanh'. The military establishment had signed 'in blood' to guarantee the security of the outpost, but Johnson did not want to allow them the option of using the weapon of last resort. Westmoreland, though, did not want to rule the concept out. He was thinking along the lines of tactical nuclear weapons—battlefield bombs that could be fired from artillery or dropped from jets and could be used relatively close to friendly troop positions. A small group was hastily established to study such a move, but Johnson closed it down as soon as he heard of it. Visions of MacArthur threatening to obliterate cities in China and North Korea with President Truman's A-bombs no doubt swam clearly into view. After the war, Westmoreland would consider that the nuclear defence of Khe Sanh had been a viable option, and that to 'fail to consider this alternative was a mistake'.

The Logistical Effort

Khe Sanh depended for its very survival on aircraft from the three US armed services. In Operation 'Niagara' the onus was on strike aircraft that included, besides the B-52s, A-4 Skyhawks, A-6 Intruders, F-4 Phantoms, F-8 Crusaders, A-1 Skyraiders, F-105 Thunderchiefs and F-100 Super Sabres. But, without the

Air Force's fleet of C-130 Hercules and C-123 Providers, Khe Sanh could not have held out, despite the bombing campaign. Route 9, the only road to the coastal enclaves, was hopelessly riddled with hostile forces ready to spring an ambush. When the ammunition dump exploded in the opening hours of the siege, approximately ninety per cent of Khe Sanh's ammunition was destroyed. Immediately Brigadier-General Burl McLaughlin of the US Air Force, who was made responsible for the air supply, ordered small Provider cargo planes into Khe Sanh to rearm the Marines trapped there. The C-130 Hercules, the standard workhorse of air supply operations, could not be used since the exploding ammunition dump had destroyed the end of the runway at the base on 21 January: now only 600m long, it was too short for the landing and take-off run required by the Hercules.

Other supplies besides ammunition were also in demand. Food, medicines, raw materials for bunkers, troop reinforcements and spare parts were all flown in. The lack of an adequately sized runway was not allowed to interfere with this operation. Methods were designed to overcome the (relatively huge) obstacles that both the situation and the North Vietnamese Army had created for the Air Force. Parachute drops were made, but often these were inaccurate and tended to drift, sometimes outside the drop zone on the edge of the Khe Sanh perimeter. Troops dispatched to retrieve the contents of air-dropped pallets would often come under fire and the drops became too hazardous for this reason. While the Navy engineers (Seabees) began repairing the runway, more unlikely methods of resupply were developed. Two successful methods were used. LAPES (Low Altitude Parachute Extraction System) employed parachutes that were attached to a cargo pallet by cable to drag it out of the back of a Hercules as the plane flew low over the airfield. The cargo would slide out of the hold and drop the three metres or so, decelerating from over 200kph to zero in just a few seconds. As they careered across the aluminium matting, the pallets occasionally caused damage, and they were also prone to skidding wildly in some unforeseen direction. On 2 March one Marine was unfortunately killed when one such LAPES pallet smashed into his bunker alongside the airstrip. A second method involved a similar procedure, but, instead of a parachute, a hook trailed from the cargo out of the aircraft and engaged an arrester wire that had been stretched across the runway. As the Hercules maintained its flight path, the arrester wire pulled the cargo pallet out of the plane and to the ground, holding it safely. This was GPES (the Ground Proximity Extraction System).

By the end of January the runway was again open to the Hercules and supplies came in at an increased rate. A Hercules cargo hold tripled the available space offered by a C-123 Provider. Marines at Khe Sanh disparagingly called the C-130s 'mortar magnets', and after two were lost and several others damaged it was recognised that the risk both to air crews and aircraft had become so great that it was thought best to use airborne delivery entirely. Providers still made landings since they could be off-loaded and turned around in much less time than the C-130, but three C-123s were nevertheless destroyed at Khe Sanh. The NVA gunners had zeroed in on the touch-down and off-load points of the landing operation, and always opened up when any aircraft began its descent. Royal Air Force pilots, flying C-130s into Sarajevo airport during the Bosnian conflict in the early 1990s, carried out what they referred to as the 'Khe Sanh approach'. It involved a medium-altitude approach followed by a sickeningly steep final approach to the runway, while firing anti-missile flares, all at moderately high speeds. It has become the standard procedure for landing large cargo planes in a hostile environment.

After the last of the three destroyed Providers was shot out of the sky on 6 March, a greater emphasis was placed on the use of helicopters for air supply. For the Marines stationed out on the hills, this would be the only method of re-supply to which they had access. In an operation termed 'Super Gaggle', a large flight of Marine CH-46 Sea Knight helicopters would 'chopper in' up to 1,800kg of supplies each, slung from nets beneath them. These drops were also prone to drawing fire and A-4 Skyhawks usually accompanied the flights, ready to pound enemy positions with rockets, napalm, bombs and cannon-fire. Seventeen helicopters were lost to enemy fire during these hill re-supply missions.

In general, the logistical effort triumphed over its single obstacle: placing supplies on a runway that was under continuous enemy fire. The various aircraft involved eventually delivered 12,400 tons of supplies to Khe Sanh, and a large proportion of this was ammunition. C-130s made 273 landings and C-123 Providers made 179. There were 496 parachute drops by C-130s over the combat base, while C-123s made 105 air drops. Only the C-130 Hercules carried out LAPES and GPES operations, a total of 57 in all.

The Siege is Lifted

For most of the Marines, life at Khe Sanh consisted of almost unending periods of boredom. This was interspersed with bouts of intense fear and dread as another heavy artillery barrage pounded the base, or some activity beyond the wire seemed to signal an imminent communist attack. During the day troops tried to catch up on much-needed sleep, relaxed or repaired bunkers. At night it was usual for a one hundred per cent watch to be posted, every man ready and waiting for the expected attack, scanning the perimeter for some kind of warning. On the morning of 7 February an event occurred that reduced morale at Khe Sanh to a new low. The Special Forces camp at Lang Vei, cut off near the Laotian border was overrun—by tanks. Of the 400 defenders, 316 were killed, and the tanks (actually PT-76 tracked reconnaissance vehicles) helped to destroy much of the perimeter defences and assaulted the Lang Vei command bunker. At Khe Sanh, barely 8km away, the Marines could not doubt that their turn was next. One CBS correspondent optimistically reported: 'The Marines are long on courage and short on dug-in positions.' But the fear that Khe Sanh was about to fall was tangible amongst the troops manning the bunkers. 'We're gonna get whacked,' said one disgruntled Marine. 'We're gonna get hurt bad, real bad.'

On the hills life was just as hard, if not harder. There were fewer fortified positions and a constant exposure to both NVA artillery and infantry attacks. But the hill positions were by far the most crucial positions of the war, even if the casualties it took to hold them became excessive. On Hill 861 a Marine platoon was ambushed while on patrol and almost totally wiped out. To the west, on Hill 881S, a company that had started with 185 men took so much fire that 167 members of the company were killed or wounded. But both 861 and 881S were bulwarks of the Khe Sanh defence. Each one of the surrounding hills was manned by elements of the 26th Marine Regiment and each became besieged in its turn— each a miniature version of the drama unfolding down at the Khe Sanh base. Resupply was made even more hazardous by the lack of proper landing facilities. On Hill 881S a medevac helicopter gaining speed for take-off was destroyed by an NVA mortar round on 22 January. More than twenty wounded Marines were killed in the wreck. The 'Super Gaggle' helicopter re-supplies increased both morale and fighting effectiveness and enabled the weary Marines to remain strong enough to fend off the slackening NVA assaults.

As March progressed, the hill fights wound down, with communist attacks becoming less and less determined. Continued artillery and napalm strikes had stripped almost every vestige of jungle growth from the hills to create a barren and alien landscape, marked here and there with craters, ravines and tree stumps. But without its all-important cover, and losing troops on an hourly basis, the North Vietnamese offensive eventually slackened and finally ended, its troops melting away back over the border into Laos or eastwards towards the coast. As resistance faded, MACV organised an overland relief effort to link up with the Marines and South Vietnamese troops at Khe Sanh. Begun on 1 April, it was code-named Operation 'Pegasus'. Marines from the 1st and 3rd Marine Regiments moved along Route 9 while elements of the 1st Air Cavalry Division conducted leapfrogging airmobile operations, emplacing artillery to cover the route and assaulting communist positions. Landing Zones were established all along the road, enabling the force to be supplied and reinforced quickly if required.

As the 'Pegasus' troops entered the Khe Sanh valley on 4 April they encountered rigorous opposition from North Vietnamese regulars. A dominant hill in that area, Hill 471, was fought over until NVA troops were dislodged. Enemy activity continued to harry the force as it opened up Route 9 and repaired the road and its bridges. Finally, on 6 April, the Air Cavalry met up with Marines from the Khe Sanh combat base. With no remaining NVA left to lay siege to the shattered firebase, the Marines were none too pleased to have been 'saved' by the Army. General Westmoreland had said that 'Pegasus' would not be a rescue, rather it was a westward search-and-destroy operation that would link up with the Marines in the Khe Sanh valley. But for the reporters and television cameras it was a relief column and a rescue mission, even though there were no enemy huddled around the wire lobbing in mortar rounds. The battle for Khe Sanh was over. Two months later, with little fanfare, Khe Sanh was dismantled, its bunkers bulldozed, blown up or burnt. Anything of value to the communists was ripped up and smashed. In only a few hours the Marines did to Khe Sanh what the North Vietnamese gunners had been trying to do for 77 days—demolish it entirely. All that was left as the last trucks rumbled away from the rust-red plateau and the last helicopters lifted off the remaining engineers was the airstrip. The expense of dismantling it was not thought worthwhile, and, like the French, the Americans left it behind as a mute testimony to a cause and a war that would become part of history.

In total, approximately 600 allied lives were lost in the defence of Khe Sanh, and to abandon it utterly sickened some and gladdened others. The Marines had fought for a scrap of land, a hill-top fortress, and had been repeatedly told of its immense strategic importance to the defence of South Vietnam. To evacuate the base after so much effort had been expended to keep it made most Marines bitter and angry. For Westmoreland the survival of the base alone was a victory that he could be proud of. Was it a victory? Despite the Marines' facing perhaps 35,000 NVA, only 1,602 bodies were counted in the wire and on the hillsides. Perhaps two or three times this figure were actually killed, since the high-explosive bombs and shells will have shredded many bodies and pulverised their remains into uncountable fragments. Like all the battles of the war, the siege of Khe Sanh had ended inconclusively. Today, Khe Sanh is still a subject for discussion, and few operations of the war have been wracked by such controversy.

Khe Sanh and the Firebase Psychosis

Even before the siege of Khe Sanh had ended, military strategists, politicians and reporters all wanted to know: what had just happened? According to General Westmoreland, General Giap's divisions had intended to capture the whole of Quang Tri province, south of the DMZ, but had been stalled at Khe Sanh and forced to engage the garrison there. By relentless pounding from supporting artillery and from the aircraft of Operation 'Niagara', Giap's forces, as well as his hopes of victory, had been smashed (military estimates of enemy dead were between ten and fifteen thousand). Soon after the siege of Khe Sanh had begun, the nationwide Tet Offensive erupted in all major towns and cities, involving thousands of Viet Cong irregulars in daring attacks. Westmoreland was convinced that this crucial large-scale conflict was merely a diversion for the siege in Quang Tri province. After the war this theory was widely decried: the sheer scale of the Tet campaign (discussed in the following chapter) could in no way be called a 'diversion'.

In all probability, Westmoreland's theory was partially correct. The NVA divisions would have cut across South Vietnam to the coast, seizing Quang Tri city and linking up with Viet Cong units battling in Hue. But Khe Sanh itself was not the important linchpin imagined by him at the time. Rather it was the final climax of the border battles that had been designed to pull entire troop divisions away from the cities and out to the borders with Laos and Cambodia. The *real* thrust of the campaign was to be the Tet Offensive. Giap's strategy of bluff had worked, and this was proved by Westmoreland's wartime statement that Khe Sanh had been the communists' main target all along.

The General was criticised for garrisoning and fortifying what was essentially just another firebase to create a huge combat base needing extensive re-supply and combat support. It was said that he was tying down thousands of troops that could have been more fruitfully employed countering the Tet guerrillas. In other words, he had fallen into Giap's trap. But, in doing so, Westmoreland did in turn tie down 35,000 well-trained and well-armed North Vietnamese regulars who could have turned the tide for the revolutionaries in the north of the country. The NVA was poised to sweep southwards and take advantage of any success gained by the Viet Cong in their surprise attacks. When these successes failed to materialise, the military leadership in Hanoi must have hoped to salvage something out of the situation and declined to withdraw its forces from Khe Sanh.

The siege was not a singular event, a one-time strategic mistake that had never occurred before nor was likely to occur again. There were many Khe Sanhs across South Vietnam from 1965 to 1972. The problem revolved around one of Westmoreland's chief military innovations: the fire support base (FSB). He was to later call the Army and Marine dependency on the ubiquitous artillery fortifications a 'firebase psychosis'. And Khe Sanh was to be an example of this psychosis writ large, a gross distortion of reality that had inverted the rules of war. The siege perfectly illustrated the excesses of the American war in Vietnam, its huge errors and its failures, becoming almost a microcosm of the war as a whole. We have already discussed some of the war's tactical disadvantages, mainly hinging on the reliance of firepower at the expense of manoeuvrability, and in Khe Sanh we can see many of the elements of this controversial approach.

Khe Sanh was in essence a large FSB, a standard fortification of the war that supported infantry patrols with speedy artillery fire as they slogged through thick jungle or waded through paddy fields. Few foot patrols or infantry operations took place outside these firebase 'umbrellas', which seriously limited pursuits and encircling manoeuvres. What Westmoreland called the 'firebase psychosis' referred to both these installations and also to helicopter landing zones, which often became temporary field bases.

Khe Sanh was supplied almost totally by air, a common method of re-supply for both FSBs and other combat bases in the field across Vietnam. This illustrated a common philosophy during the war: if you can't go through a piece of terrain, go over it ! This made American bases easy to surround and put under siege. At some time, almost every CIDG camp and large firebase came under attack from communist forces beyond their perimeters. Their isolated locations added to their vulnerability and dependency on air supply. Airstrips played a crucial role in the survival of firebases so equipped. Consequently a great deal of effort was put into defending them. A kind of self-fulfilling mission thus evolved for some of these outposts. Army Captain (later General) Colin Powell once asked his ARVN opposite in 1963 why the lonely jungle outpost of A Shau had been sited so far from friendly base areas. 'Outpost is here to protect airfield,' said the ARVN Captain. 'What's the airfield here for?' asked Powell. 'Airfield here to resupply outpost.' Such a circular argument might easily have issued from the lips of an MACV press officer defending the Khe Sanh strategy.

That defensive strategy rested mainly on aerial bombardment, yet another broadly typical feature of most ground contacts in-country. Air support was almost always available, if the weather permitted, to strafe and bomb enemy troops. Operation 'Niagara' transformed the tactical air support mission into a 24-hour, seven-days-a-week industry. It honed and enlarged on a system that had been functioning daily since the first warplanes had arrived in Vietnam. The torrent of bombs from the sky was relentless. There are several locations in present-day Vietnam, including the area around Khe Sanh and Con Thien, that are still littered with unexploded ordnance, and adults and children die every year in bomb accidents. Saturation of the perimeter of a firebase or defensive position from the air provided the greatest amount of firepower quickly and without a serious risk to pilots.

Finally, as we have seen in the previous chapter, Khe Sanh illustrated more than any other battle that territory was disposable, important to the point of madness one day and useless and of no strategic value the next. There were many hills fought over in various wilderness areas of South Vietnam that were referred to merely by a number. Most became violent battlegrounds purely because the enemy was there in strength and had to be dislodged. Khe Sanh typified this strategy, beginning life as an unimportant CIDG camp, suddenly becoming the western anchor of allied defence and then reverting to uninhabited terrain, a worthless red-dust plateau, scored and burnt by the conflict and its aftermath.

Chapter 7

TET AND THE TV WAR

'It is questionable whether a democracy can fight war successfully without censorship,' said Ambassador Ellesworth Bunker, who had taken over from Henry Cabot Lodge in 1967. He concurred with General Westmoreland in his deliberations over the role of media reporting in the Vietnam War. How could effective reporting be carried out when (according to Westmoreland) there were 700 reporters in South Vietnam roaming about at will searching desperately for a sensational story that would catch the eye of the public back home? Secretary of State Dean Rusk cautioned that in the event of Congress committing troops to another war, 'it must address itself to the censorship problem at the same time'. After the bloody Tet Offensive in early 1968, the pervading mood amongst both the military staff and those in Washington was one of bitterness against the press. Increasingly, the Saigon press corps was seen as an enemy on a par with the Viet Cong and North Vietnamese and many in the military were blaming the media for crippling the war. Accusations that it had worked against the American commitment in South Vietnam and not with it were common. When American troops had pulled out completely by 1972, the press actually caught the blame for losing the war entirely. Were these accusations justified?

Journalists who made the trip to Vietnam found that they had an almost unlimited freedom to report. With helicopter transport available to any part of the country, including some of the hottest front-line areas, the journalist had unprecedented opportunities. In some cases requests for transport would be met by eager commanders laying on a helicopter just to get a reporter into the action immediately. At least one of the print journalists carried around a camera specifically for the benefit of looking the part and catching the eye of unit commanders. Press camps were organised that were a world apart from the firebase amenities that the troops (rarely) enjoyed. These camps included telephones and opportunities for regular military flights to Saigon. No other war had been able to provide such rapid and frequent transport facilities into and out of combat zones. This meant that reporters were not restricted to a single place or unit, but could obtain stories from almost every possible in-country location. Uniquely, there were very few official reporting restrictions, and the existence of Gulf War-style press pools, each with its own Public Affairs Officer, would have been quite unthinkable. Considering the 'Press Lost Vietnam' syndrome that is perpetuated in the military even today, the freedom granted to journalists in that war was ironic.

George Orwell, in his novel *1984*, wrote of a totalitarian state that waged a perpetual war against its neighbours. Every defeat in this war was portrayed by the government as a resounding victory, and the citizens were forever unaware of the true nature of the conflict that was being fought by, and for, them. Orwell had singled out the levers of power, the mechanism for almost total control of people and politics—the media. In the spring of 1968 a similar sleight of hand is said to have taken place that utterly reversed the outcome of the greatest campaign of the Vietnam War, the Tet Offensive. No one is suggesting that the corridors of Washington in 1968 were home to a despotic totalitarian government: in fact, President Johnson's administration was to become one of the first victims of this paradoxical reversal. According to critics in the post-Tet period, the outcome of the allied struggle against the communists during the Tet campaign had been portrayed to Americans not as the victory that it was. In a bizarre inversion of Orwell's victory propaganda, it had been depicted as a defeat, and it resulted in America's pulling out of South-East Asia altogether. Perpetrating this misinformation campaign were key journalists and news reporters, who represented a new anti-establishment movement. But there are those who dispute this now widely accepted theory and who categorically deny that the media should take the blame for the fall of South Vietnam.

From the very beginning of Johnson's commitment to the war in Vietnam, a credibility gap had opened up between his government and the people of America. The truth behind the Tonkin Gulf incident, the body counts, the real failures of the pacification programme and the secret wars being fought over the borders in Laos and Cambodia should have occupied this gap, bringing Americans closer to the reasons, the decisions and the rationalisations. Where these facts had been there now existed an information vacuum, and it was soon to be occupied by the ever-hungry American media. Working not on the government's behalf but on their own, the reporters filled the credibility gap and seemed eager to find their own motives and assessments of the Vietnam situation. A prevailing mood of suspicion and distrust was working its way into the media on both sides of the Pacific. Few believed either the body counts or the numerous MACV press statements claiming total communist eradication from some region or other. When enemy-held hills were claimed to be of 'vital strategic importance', most journalists knew instinctively that they would be abandoned almost as soon as they were taken. And any officer in the Command who claimed to be able to see the mythical 'light at the end of the tunnel' was met with choking disbelief—more because of that phrase's hoary antiquity than its blatant lack of truth.

The Tet Offensive: 31 January 1968

The siege of Khe Sanh, although vast in scope, formed only part of General Giap's 1967–68 winter/spring offensive. Although Westmoreland believed otherwise at the time, that great battle in Quang Tri province had actually been a feint, and a continuation of the 1967 border battles that aimed to test allied resolve and efficiency. Simultaneously it flexed communist muscles in preparation for the fighting to come. Giap's 'Second Wave' was an all-out urban offensive on every major population centre. It was carefully calculated to inspire a spontaneous Vietnamese uprising against both the Americans and their 'puppet regime'. The success of the 'Second Wave' attacks depended on many things, but most of all on two assumptions, the first being that the ARVN, 'the army that will not fight', would collapse or side with the guerrillas rather than give battle. It also required that the urban Vietnamese rise up in support of the communists, showing their defiance of the Saigon government and their support of Hanoi in a popular revolution. Given the immense size of the Tet Offensive, and the fact that it would deliver a devastating hammer blow to communities across South Vietnam, striking everywhere at once and without warning, these assumptions seemed sound. Had a senior American officer been in on Giap's meticulous planning, he might well have agreed. But in war, just as in life, plans can be thwarted and assumptions proved wrong.

The coordination of the communist attacks, involving more than 80,000 troops from Quang Tri in the north down to Quan Long in the Mekong Delta, was in itself a stupendous feat, and one that did not run smoothly. In the early hours of 30 January, exactly 24 hours before the main fighting began, eight towns in the Central Highlands and along the coast were assaulted by Viet Cong forces using rockets, mortars and infantry. Nha Trang was hit, Hoi An was hit, the highland city of Ban Me Thuot and the cities of Pleiku and Qui Nhon were hit and Da Nang suffered attacks from a communist sapper unit. The soldiers had mixed inextricably with the Vietnamese peasants and townsfolk and achieved utter surprise in carrying out their attacks. In retaliation, the allied response was remarkably quick and efficient, and few of the attackers survived to see the 31st. There had been rumours and intelligence reports of a suspected nationwide offensive erupting sometime around the Tet New Year holiday, and for many in the Command it looked as if it had been easily contained—perhaps too easily.

Reading the failed offensive as a warning, American and South Vietnamese forces were immediately put on full alert and had their leave cancelled. For the South Vietnamese President, Thieu, the mobilisation of his army was going to be difficult. The Tet Lunar New Year holiday was the most important and revered festival of the Vietnamese calendar, and up to fifty per cent of the ARVN troops were away on leave, visiting relatives, celebrating in the bustling city streets or indulging in quiet prayer at a local temple. The sacred holiday officially began on 31 January and lasted for several days. During that time virtually all work stopped, and warfare stopped along with it. Little fighting had been conducted during previous Tet holidays in all the long years of struggle against the communists. Few but the most paranoid of intelligence analysts doubted that 1968 would be any different; an official cease-fire had even been arranged between the two sides. Unfortunately for Thieu there was not enough time to recall troops on leave in sufficient numbers. The hastily mobilised American and ARVN units would have to face the onslaught alone. General Westmoreland's chief of intelligence predicted that the next wave of communist guerrillas would attack 'tonight or tomorrow morning'.

MACV had 24 hours to prepare for the Tet Offensive, hardly long enough but infinitely better than no time at all. What motives and plans the regional communist officer responsible for pre-empting the Tet Offensive had may never be known. Some confusion over the timing of the attacks may have existed, since Ho Chi Minh had decreed that, for 1968 only, Tet would officially begin a day early, on 29 January. This allowed the North Vietnamese to begin their holiday celebrations on 28 January (the eve of Tet, always a time for festivities) and end them on 30 January. It was a three-day period that mirrored the Tet holiday of the South. Ho Chi Minh's aim was to prevent the North Vietnamese from being caught totally unprepared as American warplanes retaliated with bombing attacks as they had done in the past. Whatever the reason was for the mix-up, it enabled the allies to prepare for Tet, the coming storm. When it did eventually arrive on the morning of 31 January, the Tet Offensive shocked and amazed both privates and generals with its sheer size and unexpected ferocity.

One of the first attacks made against the Americans—and one of the most psychologically damaging—was a fifteen-man 'suicide' raid on the US embassy in Saigon. These specialised commandos, termed sappers, were the communist élite troops and were often expendable Viet Cong irregulars. Although the name 'sapper' used to mean, historically, a military engineer, the VC sappers in Vietnam were highly trained explosives experts, skilled in breaching fortifications, gaining access to the inner defences of a position and engaging in dirty hand-to-hand combat if necessary. For weeks, and even months, teams of sappers would study their targets in person and coordinate their attacks using a scale model built on a sand table. They were often referred to as 'suicide squads', although these troops never considered themselves such. A *Thuong Si* (Master Sergeant) who survived a raid on the Go Hoi airfield in Quang Ngai province remembered how afraid men in his unit had been, 'but we couldn't give up the attack, even though we knew what the chances were of getting back'. On that raid the assistant company commander had pulled out of the mission as the men were halfway through the wire: he had lost his nerve and fled.

The embassy attack proved to be a deadly venture for the sappers: the first two through the breach in the concrete wall were killed, but others moving up behind were able to get into the heavily defended compound. It took several hours for military policemen and airborne troops to kill all of the Viet Cong, and in doing so numerous allied fatalities had been incurred. Although the guerrillas had not been able to penetrate the chancery building itself, the camera crews and reporters who quickly flocked to the scene were convinced that the American embassy had been seized. Erroneous reports from the military police in the area were responsible for this belief. Uncorrected reports to this effect were filed with news agencies in the US, resulting in sensationalist reports gracing the front pages of the American newspapers. After the combat, General Westmoreland visited the chancery building and attempted to put the record straight, but several newsmen could not be persuaded that the American embassy was not now under communist control. However, even though the Stars and Stripes still flew over the embassy, the attack had signalled a grave warning to a troubled America. 'What the hell is going on?' Walter Cronkite, veteran newsreader and reporter, is said to have exclaimed. 'I thought we were winning this war!'

American forces were committed to Vietnam, so the public had been told, to aid the South Vietnamese in the defence of their own land. They would provide military training, assistance and actual combat units to that end. And, as 1967 drew to a close, the politicians and the generals had sounded optimistic that a victory was on the horizon. Why, then, had the nerve centre of US operations in this foreign land, the embassy, come under a close-quarter assault and almost fallen? The psychological impact of the fifteen-man raid had far exceeded its military value: no other Tet attack achieved as much as did that little sapper platoon. A example for the 1990s might be the way in which the Irish Republican Army (IRA) brought the conflict in Northern Ireland home to the British public by firing a mortar barrage at the Prime Minister's home at Number 10. It was an immediate statement of both vulnerability and resolve.

In other parts of Saigon, in the towns and cities, and around military camps across South Vietnam, surprise attacks followed. Each added further to the psychological damage already done by the embassy raid. Saigon seemed like a city under siege, and its people were jolted from their holiday revelries. Viet Cong and NVA units had occupied several locations, including a cemetery and a racetrack in the Chinese ghetto of Cholon, and the fighting to remove them was furious. Satchel charges, bombs and mortars exploded in the streets, causing chaos and casualties. President Thieu's palace came under attack from a sapper unit masquerading as a group of ARVN soldiers, but they were quickly repulsed. The South Vietnamese Joint General Staff building and the Bien Hoa air base were also strongpoints of the Tet offensive in the city. At the nearest airport, Tan Son Nhut, a more determined struggle was under way that morning. Thirteen aircraft were blown up by members of a communist sapper battalion, and four battalions of infantry moved in to take the air base. This attack, too, was halted following a fierce exchange. Communist losses were put at 962 at the end of the battle for Tan Son Nhut, while the allies had lost 55 men, mainly ARVN and US Army troops that had supported the Air Force security units.

Elsewhere, the nation fought for its survival. The war was no longer a long-distance affair conducted by soldiers in remote farming and wilderness areas. It had come to many important towns and cities, including 36 of 44 provincial capitals, 64 of 242 district capitals and five of six major cities. Most of the fighting came in the form of mortar and artillery barrages, but in thirteen cities communist infantrymen exploited the lax holiday atmosphere to secrete themselves deep within the population. On buses, bicycles and in taxis the soldiers had arrived days before with their bundles, and secret meetings had taken place with other guerrillas in hotels, warehouses and garages. On the eve of Tet the weaponry had been unwrapped and the final plans made. Little interest had been taken in these strangers, for the cities were full of them.

Devastating though the shock of the Offensive had been, the quick reaction of American units and their efficiency in clearing contested positions was commendable. General Westmoreland poured troops into the Tet battles, with the result that, within two weeks, it was estimated that 38,000 guerrillas had been captured or killed. This amounted to roughly 45 per cent of the total committed. American combat losses in those weeks were heavy, and as the fighting wound down at the end of February the number of US soldiers killed or missing in action amounted to 1,547. A significant amount of the close-quarter carnage had taken place during the fighting for Saigon, and also for Hue further north.

The Citadel

Hue was the old imperial capital of Vietnam, and the fighting there was intense and prolonged. The communist assailants, including large elements of Viet Cong and NVA regiments, had dug in within the Citadel. Resembling a walled fortress, the Citadel was packed with palaces and temples and lay along the banks of the Perfume River. Impressive and impregnable, each of the Citadel's four walls was almost 5m high, over 18m thick and 3km in length. Luckily for the South Vietnamese, the ARVN 1st Division had moved its HQ and supporting troops into the Citadel following the premature attacks on 30 January. When the communists had penetrated the defences of the fortress city they found that they were unable to secure it, and were surprised by the stubborn and spirited ARVN defence. Other NVA and Viet Cong units dug in around Hue. South of the Perfume River the enemy build-up was extensive.

The allied counter-offensive took 25 long and bloody days to force the guerrillas out of Hue. Committed to this siege were three US Marine battalions and an ARVN division. Fear of laying waste populated areas and important cultural centres meant that artillery and air strikes were little used. Direct fire support came in the form of M79 grenade launchers, M40A1 recoilless rifles and the heavy guns of Marine M48 tanks; these weapons were all that could be safely brought to bear. Every metre of ground taken in the battle to cross the Perfume River and recapture the Citadel was gained by hand-to-hand fighting. It was unlike anything the young soldiers had experienced in Vietnam so far, and more reminiscent of the urban battles in Nazi-held cities during the Second World War than the rice-paddy war they were used to. *Thien Tuong* (Brigadier-General) Ngo Quang Trong's ARVN troops fought desperately, and the élite 'Black Panther' Recondo company, caught within the Citadel, was hopelessly outnumbered and forced to pull back. Nasty, dirty and savage street fighting followed as the 1st Marines battled to overcome the defenders. NVA resistance was stiffer than expected, mainly due to the fact that the communists had never before enjoyed such a superiority in fortified positions.

Few of the Marines had been trained in, or had had experience of, urban warfare. But they and their comrades up and down Vietnam were learning—fast. The standard tactic of search-and-destroy operations had consisted of beating the bush until the unit came under fire, then exchanging automatic fire to pin down the enemy as artillery and jet bombers did the real destructive work. Giap's master strategy, although at once dispersing his forces counter to established military thinking, was able to neutralise the true American advantage—firepower. The US military was being forced by the Tet strategy to fight within the cities and towns, and in amongst the people on whose behalf the war was being waged. It was a gamble, and in Hue it seemed to pay off. Tactical considerations during the fight for Hue were never more than a street away. The fighting was made hellish by snipers who had dug in behind solid concrete walls, by deadly fixed or mobile ambushes at doorways, windows or intersections and by the ease with which the enemy could manoeuvre out of sight of friendly observers. Casualties mounted until, on 7 February, the restrictions on air and artillery support were lifted. On 12 February the Marines began the bitter struggle for the walled Citadel; from 14 February bombs and napalm were dropped against its walls and on to the enemy soldiers hiding inside.

If anything, the fight for the Citadel was worse than what had preceded it. Snipers picked off individual Marines, easily hidden booby traps in the rubble or buildings caused shocking injuries and mortars rained down sporadic barrages on the allied assault troops. All the time automatic fire raked the constricting streets, turning them into fire lanes and shooting galleries. Grenades and tear gas for house-clearing were quickly distributed and used, and the automatic-firing, lightweight and relatively compact M16 rifle found new adherents in the Marine Corps. On 25 February the battle for Hue was officially declared to be at an end: the communists had been routed and the Marines, after the painfully slow and tiring advance from wall to wall, had eventually captured the Imperial Palace. The last battle of the Tet Offensive had ended and the allies had won a resounding victory over Giap's forces. Or had they?

Victory or Defeat?

The casualty figures looked impressive when they were sorted and compared. Communist losses totalled over 40,000 (equal to the entire NVA force surrounding Khe Sanh), while the allies had suffered 4,300 combat deaths. Some commentators estimated that approximately half of Ho Chi Minh's Viet Cong army had been wiped out during the fighting. What remained of the secret networks of the VCI would be easily dismantled with help from the information gleaned from prisoners. This meant that the blow to the communist effort had been immense. Little of the guerrilla movement remained in the South with which to carry on the liberation war. Giap's central assumptions, that the ARVN would crumble and flee, and that the Vietnamese people would rise up in support of the communists, were proved wrong. Like the Americans, the Viet Cong had failed to make any progress in the battle for hearts and minds. Tet proved more than anything else that the civilians were sick of fighting, destruction and the senseless killings, no matter who was doing it to whom, or for what cause.

The campaign also proved that, when it had its back up against the wall, the South Vietnamese Army could fight as well as any American unit. Rather than abandon the fight and throw down their weapons, the soldiers had fought with a determined resolve and a great deal of courage that surprised American officers (and probably a number of ARVN officers too). A proportion of this sudden determination may have originated from the fear of being summarily tried and punished by a communist victor after the battle. It is this emotion that drives armed robbers and terrorists, fearing the weight of established justice, to fight a suicidal battle till the end. The 'Vietnamisation' project, which aimed to let the Vietnamese shoulder the full burden of the war themselves, was implemented successfully following the Tet Offensive Both the US government and public had been impressed by the ARVN's performance in battle and became convinced that it had the ability to stand alone against North Vietnam.

On paper, then, the allies had won a clear-cut victory over the communists. But the dissection of the campaign, even as it was being fought, was not restricted to paper: it flowed messily on to the world's television screens. The TV images that were depicted in some instances seemed to contradict the optimistic reports of military commanders on the ground. The consensus of opinion amongst the Saigon press corps seemed to be that Hanoi had successfully pulled off an audacious attack equal in scale to Pearl Harbor, and that any US talk of complete victory was a lie. In some ways the journalists were not wholly to blame for this distortion. MACV, the Pentagon and the President himself all helped to create the credibility gap that had ruined press–military relations. Every in-country operation, whatever the outcome, had been described by Army or Marine press officers as a major step forward. Victory, the American public was told, was just around the corner, and the light at the end of the famous tunnel grew ever brighter. Fear of public vilification of its actions forced the Command to whitewash any reports that would hinder support for the war. The killing of civilians by American troops, incursions into Cambodia and Laos, the murder of US officers by their own troops, drug use, Phoenix and the utter devastation of villages and cropland were all played down or covered up. For years the Command had played the Orwellian game of convincing the public that two plus two equalled five, of trying to make what had happened on the battlefield fit into the timetable of victory that General Westmoreland had already set out. With the repulsion of the Tet Offensive the military had gained a decisive (perhaps *the* decisive) victory of the Vietnam War. There had been no need to juggle the numbers this time, but the credibility gap had opened up too far and it seemed impossible to cross. Newsmen in Saigon looked for signs of defeat everywhere, and when they looked hard enough they seemed to find them.

It was this pessimism that became the focal point of Peter Braestrup's two-volume study of Vietnam War reporting entitled *Big Story*. This acclaimed Freedom House publication carefully analysed the role of American journalists in South-East Asia and concluded that they consciously worked against the military and political establishment to undermine the war effort. It specifically targets news coverage of the Tet Offensive and argues that unfair and biased reporting of the conflict turned the majority of Americans against the war in Vietnam. As a side issue, the study also points to an adversarial theme in much of the reporting during Tet. Braestrup believed that, unlike any war before or after Vietnam, the most vital aspect of the campaign was to be fought in the newspapers and on the television screens of America. It was not just the outcome of the street fighting that was instrumental in deciding the overall victor, argued Braestrup, but also the reaction of the American media and its public. It was to be a war of words. Both the troops on the ground and the generals and politicians who sat around their tables were to be spectators to the event, as it unfolded in the aftermath of Tet.

Friction did exist between the media industry in America and the established government structure. Samuel Huntington, part of a Trilateral Commission in 1975, argued that the media organisations 'became a highly creditable, never-tiring political opposition, a maverick third party which never need face the sobering experience of governing'. At this high level, the newspapers and television stations saw themselves as watchdogs of government propriety, and inside Vietnam individual reporters were depicted as representatives of this mission— as sentinels looking after the (American) public interest.

Only recently have 'counter-critics' emerged to bury this idea of a rogue fraternity dedicated to ending the Vietnam War through media manipulation. Braestrup's *Big Story* argument is compelling, but it rests on flimsy and contradictory evidence. Some of this evidence is even provided by Peter Braestrup within the text of his own book. And the role of this study has been crucial in supporting the arguments of those who seek to illustrate the destructive power of an unchecked press. Perhaps the central argument of the work revolves around the claim that journalists painted such a bad picture of the Tet outcome that the public turned against the war. In fact, as a poll published within the report indicates, there was little relation between the anti-war movement and Tet. Public resolve did not falter and crumble as Braestrup insists but actually strengthened as a firm mood of retaliation against the Viet Cong swept through America. Only when President Johnson failed to follow up the gains made during the campaign did the public became disenchanted with both the President and his handling of the war.

The influence of policy-makers and government advisers through the press and television reports formed another pillar of the Freedom House study. Was the government misled by the media? Again the evidence is flimsy, for it is difficult to believe that the 'wise men' of the White House and Pentagon were more easily swayed by watching TV news broadcasts than by their own intelligence analyses, military reports and statistical and electronic information. Johnson's highest echelon of advisers had already become disenchanted with the progress of the war. General Westmoreland was to remain stubbornly optimistic, but back in Washington 'intelligence estimates were much more pessimistic', according to insider George Herring. Secretary of Defense Robert McNamara was already totally despondent about the outcome of further US intervention and had tendered his resignation to Johnson before the Tet Offensive had even begun. This move was motivated by his feelings that the war was being lost, and that it could never be won. During the campaign the chairman of the Joint Chiefs of Staff, General Wheeler, declared that much of rural South Vietnam had been lost to the communists. He did not need the newspapers to tell him this: his own intelligence reports were already available. One CIA report from early March feared the collapse of the ARVN and the total loss of control over large parts of the countryside—and this was after the Offensive had been crushed.

Contrary to the Freedom House as well as the popular view, then, the American media did not induce mass pessimism into Washington. Rather the media tended to reflect the mood of the government and picked up on the concerns and worries about the months and years to come. Up until January 1968, and barring several brief episodes that had been rent by the credibility gap, the reporters in Vietnam and the networks back home had followed a distinctly patriotic and supportive line. This changed during and after the Tet Offensive, partly as a reaction to the doubts surfacing in the establishment and partly to the close-in nature of reporting during Tet. A journalist had only to step outside his hotel lobby to see death and destruction being wrought before his eyes. Although exposed to the harsh realities of urban warfare, most continued their strong support for the American counter-offensive.

The repeated claim that the victory of the Tet Offensive had been inverted and reported as a defeat actually has little support. Walter Cronkite, for many years lambasted as the key conspirator in the post-Tet débâcle, actually said, during a broadcast on 14 February, that 'first and simplest, the Viet Cong suffered a military defeat'. Throughout the media this sentiment was echoed: Howard Tuckner, for example, stated that 'Militarily the allies won'. When the newspapers claimed that the pacification operations in the countryside had been 'killed dead' and 'torn to shreds', they were not, as Braestrup concludes, being overly pessimistic. Various Pentagon summaries openly declared that the war in the villages had been thrown back to pre-1965 levels, and that the pacification effort had been effectively terminated by the tremendous Viet Cong campaign. Robert Komer, MACV's foremost pacification expert, stated darkly that the recent offensive had posed a 'considerable setback' for the American village pacification programme.

For the majority of the journalists, the Tet Offensive had been a great shock that seemed to make a mockery of the military's oft-voiced and over-optimistic analyses. But it had been just as much a shock to General Westmoreland and General Wheeler, even though Wheeler had briefly warned of an impending attack sometime around the Tet holiday. Capitalising on this surprise element, many journalists saw the Tet campaign as a spectacular *tour de force*, and the opening attack of a renewed offensive. In truth the Tet Offensive had been a last-ditch measure on a grand scale, an attempt to leapfrog established military thinking with an audacious and potentially costly gamble. It resembled the Battle of the Bulge more than it did Pearl Harbor, an all-or-nothing strategy to win a losing war. Playing a crucial part in the reports coming from the Tet combat zones were the graphic descriptions (and depictions on television) of urban violence and destruction. Parts of Hue resembled Berlin as it looked just before that city fell to the victorious allies in 1945. It was these images of urban devastation that seemed to portray the end of Hue. The unfortunate civilians that had called Hue, Saigon and the other South Vietnamese cities home became the central victims of the Tet carnage. There were approximately 14,000 civilian dead by the end of Tet, some as a result of enemy pogroms in Hue and elsewhere (over 2,800 civilians were tortured and executed by the VC at Hue) and the rest killed by allied artillery and air strikes.

Big Story painted the picture of a journalistic clique working against the American mission, with a heavy and overt bias in favour of the enemy. It is therefore surprising that the actual reporting did not capitalise on the widespread, even systematic destruction of civilian areas by the United States armed forces. Rather than pessimistically report the actual extent of this suffering, the American media glossed over it and shrugged it off. On 12 February reporter Don Webster accompanied the Marines as they fought the Viet Cong in Hue. With innocent civilians dying or being wounded on an hourly basis, he expressed his hope that 'the Vietnamese people will blame the communists rather than the Americans for whatever damage is being done'. Rather than occupying neutral ground from which to survey the conduct of the war on both sides, the US media documented the liberation of the cities from a purely American military viewpoint.

A CBS report during the fight to recapture Hue University featured one dour Marine colonel about to send his men into 'house-to-house, room-to-room' fighting. His assessment of the situation was all too grim: 'We're hoping we don't run into any civilians in there . . . if there's somebody in there right now, they're Charlie as far as we're concerned.' But the tone of the piece was of grudging acceptance of these civilian deaths. After all, were not civilian casualties part and parcel of every war? General Vo Nguyen Giap had calculated correctly that the urban environment would throw the American forces off balance and put the defensive military mission into direct conflict with the civilian population that it was there to protect. It was this direct conflict which seemed to contradict the American *raison d'être*—protecting the South Vietnamese from aggression. In chasing down and destroying Viet Cong concentrations that had fled to towns in the Mekong Delta, the actual towns were destroyed too. My Tho and Ben Tre were particularly badly hit, with the dead and wounded outnumbering captured weapons by a factor of five.

All the talk of Khe Sanh being America's Dien Bien Phu proved hollow. Dien Bien Phu was a military defeat, yes, but it struck a note that reverberated down through the decades because of its enormous *psychological* impact on the French government and people. For the French that momentous battle had become an end-of-war landmark, a statement that declared 'enough is enough, the killing has gone too far'. Khe Sanh held out and the NVA were successfully kicked back into Laos, but Lyndon Johnson got his 'dinbinfoo' anyway. It was Tet. In the end, the two enduring images of the Tet Offensive were not ones of allied victory, the raising of a flag 'Iwo Jima style' or rows of enemy dead lined up with their captured weapons: they were of the near-tragedy of the commando raid on the American embassy in Saigon, and of the impromptu execution of a Viet Cong officer on a street corner.

Eddie Adams, a photographer working for Associated Press, watched with camera ready as the Saigon Police Chief Nguyen Ngoc Loan had the bound Viet Cong led into the street and then lifted his snub-nosed revolver to the man's head. The picture Adams took captured the fear and terror of the man in the instant before death, as well as the casual, almost nonchalant actions of his executioner. Caught on TV camera, the man's death was shockingly graphic, simple and quick, a piece of film Stateside viewers could never forget. Pictures show, not tell, and the American public were shown a South Vietnamese officer executing an apparent civilian, dressed in chequered shirt and shorts, without trial or appeal. Both the embassy firefight and the street shooting became testaments to Tet, vivid illustrations of a war going wrong: defeat and brutality.

It was to be the Helicopter War, the Electronic War, and also the Special Forces War, but the Vietnam War had one other appellation—the Television War. For the first time the true horrors of the battlefield were piped directly into the living rooms of American families. It was immediate, colourful and gripping. But the impact of such saturation coverage is still contentious. Did it maintain popular interest in the war, or did it switch it off? Some people have likened the daily coverage of the Vietnam War to that of the interminable conflict in the former Yugoslavia. By virtue of their frequency and apparent similarity, the reports lose much of their impact, dulling the interest and becoming almost blandly monotonous. It is doubtful that the TV camera did, in the end, make a difference in the pro- and anti-war debate. Media networks were careful not to air film that contained disturbing footage, since by doing so they would attract the ire of either the government or the viewing public.

Walter Cronkite, stalwart anchorman for CBS and the nation's most respected newsman, came under fire from Peter Braestrup for his comments on the Offensive. But as Cronkite spoke he voiced the concerns of the government and the nation. 'Who won and who lost in the great Tet Offensive?' Cronkite asked the camera on 27 February. 'I'm not sure.' The verdict of the press, then, was that Tet had been, if not a total victory for America, then a stalemate. The trusted anchorman continued, with an analysis of the war and the prospects for the future: 'To say that we are closer to victory today is to believe, in the face of the evidence, the optimists who have been wrong in the past . . . it is increasingly clear . . . that the only rational way out then will be to negotiate . . .' Walter Cronkite ended his piece to camera reaffirming the American role in Vietnam 'as [that of] an honourable people who lived up their pledge to defend democracy, and did the best they could'. Few could doubt his patriotism and his concern for the war effort, but President Johnson, watching the CBS broadcast from the White House, turned at that end of the broadcast to his press secretary and solemnly declared: 'If I've lost Walter, I've lost Mr Average Citizen.' Had the press turned Tet from a resounding victory to a stalemate or defeat? Yes or no, the tide of war was about to turn. While General Westmoreland smelt victory for South Vietnam, many in MACV and Washington smelt defeat.

Post Tet: Final Casualties

General William Westmoreland was optimistic about the damage allied forces had inflicted upon the Viet Cong and their infrastructure. Although there were attempts by the enemy to re-start hostilities (notably in May and August of 1968), the South Vietnamese looked hopefully toward the future. The ARVN increased its recruiting drive, accepting men of all ages 'for the duration'. Self-defence forces, the Regional and Popular Forces, were expanded and rearmed to deepen the layers of defence against further communist attacks. In addition, the American commitment in men and material continued to increase throughout 1968 in an effort to consolidate the Tet victories.

Vietnam was not Washington's sole concern, however. The Cold War raged on, and commitments to the countries of NATO and other parts of the world continued apace. General Wheeler, the Chairman of the Joint Chiefs of Staff, was responsible for coordinating America's military commitment across the globe. And with only a single division available for the strategic reserve, Wheeler rightly felt that more troops were needed to compensate for the vast drain on military manpower and resources that was Vietnam. In an attempt to rebuild his strategic reserve to counter any foreign aggression around the globe, Wheeler urged General Westmoreland to call on President Johnson for the mobilisation of America's reserve forces. Westmoreland in his turn hoped to use additional troops to launch follow-up attacks across the Ho Chi Minh Trail into Laos and Cambodia. Such a strategy could end a war that had been so tightly constricted within the narrow and unnatural confines of South Vietnam alone. This troop increase would amount to 206,000 men, with half being deployed inside South Vietnam and half for Wheeler's strategic peacetime reserve. Johnson did not immediately make a decision on this increase but organised two study groups to assess the impact of these troops on the war effort and to determine their effectiveness. Both cautioned against any deployment of reinforcements. There the matter rested—for now.

The *New York Times* went to press with the story that Westmoreland was requesting further troop increases whilst he simultaneously declared Tet a victory for the allied war effort. The article mentioned nothing of the proposed change in strategy from one of attrition to one of manoeuvre and interdiction. Some criticism of both the political and military effort followed and was picked up by others in the press and television. If the Tet Offensive had been such a clear victory for Westmoreland, why was he requesting an increase in America's troop levels? President Johnson's decision to promote General Westmoreland to the Joint Chiefs of Staff also caused some confusion. Although the move had been decided upon in mid-January before the Tet Offensive had even begun, it was seen by some in the media as a clear signal that Westmoreland's services were no longer required and that he was being promoted out of harm's way. His second-in-command, General Creighton W. Abrams, took over as commander of US forces in South Vietnam. Other changes were in the offing.

Robert McNamara, who had been responsible for America's intervention in the conflict, had now begun to have grave doubts about the progress of the war, how it was being fought and indeed whether it should be fought at all. In November 1967 Johnson accepted his resignation, and the President was happy to let his Secretary of Defense go, since he did not want a converted critic of the war to retain control of it. The hawk had become a dove. His replacement, from 29 February 1968, would be Clark Clifford, a close adviser of Johnson's who felt at ease with people rather than computers and their reams of statistics. McNamara's timing coincided with Tet, with Westmoreland's replacement and with President Lyndon B. Johnson's most startling public announcement of the war—his own resignation. On 31 March 'LBJ' faced the television cameras in the Oval Office and declared to the people of the United States that he would not run again for President. His motives were not, as the majority of the media portrayed it, driven by guilt for the Tet Offensive. Although the anti-war movement claimed it a victory for their cause, Johnson's overriding concern, according to both Dean Rusk and Clark Clifford, was of failing health. Concerns were growing that the President would not survive another term. In the nationwide elections later that year, the Republican candidate, Richard M. Nixon, became America's next President and in doing so, the commander-in-chief of its military might. Nixon would not flinch from using it.

In retrospect, 1968 was the climactic year of the Vietnam War, a turning point that would be followed by intense re-evaluation and a decision to pull out. Despite initial victory in the streets of South Vietnam, the cost had been high. Almost half of the American manoeuvre battalions had been deployed in the north to support the expected NVA invasion through Quang Tri province, and most of the capable ARVN units were dug in around the cities. The countryside, therefore, had been abandoned to the remnants of the Viet Cong, and following Tet a huge effort had to be made to move back into these areas. Pacification had been the real victim of the Tet attacks; Robert Komer's CORDS programme was to be the answer. Meanwhile the desperate street fighting, the sickening images of civilian suffering and death and the never-ending story of Khe Sanh seemed to provide the government and the people with an opportunity to re-assess their commitment to the war. The TV portrayal of the entire offensive as a renewed (and heightened) campaign of aggression, and not as the desperate act of a losing side, reflected real fears in the government and the nation as a whole. Unfortunately, as it became clear that Johnson could not or would not retaliate strongly against the North, the general public decided that it wanted to see less conflict on its screens, not more. It wanted the troops home—for good. Pressure on Johnson from the anti-war movement had been intense in the post-Tet period, and he felt obliged to call a halt in the bombing campaign, simultaneously giving the North an opportunity to respond to his peace overtures. These were directed against an enemy that had suffered a resounding defeat on the battlefield and had every reason to enter negotiations. Surprisingly, North Vietnam accepted Johnson's offer of peace talks in Paris, thus beginning a seemingly endless round of diplomatic meetings that would only end, years later, when North Vietnamese soldiers invaded the South once again—but stayed there for good.

Massacre at My Lai

The year of Tet was also the year of My Lai, an incident that was to become the most infamous episode of the American commitment. For the anti-war groups, the My Lai atrocity seemed to provide a shining example of US injustice in South-East Asia; for others in the media it was an aberration. Interestingly, the soldier responsible for bringing the murders to light did not trust the Army hierarchy. He went, instead, to the government and free press. Attempts by the Army to whitewash the affair meant that its own investigators could not be trusted.

My Lai-4 was a sub-hamlet, part of a larger gathering of hooches and out-buildings in northerly Quang Ngai province. Although American patrols had swept through it in the past, it was the search-and-destroy mission led by a lieutenant, William L. Calley, on 16 March 1968 that would forever sear the history of My Lai. His platoon entered the southern part of the village and opened fire immediately on anyone who tried to flee. Those remaining to confront the Americans were killed face to face, with bayonets or bursts from the GIs' M16s. Women and girls were raped, livestock were slaughtered and the hooches of My Lai were burned to the ground. Terrible atrocities were committed by the 1st Platoon (and later by the 3rd Platoon, who joined it), which amounted to sickening displays of the unit's anger and frustration. Civilians had been killed on operations before, sometimes on purpose or by wilful neglect but more often by accident. After My Lai, however, the company commander, Captain Ernest Medina, nonchalantly declared that the 16 March mission had netted 90 Viet Cong dead at the cost of one US serviceman wounded (although this later proved to be self-inflicted). But the dead were all old men, women and children! How could they be the enemy? What justification did the lieutenant have for horrifically torturing and massacring an entire village of South Vietnamese friendlies? Somewhere between 172 and 347 civilians were murdered by US servicemen at My Lai, the greatest American atrocity of the war.

Months after the massacre, some of those involved began to thinking more seriously about what they had done. A few opened their hearts to Ronald Ridenhour, a soldier uninvolved with the incident who had taken an interest in the rumours and half-whispered tales of My Lai. What he compiled was a damning indictment of an Army unit let loose without moral or military constraints, free to do what it liked with little fear of retribution. Ridenhour was determined to bring the bloody atrocity to light. He dismissed the Army's investigation branch as a potential ally, fearing that, as a representative of the service, it would attempt to cover up the entire affair. Ridenhour completed his tour without approaching the authorities with his evidence, but once in the United States he prepared a summary of the My Lai incident and mailed it to thirty of America's most influential senators and congressmen. My Lai quickly became news. A year and a half after the massacre in Vietnam, Lieutenant William L. Calley was placed under arrest and charged with murder. Other members of his platoon were also charged, and a handful of officers were put on trial to be charged with offences including attempted cover-up and violating the customs of war. Calley's story leading up to the My Lai incident illustrated the moral vacuum in which most soldiers were operating. The account he gave of his tour included numerous inconclusive patrols that were typical for units in the field. Coming under fire, the company of which the 1st Platoon was a part was unable to locate its source. Booby traps chopped up its men and destroyed morale, but the patrolling continued. There were more firefights and more mines, yet no significant contact had been made with an enemy force. The stage had been set for the deadly sweep through My Lai. Frustration, anger and revenge were the motivating factors for the mass murder, and Calley was not experienced enough to control his men. In fact he had actively participated in the sick murders.

Calley's emerging testimony of the My Lai massacre brought home the difficulties and problems of fighting an *idea*—communism. Throughout the Vietnam War there had never been a satisfactory definition of a communist, which therefore made the suppression of communism a difficult and frustrating task. If the village menfolk were Viet Cong, were the women and children? If the villagers showed support for the Viet Cong yet did not engage in subversive activities (such as stockpiling weapons and supplies), were they communists? And what about the ubiquitous tunnels and bunkers? Were they Viet Cong fortifications or just air raid shelters for the beleaguered and often-bombed civilians? Difficulties in differentiating friend from foe, supporter from victim, are part and parcel of guerrilla warfare. Time and again the rural population became the pawns in a larger game, expendable assets that were useful to one side or the other only for the political support they could provide. At the village of Cam Ne in 1965 Marines had burned the hooches there and laid waste the village. This was despite the fact that the Viet Cong who had opened fire on the patrol 'were long gone', as CBS newsman Morely Safer reported. My Lai was Cam Ne multiplied a thousandfold. The troops had known that the children, the sullen-looking old men and anxious-looking women were not combatants, but someone had laid the booby traps and allowed the Viet Cong to shelter there and fire on the Americans. If the villagers had not been communist supporters in the past they were now, or *could be in the future*. And so the destruction could be justified.

At other times and other places, a similar attitude was adopted by patrolling infantrymen. Marines entering the village of Thuy Bo in 1967 were pinned down throughout the night by a fusillade of Viet Cong machine-gun fire. When dawn arrived and the troops warily moved into the village, they found not a single trace of enemy activity. Both Marine companies involved had suffered a number of casualties during the night's combat, and morale was very low. In anger they burnt Thuy Bo to the ground, blew up shelters and shot anyone they found inside them. In total, the commander of the mission, Captain E. J. Banks, reckoned that no more than fifteen villagers had been accidentally killed. A communist spokesman after the war claimed that as many as 145 of the villagers had been massacred. One anonymous GI, after cataloguing a list of civilian murders that he and his unit had routinely carried out, excused himself by saying, 'You may be sorry that you did. But you might be sorrier if you didn't.' In fact, there were infantrymen who had been specifically *ordered* to 'kill everyone and everything', according to interviews conducted by John Pilger. On a distinctly larger scale, Operation 'Speedy Express', a search-and-destroy mission conducted by the 9th Infantry Division, boasted a final body count of 11,000—surely an unprecedented success. Or was it? A military spokesman later admitted that 5,000 of that total had been 'non-combatants', turning 'Speedy Express' into little more than wholesale slaughter. How many My Lais and 'Speedy Expresses' remain unreported? And how many civilian murders have been disguised as part of a statistical body count?

The My Lai verdict split the nation. The war's detractors were convinced that what Calley and his men had done formed the tip of an iceberg, and that they were to be the Army's scapegoats. Others believed that he had been an American officer just doing a tough job in a war that lacked proper front lines. At the end of March 1971 William Calley was sentenced to life imprisonment with hard labour for the murder of 22 South Vietnamese citizens, one of whom was a two-year-old child that Calley had shot himself. The sentence was quickly reduced to one of ten years, but there was little chance of Calley remaining in prison for that length of time. In the end he was paroled only three-and-a-half years later, coming out before the end of 1974. He was the only member of the

1st Platoon to be found guilty of murder. His officers were all acquitted, since the jury was not convinced that they had known what was going on inside My Lai at the time, despite the fact that both Calley's battalion commander, Lieutenant-Colonel Frank Barker, and the brigade commander, Colonel Warren K. Henderson, flew low enough over the village to see the highly unusual activity. US troops were chasing wounded civilians and lining up a huge group of frightened women and children in front of a ditch ready for execution. Rapes, bayonet attacks and indiscriminate fire at fleeing villagers could not have gone unnoticed by Calley's superiors. One of the Americal Division's* staff officers, Major Colin Powell, would feel the heat of My Lai twenty-five years on as he teetered on the brink of running for the 1996 Presidential elections. In 1989 he had achieved the United States' pre-eminent military position as Chairman of the Joint Chiefs of Staff, and upon his retirement he faced a carefully cultivated clamour for his candidacy. But Powell knew full well that as part of the traditional 'opposition research' plaguing modern Presidential campaigns he would undoubtedly come face to face with charges of conspiracy and collusion in the attempted cover-up of the My Lai massacre.

Obviously My Lai was not an isolated incident: other atrocities by American soldiers were reported, and many more were not. In total, from 1965 to 1975, and excluding My Lai, 291 American servicemen were found guilty of serious crimes against South Vietnamese civilians. As the My Lai case was preparing to come to court, changes were made in the way that such incidents could be reported within the Army. But nothing could be done to prevent officers attempting to cover up an embarrassing atrocity, which suggests that many incidents after 1970 did not reach the media. One cannot utterly condemn the American record of human rights in South Vietnam without comparing it to that of the Viet Cong. US atrocities were not the norm but violations of both MACV and US military law, while the VC made torture, indiscriminate murder and mass execution legitimate weapons in their struggle for domination. The American Phoenix Program, which anti-war critics roundly condemned as a policy of mass murder, was actually a selective, intelligence-orientated method of removing key VC operatives. The Viet Cong long-term terror campaign, on the other hand, was responsible for over 60,000 civilian deaths, most of the victims being civil servants, schoolteachers, village elders and doctors. Murder had become a part of communist policy since the earliest years of the struggle and this policy was fully enacted in 1968 for the execution of perhaps 3,000 people following the fall of Hue. Luckily for the inhabitants of Saigon, the Tet Offensive was vigorously repulsed. On the bodies of communist cadres shot down in the streets was found documentation listing intellectuals in Saigon who were to be rounded up and shot, Hue-style, as soon as the city had been captured.

---

*The Americal Division fought the Japanese during the Second World War and was reactivated in 1967 to help the Marines defend northern South Vietnam. It was an amalgamation of three independent Army brigades, formed specifically for the task.

My Lai was an aberration of the normal US rules of war; it contradicted the MACV Rules of Engagement, as well as the Uniform Code of Military Justice which governed military conduct during wartime. But it illustrated, like nothing else, the quandary in which the American infantryman was placed. Plucked from the streets of an American city to fight a jungle war in a foreign country, the infantryman was as confused as the politicians when it came to identifying the enemy. In fact, many of the young soldiers were coming to question the entire reasoning behind the conduct of the Vietnam War. And, as My Lai indicated, morale was sinking ever lower.

Chapter 8

MORALE AND THE GI

Warfare is universally tough, dangerous and frightening, and Vietnam was no exception, with enough fear, carnage and squalor to go around. But, more than in other wars, the American soldiers proved to be a reluctant breed. Morale had become a problem almost as soon as troops were in-country. There seemed so many insurmountable obstacles, and so many frustrations in the GI's tour, that he became, like many of the civilians and government officials back home, thoroughly disenchanted. He was often blandly ignorant of its aims and methods. Especially hard hit by this wave of disillusionment were the young draftees, most of whom were still teenagers, unused to military life, to foreign climates and to the concept of being killed by the people they were there ostensibly to protect.

Although the morale of troops was seriously challenged by the nature of the conflict and by the US Army's reaction to it, nothing did more to shatter any sense of purpose and meaning than the July 1969 announcements of troop withdrawals. President Nixon wanted to hand over the war to the South Vietnamese, not all at once, but through a policy of 'Vietnamisation' that included the rearming and re-training of the ARVN. For those staying behind, the war had taken a turn: now it was 'their' (the South Vietnamese') war, just as it had been prior to 1965, with American forces providing just a supporting role. No one wanted to be the last GI killed in Vietnam, and everyone knew that although the American troops were pulling out of the war, it was a war that still had not been won. Imagine the state of military opinion if Eisenhower had been forced by the White House to pull out of Nazi-occupied Europe some time after the D-Day invasion. In Vietnam, following the 1969 announcements, the prevailing mood amongst the American soldiers was almost unanimously one of self-preservation. Units would become despondent and very reluctant to force combat with the Viet Cong or NVA. And with fewer and fewer incidents of combat encounters with the enemy, the GIs kicking their heels in FSBs and rear-echelon bases often vented their frustrations in questionable, and sometimes illegal, activities.

There were approximately 543,400 American troops in South Vietnam in early 1969—half a million men who were ready and able to follow up on the post-Tet gains and take the fight to the communists. But Tet had shown Washington that the war was far from over, and that although the majority of the Viet

Cong guerrillas had at long last emerged from cover and been shot to pieces, the North Vietnamese Army remained poised all along the border, in Cambodia, Laos and North Vietnam. In January 1969 Richard Nixon succeeded Lyndon B. Johnson as President of the United States. He would bring a radical new approach to the Vietnam War that focused on 'withdrawal with honour', not on fighting and winning the war on behalf of the Saigon government. But President Nixon, like his predecessors, still could not afford to let the nation fall to the communists. Meanwhile the American public was split on the Vietnam issue: one poll in March revealed that a third of the public favoured a tougher line against North Vietnam, a quarter favoured withdrawal and, of the remainder, half were satisfied with current policy while half had no opinion.

Nixon opted to reduce America's commitment while shifting the burden of the war on to the shoulders of the 'Asian boys' (as Johnson had referred to the ARVN). The new President realised that every war was a contest of willpower, and that both Congress and a large portion of the American electorate had already turned against this particular conflict. From the end of the year onwards, support, not combat, would be the brief of virtually all US forces in South Vietnam. Before that, though, the year 1969 was still a period of intense combat activity for the American military. More US troops were now stationed in the country than at any other time in history. Combat operations continued apace, with names like 'Dewey Canyon', 'MacArthur', 'Kentucky', 'Apache Snow' and 'Idaho Canyon'. Of crucial importance to the Vietnam War was Operation 'Menu', the highly secret March 1969 bombing of NVA troops who were comfortably ensconced in Cambodia. 'Menu' was a successful attempt to hamper the communist supply lines and allow a breathing space for the withdrawing US troops.

The Reluctant Army

Although a portion of the blame for the disintegration of American military morale can be placed at Nixon's desk with his 1969 announcements, the problem ran far deeper. A catalogue of injustices, hardships and contradictions assailed the infantryman newly arrived in-country. These injustices began with the iniquitous draft. The majority of American combat units were composed of a distinct slice of American society, not a heterogeneous slice but one of poorer, less educated and working-class individuals. The middle classes were barely represented amongst the enlisted men, and the youth of the upper classes (apart from select families with a military tradition) did not serve at all. The mechanism for implementing such an unequal bias was the Selective Service System, which was designed to fulfil military manning levels by the (supposedly random) conscription of young men into the armed services. In total, 2,215,000 men were drafted for service in Vietnam. There were a multitude of draft deferments available that would allow a potential draftees to sit out the war in the United States, and it was the nature of these draft categories that defined the unequal and unfair manning of the armed forces.

Fighting Japan and Germany in the Second World War had been a national effort: married men, college students and those who objected in principle were all called to arms. In Britain only the most important of occupations were classed as reserved and these included heavy industry, the railways and mining. In comparison, the list of Vietnam-era draft categories was almost endless. Conscription could be avoided by being eligible for one of the following main categories:

I-A-O Conscientious objector available for non-combatant military service only.

I-C Serving member of the armed forces, the Coast Geodetic Survey or the Public Health Service.

I-D Member of the military reserve (National Guard) or student taking military training.

I-O Conscientious objector available for civilian work in hospitals or other service contributing to the national interest.

I-S Student deferred by statute (the most widely used method of avoiding the draft).

I-W Conscientious objector performing civilian work in hospitals or other service contributing to the national interest.

II-A Deferred because of civilian occupation (for example, teachers, engineers and police officers)

II-C Deferred because of agricultural occupation.

II-S Deferred because of special studies in research.

III-A Deferred because registrant has children or has dependants who rely on him.

IV-A Registrant has already completed military service, or is a sole surviving son.

IV-B Deferred by law.

IV-C An alien (actually there were many resident aliens who found themselves drafted into the war)

IV-D Minister of religion or a divinity student.

IV-F Unfit to serve on grounds of physical, mental or moral character (deferments were sometimes fabricated by ingenious registrants; homosexual leanings, madness or more commonly a medical problem could be faked).

V-A Registrant over the age of liability for military service.

When a registrant failed to fall into one of these draft board categories he was classified as I-A (available for military service), which virtually guaranteed his conscription into the armed services in the near future. He was then almost certainly Vietnam-bound. Some young men, fearing that the draft could at some unknown point in the future whisk them to the Vietnam battlefield without notice, took precautions. Some joined the Army, Navy or Air Force as regulars, serving for a minimum of three years. This reduced their chances of going to South-East Asia considerably, but of course joining the armed forces as a professional did not appeal to all. Others pre-empted the draft board when they found out they were classified I-A and volunteered immediately for service. By doing so they got their tour over with quickly, which was preferable to waiting months for the call-up papers and having their careers fouled up in the process.

For many young men marriage or college enrolment became the quickest, easiest and most socially acceptable ways to avoid the war. But a minority opted to fight the selection boards and went into exile abroad, usually to Canada or Sweden. Others went into hiding in the US, finding protection from sympathetic family members or organisations set up specifically to hide draftees. There were 570,000 men who were technically classified by the government as 'draft-dodgers'. This meant that they had refused to register, or that they had moved abroad with the sole intention of avoiding the draft. Those unable to gain a college entry were often prime targets for the local boards. Most students came from relatively well-off families and so it was often the poor and uneducated youths who fought in South-East Asia on their behalf. Hispanic and black communities especially suffered the attentions of the draft boards to a greater degree than the white urban communities, opening the government to the charge of employing a racist recruiting policy. Martin Luther King, America's foremost civil rights activist, argued that 'negroes are dying in disproportionate numbers in Vietnam'. And when the percentage of blacks in the United States was compared to the percentage fighting in Vietnam combat units, he was right.

Part of the problem was Robert McNamara's own 'Project 100,000'. Established in 1966, the programme was an undisguised move to dispose of America's most unpromising youths (the 'subterranean poor', as he had referred to them) by pushing them into the armed services. It was said that they would learn new and valuable skills which they could take back to their communities. Rehabilitation was also the central excuse for offering petty criminals the choice of Vietnam or jail. No army that recruits by duress, either through the law or through this courtroom blackmail, can boast of efficiency and good morale.

Many draftees fared badly in the Army (and also in the Marines later on, when the normally volunteer-only service had lost so many men that it too had to turn to the draft board for replacements). With most Vietnam combat units severely undermanned, the pressure on training centres to turn out as many recruits as fast as possible was overwhelming. Studies conducted by the Pentagon at the height of the conflict indicated that the death rate for draftees was twice as high as that among regular trainee soldiers. Rock-bottom recruit morale, a low aptitude for soldiering and a high-speed training programme were no doubt the main causes of this awful statistic. The majority of these deaths were caused by accidents, and a small minority were the result of suicides. Those scoring badly in the obligatory written examination were almost certainly destined for an infantry combat unit. Few learnt skills that would be of any use outside a sub-tropical combat zone, despite the promises of 'Project 100,000'. Even then, there were not many veterans outside the Special Forces who could claim that their Stateside training had actually given them the skills that they really needed to survive in the Vietnam jungle. Rather, the training provided a crude but effective form of indoctrination. 'They cut your hair and took your brain, too,' said one Marine veteran.

It was not just 'ghetto kids' but also various religious minorities that received an unfair amount of attention from the draft boards. Black Muslims, looking to the boxer Muhammad Ali as a role model, declared their lack of allegiance to the US government and were jailed for refusing to fight the communists. Jehovah's Witnesses were similarly persecuted for refusing to recognise the authority of the Selective Service System. A number were jailed, pushing up the total of imprisoned conscientious objectors to 3,250.

Such a disparity in the economic and educational levels of those who were drafted and those who were not soon came to the attention of the media. Pressure on the Department of Defense increased to such an extent that changes had to be made. In 1967 the deferment for graduate students was abolished, and it was not until 1971 that college students at last became eligible for the draft. By 1969 the method of allowing local draft boards, which were manned by civilian volunteers, to choose those who would fight overseas was changed. In its place a lottery draft system was organised that attempted to make the selection of draftees wholly random. Despite this, the system retained its bad image and the draft, inequalities and all, was dispensed with completely by the end of 1972. It has been pointed out that well over half of the men who served in Vietnam had actually volunteered rather than been dragged there against their will. But it must be remembered that this figure incorporates totals for the Air Force and Navy, both of which worked almost entirely on a volunteer basis. Young draftees usually went directly into the infantry, or, if they were very lucky, the artillery, military police or some supporting rear-echelon unit.

Second World War infantrymen had an average age of 25, whilst the Vietnam-era 'grunt' (a nickname that symbolises his low status in the Army and his knowledge of the same) was, on average, nineteen years old. These teenagers were plucked from their relatively comfortable lifestyles and deposited with little foreknowledge into a hostile and utterly alien world; some of these men had never stepped outside their home towns before. All grew up quickly, and experienced things that few Americans could ever imagine. The smooth faces of teenage boys were marred by the dull hard eyes of men who had seen too much death and too much horror. This empty gaze soon became known as the 'thousand-yard stare'.

News reports that detailed some of the horrors of the war reached American audiences, and in response the number of young men opposing the draft, and the war in general, grew. A draft avoidance movement sprang up to help those desperate to avoid the call-up; its members publicly burned draft cards, burgled draft offices and burnt the personnel files that they had stolen. Little sympathy existed for draft-dodgers, however, and public opinion branded them as traitors and cowards, especially in the early years of the war. An older generation that had lived through the Second World War nursed only contempt for the younger generation that seemed to have no respect for the American government or its role in the world.

The weakening public resolve that followed the 1968 Tet Offensive paved the way for a passive acceptance of draft-dodging. More and more it was seen as a legitimate form of protest against the Vietnam War. Parents became more willing to move over the border for the welfare of their sons, or to fund them through college. With the American mission in Vietnam at an end in the mid-1970s, draft-dodgers were able to benefit from President Gerald Ford's clemency programme. Military and federal charges pertaining to them were dropped, but there were still often legal wrangles to be negotiated. Finally, in 1977, President Jimmy Carter announced a general amnesty that allowed most of the exiled draft offenders to return to the United States.

Educated men did serve in Vietnam, predominantly amongst the officer corps. But when it came to their tours of duty they seemed to have an unfair advantage over the NCOs and enlisted ranks. For all enlisted and non-commissioned soldiers a tour of duty in Vietnam lasted exactly one year, and the date set for return to the United States was referred to officially as DEROS (Date Eligible for Return from Overseas). Midway through the tour came five days of rest and recreation (R&R) leave, usually taken somewhere in the Orient. At the end of his tour a soldier would climb aboard the airliner (evocatively christened the 'Freedom Bird') for the trip home. In an attempt to cycle as many officers through Vietnam as possible, the US Army command organised six-month tours for those officers serving in combat commands. Field experience in a combat zone was thought invaluable for the Army's officer corps, especially since the duration of the war was not predicted to be very long. To dissuade criticism of this policy, the Army also claimed that the six-month tour prevented the officers from cracking under the strain of command. Whatever the reasoning, these short terms that were offered to the commissioned officer corps added to the low morale of the average soldier in-country.

Units saw a constant rotation of young officers, which often resulted in a very poor relationship between an officer and his men. To make matters worse, the brief six months of field experience had to be exploited for maximum advantage. Career-orientated officers could misuse their command by 'ticket punching'—putting the unit into adversely dangerous situations merely on the pretext of demonstrating their leadership ability. The notorious body count helped to fuel this problem. Promotions and awards were eagerly sought to the detriment of unit efficiency. Not that the one-year tour of duty was in itself a perfect system: if anything, these short terms were disastrous for American morale in Vietnam and have been abandoned (one hopes) for good. In retrospect, the probems associated with sending a Private First Class into a combat zone for a single year, then replacing him, are obvious. At the time, however, General Westmoreland was convinced that this rotational approach to service would keep morale at a high level. Soldiers were never more than twelve months away from civilian life and so their commitment, it was hoped, would be deeper, and their willingness to fight stronger, than if they had been wedded to the war 'for the duration'. Westmoreland's main hope was that the one-year tour would keep public dissent low, since it meant that there were troops constantly returning home.

The drawback of the one-year tour was the utter lack of cohesion that it caused within many combat units. 'Trickle-posted' soldiers would often arrive at their units on their own, and replace a man who had reached his DEROS, or been wounded or killed. This constant influx of 'new guys' not only destroyed the platoon's important camaraderie but diluted its experience and fighting efficiency. Veterans in-country (those who had several months' experience under their belts) referred to these new recruits disparagingly as FNGs, or 'F—ing New Guys'. Fresh from an Army training centre, the 'new guy' was virtually shunned as he stumbled about for those first few days or weeks, learning the ropes and trying not to get killed. Amongst those units exposed to combat the most, 'new guys' were considered a dangerous liability. They knew nothing—about fighting, about Vietnam or about life, and no one took the time to teach them. The more experienced soldiers tended to stick together: they knew each other's strengths and weaknesses, their personalities and skills. It took time for the new recruit to become one of the group, usually by which time another recruit had appeared. And *that* man was now the FNG! And, just as the soldier mastered the art of jungle warfare and of staying alive, his DEROS arrived and he was whisked away from the battlefield to be replaced by another FNG. Units did not get better and better, as they often did in Korea or the Second World War, they remained a constant mix of hard-core veterans and inexperienced and frightened 'new guys'. This prompted one commentator to state that 'America did not fight a ten-year war, it fought a one-year war ten times'. Excepting regular career soldiers ('lifers'), who were thin on the ground in most infantry platoons, the unit had at maximum the experience of only a year in-country. Such a system was inherently responsible for much of the American lack of resolve on the battlefield, and ensured that Vietnam would always remain an alien and unfathomable land. Any attachments to the country and its people would be fleeting—most GIs just did not want to get involved.

The problems afflicting a 'new guy' recurred when a soldier faced the end of his tour and became a 'short-timer'. Much of an average soldier's focus was concentrated, not on the patrol at hand or the operation in which his platoon was involved, but on his DEROS and the trip back home. Etched into the mind, and on to helmets and flak jackets, the short timer's calendar ticked away silently until he was almost due to leave Vietnam. Being 'short' sometimes meant that platoon commanders would allow a soldier to take any non-combat job that was going, from cook's assistant to supply clerk. This gesture was not altruistic but stemmed from the short-timer's obsession with survival. With a guaranteed release date and the final few days slipping away, most men were desperate to avoid combat and to make it safely back home. Like the FNGs, the short-timers were sometimes shunned by their fellows. Military-style superstition convinced the rest of the squad that if the short-timer hadn't been hit by a bullet or tripped a mine in the last eleven and a half months, then his luck was about up. No one wanted to be near him when that bullet eventually arrived or that bomb exploded. And so, again, the one-year tour greatly reduced the fighting efficiency of the unit, since in most respects the short-timers opted out of it completely. A 'new guy' was unpredictable, unreliable and less effective than his colleagues, and the short-timer suffered from similar deficiencies. Both were products of an inadequate system that seriously inhibited the American ground war. Only the US Marines and the Australian and New Zealand infantry units, recruiting on a volunteer-only basis, maintained a strong sense of unit cohesion and fighting efficiency. Unfortunately, by 1969 the Marine casualty rate had taken such a toll on the volunteer force that the service was obliged to make up the numbers with draftees. The Marine Corps had been tremendously proud of its volunteer force and knew that it got more from its men than the Army got from its draftees. 'I'd rather be over there with motivated people,' said one Marine recruit, '. . . as opposed to being in a paddy with a bunch of zeros who don't even want to be there.'

REMFs and Other Tensions

Even more sources of disillusionment existed amongst the ground troops. While the one-year tour caused frustration, isolation and dislocation, the fact that there were more non-combat American soldiers in South Vietnam than combat soldiers gave those in the field a focus for their anger. As the first truly modern war, Vietnam gave America the chance to impress the rest of the world with its massive logistic effort. The troops were to be supplied with every civilian comfort. Political and military leaders were able to boast that US troops enjoyed a standard of living unequalled in previous wars. The larger camps could provide shower facilities, a PX (Postal Exchange, or Army store), clubs, barbecues, beers, music, live shows, ice cream and TVs. At the height of the war, for example, there were 40 ice-cream plants supplying the American troops with a luxury that few VC had even heard of. By 1972 a wide range of other amenities were in place, including 159 basketball courts, 71 swimming pools and two bowling alleys. Benefiting mostly from these comforts were the rear-echelon soldiers who served a supporting role in the war. Cooks, drivers, mechanics and engineers, dentists, laundrymen, radio operators and administrators all served in Vietnam but formed part of the 'tail' that allowed the 'teeth' (the combat units) to function. Critics pointed out that the ratio between these two disparate halves of the armed servces had reached an almost absurd level. Estimates vary, but there seem to have been five or six support personnel for every soldier patrolling in the field. But construction, maintenance, administration and transportation work had to be carried out. The (relatively) plush base camps were an outgrowth of this rear-echelon problem. Few grumbled more about the unequal share of the pain and discomfort of war than the soldiers out on patrol. To them the men living it up at base camp were REMFs, or 'Rear Echelon Mother F—ers'. It was a popular term, and one that illustrates the level of contempt that the gun-carrying soldier had for his air-conditioned colleague.

Of course, the distinctions were never that well drawn. Most large camps, air bases and headquarters came under fire from communist sapper teams or mortar barrages at one time or another. In the ultimate war without front lines, anyone could become a target, whatever his occupation. Similarly, almost all but the Special Forces soldiers spent a portion of their time on base camps in the rear and enjoyed the luxuries available there. Transported from jungle to junk food, from booby traps to basketball, the contrast sharply jarred the senses of many US soldiers. What kind of a war was it where you could watch a film each night, drink beer and eat steaks over a barbecue, get drunk, smoke a little dope and then fall asleep in a cool barrack room cleaned each day by a Vietnamese maid? It was life and death, fantasy and reality, base camps and the boonies. Senses were sharpened and dulled on a daily basis, and this seemed to intensify the war effort as a whole as something not real, as a game or a piece of fiction that could be forgotten about back at base camp. This investment in manpower and resources did have a reason. General Westmoreland hoped that troop morale would best be served by a support system that was worthy of a modern superpower, and called it 'one of the more remarkable accomplishments' of the war. In fact the sophisticated military force in South-East Asia actually *demanded* such a logistical prop. Unfortunately the rear-echelon build-up probably backfired and made it harder for the troops to put up with the discomfort and perpetual danger that they suffered while out on operations.

Compared to the local Vietnamese, each off-duty US soldier was a rich man. His free-spending R&R tours in Saigon, or along the beach fronts of Da Nang, Cam Ranh or Vung Tau often showed little respect for Vietnamese niceties. The result was friction. Many Americans considered that they were being exploited by the eager-to-please entrepreneurs, or at the very least that they were contributing to the economy. For the Vietnamese the harsh reality was that their standard of living did not seem to be improving. There were plenty of jobs available, from taxi drivers and shoe shiners to maids, waiters and bartenders. An entire army (literally!) of customers had flooded the towns and cities, but inflation quickly soared to match the availability of American dollars. Bribery and corruption became rife, and thousands of dollars' worth of military equipment from US bases and warehouses trickled into the black market economy. Criminal activities centred mainly on the Chinese Triads and the French *Union Corse*, both of which had to pay the Saigon leadership a cut of the profits. In return, free trade was guaranteed. Drugs (especially marijuana and heroin) and prostitution made up the meat of this trade. What was more, the conspicuous spending and constant carousing of the US troops seriously offended the upstanding Vietnamese. Those making money from the Americans regarded them with a certain contempt; others feared that long-standing customs and moral traditions would be eroded.

One such tradition was the treatment of Vietnamese women. A great number of poor, urban women had turned to prostitution to make a living off the back of the war. And soldiers in town for a few brief days of R&R had few other things on their mind. They would not have to search very hard to find a brothel or massage parlour that catered for their desires. More respectable women also found themselves objects of harassment, which caused embarrassment and some anger amongst the male population. That Vietnam's daughters should sink so low and suffer the degrading attentions of foreign soldiers sickened many. Vietnam was a war in which the loyalty of the population, not the rice-fields and hills, had become one of the central battlegrounds. The ignorant abuse of the South Vietnamese did little to win the much-valued 'hearts and minds'. Saigon had always been a defeat in this battle.

'Paris of the Orient' was a title that had little meaning in the Saigon of 1969. The beautiful French architecture, the leafy boulevards and the cool, calm atmosphere had given 1950s Saigon a distinctly Continental flavour. But at the height of the war the squalor and poverty that had been created blighted the city. It had become a city of paradoxes, and like Tu Do (now Dong Khoi) street, one of the central thoroughfares, it was caught between the extremes of extravagance and destitution. At one end lay Notre Dame Cathedral in all its nineteenth-century splendour, and at the other the riverside bars and bordellos fighting for attention amongst the shops. Caught in between were the haunts of the journalists and officers, the hotels, restaurants and street cafés. A huge underworld trade in drugs fed the military machine as it moved through Saigon and the other South Vietnamese cities. And as the war turned from aggressive action to withdrawal, soldiers began to turn to more and more to these chemical panaceas. The problem became very serious in the later stages of the war. In 1971, for example, the Americans had to hospitalise fewer than 5,000 men as a result of combat injuries, but in that same year over 20,000 soldiers were hospitalised for drug abuse. Drug use had spread to most units and was crippling military efficiency. Marijuana was the most popular, being smoked on R&R, in base camp and occasionally even on patrol, but a hard-core minority were hooked on heroin. Dealers in Saigon were able to secure supplies of that drug easily, since the world's heroin-growing region lay just to the north-west within the Golden Triangle. From this remote mountain fastness that overlapped the borders of Thailand, Burma and Laos, heroin was (and is still today) produced for the world market. How the CIA became intricately bound up in this awful traffic, and in mercenary operations behind enemy lines in Laos, is discussed in more detail later in the chapter.

For those drafted into it, the Vietnam War was unpopular and irrelevant. Most of the conscripted troops did only what was necessary to survive in this most hostile of environments. On a basic level, the draftees were against the war and against the system that had plucked them out of their world and dumped them into the Vietnam conflict. Later, as drug-taking and disobedience increased, some of the regular soldiers also turned against the military establishment. Mirroring this disenchantment was a huge growth in unofficial clothing and slang. Officers, who were generally more motivated and ambitious, differed in their approach to a unit's abandonment of regulations. Some cracked down hard, and forced a backlash, others let it go, allowing their soldiers to wear what they liked as long as they did their job. 'I don't care if he wears peace beads or symbols, or if he shaves,' said one Army captain. Like a number of other field officers, he rated personal appearance low on his list of battlefield priorities. It was generally older, senior officers who found the apathy intolerable. Love beads, peace symbols, helmet and flak armour graffiti, moustaches, sunglasses, and uniform modifications appalled high-ranking officers who were helicoptered in to visit units in the field. Helmets were being discarded, the sleeves of the tropical jacket torn off, or the jacket itself just abandoned in favour of a flak vest, olive drab T-shirt or even bare skin.

But it was by way of the black ink scrawlings on olive canvas or vehicle armour that a dejected soldier could express his identity, his rage, his frustration or his loneliness. Graffiti on the helmet cover sometimes just advertised the GI's name or nickname, sometimes his home state or even a calendar marking his DEROS. Indicating total incomprehension of the events surrounding them, some soldiers scribbled 'Gooks go home' on their helmets. A selection of the graffiti voiced blatant opposition to the war and the war-makers. 'Draft beer,' one young man's helmet read, 'not teenagers'. 'Make love not war' declared another. As veterans back in the US began marching in support of the anti-war movement, their war cry 'Vietnam veterans against the war', soon found its way into the graffiti of troops that were still in the combat zone. Less poetic and less pacific statements were also popular: 'F— Communism', 'Grunt Power', 'Hell Sucks', or 'Born to Kill'. A chilling piece of helmet art on one soldier simply gave his name followed by 'Blood Type O'.

Like the slogans, the troops' slang expressions also captured the mood of despondency, of unreality and of opposition to the system. When contact with the enemy was made, the soldiers would start 'bustin' caps' or 'capping'. This association of automatic weapons fire and toy cap guns gives an almost childlike aspect to the troops and their new 'toys'. But then there were many who had never had any lasting experiences outside childhood, school and Vietnam. References to the enemy were varied, but the name Victor Charles (from the phonetic alphabet spelling of Viet Cong) or just 'Charlie' were generally the most popular. Never clear whether they referred to the South Vietnamese, North Vietnamese or the Viet Cong were the names 'gook', 'dink' and 'slope'. One US APC had 'Dinks Killed' followed by a line of crosses. Presumably each cross designated a communist, not a South Vietnamese victim, but the crew itself may not even have known for sure.

The terminology of death reflected its diversity and needlessness. 'Gooks' were 'waxed', 'zapped', 'greased' and sometimes even shot. Americans were most often 'wasted', which on one level meant killed by enemy fire but for no worthwhile reason. The most common infantry activity was the search-and-destroy mission, which sometimes became known as a 'zippo raid', grimly associating it with the unassuming Zippo lighters with which entire villages were set alight. The word even became associated with the use of backpack or boat-mounted flame-throwers. It was as if the burning of hooches and the destruction of property which had been started by the Marines at Cam Ne back in 1965 had become normal, routine and almost expected. But for the troops the war was a weird, unreal fantasy-nightmare that would end on the arrival of their DEROS or at the end of a bullet or bomb fragment. Vietnam was not part of the normal universe, and normal laws of right and wrong, justice and morality did not apply. To soldiers in the combat zone, everywhere but Vietnam was 'the world'.

Frustrations and tempers frayed in units where officers worked against the men, or where racial tensions suddenly flared. With the withdrawal in progress and the large 'stay behind' army still in place, these problems intensified. Poor discipline and incomprehensible objectives meant that there were an increasing number of 'combat refusals' (or mutinies, as they are referred to in other armies) by individuals in the field. Convictions for mutiny soared from 82 in 1968 to 117 in 1969 and 131 in 1970. The trend continued. In 1971 an entire unit of the 1st Air Cavalry staged a combat refusal at the PACE firebase—an unprecedented action in the US Army. Black soldiers often segregated themselves within the unit as it rested between patrols, and occasionally this segregation turned into racial conflict. Fights could break out easily, especially when poor white Southern boys were mixing on a daily basis with urban black youths. Racial problems intensified following the assassination of Dr Martin Luther King on 4 April 1968. It seemed as if the barriers between black and white had come up, and a white officer commanding a mainly black unit could encounter serious problems. With the war winding down in the early 1970s, and the troops spending more and more time in base areas, friction developed to dangerous levels.

In October 1972 fighting on board the aircraft carrier USS *Kitty Hawk*, stationed off the coast of Vietnam, resulted in 46 sailors being injured. The fight had involved over 100 men and was followed later in the year by racial fights in San Diego, Midway Island and Norfolk, Virginia. Dr King, along with others in the anti-war movement, was calling Vietnam a white man's war that the black man was being forced to fight. It was understandable that ill-feeling existed on the battlefield. That ill-feeling occasionally led to incidents of more serious violence. A few individuals actually turned to murder in order to remove an officer who was thought to be incompetent. Incompetence in combat usually meant that people (usually the officer's own troops) were going to die. Rather than shoot the officer with an incriminating bullet, the *ad hoc* system of execution called 'fragging' was introduced.

'Fragging' began as an infrequent and improvised killing of an officer but developed into a systematic method of intimidation and execution. First, a smoke grenade was tossed into the offending officer's room. This served as a warning to the man—an attempt to dissuade him from issuing further rash orders. If the officer persisted, a CS (tear) gas grenade followed the smoke, and an anti-personnel fragmentation grenade followed that. The use of fragmentation grenades (hence 'fragging') was generally deadly, it avoided a face-to-face confrontation and it could not easily be traced to the killer. More often, only non-lethal smoke or CS grenades were used against a recalcitrant commander; or he would die anonymously in a jungle clearing or a rice paddy with 'more holes in his back than in his front'.

Part of the problem that led to the 'fragging' phenomenon was a poorly trained and inexperienced leadership, but it mainly stemmed from the participation of an army that did not want to fight. Officer murder became common enough to attract the attention of Congress in 1969, coinciding with the period of maximum American involvement and a time when the Army and Marines were being manned by more and more unwilling draftees. General military life and its discipline were obviously never popular with the draftee. However, the military need for the troops to engage in close jungle combat with the elusive North Vietnamese and Viet Cong soldiers contradicted the survive-at-any-costs code of ethics by which most draftees were living. Anything that disrupted that code, such as a green first lieutenant ordering his men into savage and suicidal combat (either for some elusive strategic gain or his own promotion prospects), would earn the soldier's animosity. Withdrawal saw an increased number of units restricted to rear-echelon duties, and 'fraggings' under these conditions were often drug-motivated: officers cracked down on drug-using soldiers and were suitably warned off, or else paid the price. The disintegration of the United States Army continued. Back in the US, Congress heard that 126 'fraggings' had been committed; in 1970 there were 383 and in 1971 another 333. One year later, with troop levels spiralling ever downwards, there were only 58 cases of murder reported. In total, almost 3 per cent of all officers' deaths were at the hands of their own troops. Yet how many other murders went undetected?

Perhaps the most infamous attempt to arrange the death of an officer took place during the battle for Hamburger Hill in 1969 (see Chapter 5). Lieutenant-Colonel Honeycutt, commander of the 3rd Battalion (part of the 101st Airborne Division), was so hated by his troops that a bounty was offered for his death. The interminable slog up the muddy Ap Bia mountain, the constant stream of dead and wounded and a soul-destroying incident of friendly fire close to the summit caused bitter outrage amongst the 3rd Battalion. For some, it seemed as if Honeycutt was working on the communists' behalf to chew up the unit. Lieutenant-Colonel Honeycutt survived despite multiple combat wounds and the intense hatred of his unit. After the fight he commended his men, 'I love every one of them,' he said.

Honeycutt led from the front and was undoubtedly a highly trained and experienced commander, but he ran his war by the book and approached his orders with a rigid mind-set. Younger and less experienced officers were also to incur the wrath of their troops. Some of these were removed by their own men with a grenade, others by their superiors. As the Vietnam War dragged on, the demand for junior officers increased dramatically. A growing number of officers were the product of Officer Candidate School (OCS), a US Army organisation that turned hopeful college graduates into second lieutenants. At times lacking the commitment, resolve and deep-rooted determination of the West Point or Reserve Officer Training Corps (ROTC) graduate, the OCS lieutenant usually found himself unprepared for the harsh realities of the Vietnam War. The US Military Academy at West Point turned out the majority of the Army's officer corps, while ROTC, a programme operating from the campuses of the nation's universities, recruited intelligent and motivated young men. But with local anti-war movements also based on campus, ROTC intakes dropped dramatically as the war progressed. OCS took officers from the college graduates as well as from the numerous NCOs who had a college education. The latter were a great success, often having valuable combat experience and the tried and tested ability to lead men in the field. The former, however, often did not fare so well. Lieutenant William Calley, initiator of the My Lai massacre, was one such soldier.

Agent Orange

Media debate concerning the American role in Vietnam continued after US troops had pulled out of that country in 1972 and also following the fall of Saigon in 1975. One issue that rose to prominence in the late 1970s was the use of the chemical defoliant Agent Orange. This incongruous sounding chemical soon became associated with a small number of disability claims made against the Veterans' Administration: some veterans were complaining of a range of symptoms that they put down to the activities of Operation 'Ranch Hand'. Little known up until that time, the chemical soon achieved notoriety and the full story of its use during the war came to light. It was a story with a dark premise, and a far darker epilogue. In their own way, the various technological changes that were transforming firearms (as discussed in Chapter 4) were controversial. However, Agent Orange engendered a massive controversy that would embroil the United Nations, the Geneva Protocol and the 1907 Hague Convention. The use of Agent Orange and the chemical's terrible legacy has even left the United States government open to a charge of committing a war crime against the South Vietnamese people.

When it first entered use in 1961, the chemical defoliant remained anonymous and unnoticed by the American news media. President Diem was working with MACV to introduce Operation 'Ranch Hand' as a method of denying the Viet Cong both cover and a source of food. Sprayed from the air, the defoliant killed almost all plant life, flattening jungle and laying bare the countryside. Enemy supply trails were sprayed, allowing US reconnaissance from the air, and the perimeters of large firebases were sprayed to deny cover to Viet Cong assault teams. Villages that had shown signs of communist sympathy were sprayed, reducing their crops to nothingness and forcing the inhabitants to relocate to 'Strategic Hamlets' that were closer to 'friendly forces'. In 1966 the project had reached its peak, and millions of litres of herbicides had by then been dropped on to South Vietnam. Agent Orange had emerged as the most effective, and popular, of the herbicides currently in use. Agents Purple and Pink had previously been in use up until 1964. The different defoliants actually received their names from the designating colours on the drums they came in. Agent Orange was also accompanied by the less well known (and less popular) Agents White and Blue.

A debate about the use of the herbicides began almost immediately, not in the press but in the government. Some of John F. Kennedy's advisers doubted the chemical's military use; others considered it the quickest and most effective way to deprive the Viet Cong of one of their greatest assets, Vietnam's jungle cover. Carefully controlled missions sprayed selective sites, and the planning and co-ordination of each one often involved not just the US Air Force but both MACV and the Saigon government. As the war began to hot up, fewer restrictions were placed on the 'Ranch Hand' missions and more autonomy was granted to their military planners. The pilots' motto, 'Only you can prevent forests', was a grim play on words of the US national parks signs that warned 'Only you can prevent forest fires'. But the humour belied a horrible truth. Agent Orange, it would later be revealed, contained a highly carcinogenic material called dioxin. The herbicide was a cancer-causing poison that could also induce malformations in newborn babies. And for nine years this deadly chemical rained down indiscriminately on hundreds of thousands of farmers and their families, as well as on South Vietnamese, American and other allied soldiers. Communist guerrillas, the main target of the spray-planes, were also frequently in contact with the chemical.

Vietnam was to be a new and challenging test area for Agent Orange but not its first. Similarly effective herbicides were used in back in the United States on a regular basis, for clearing farmland, roadsides and other areas of unwanted vegetation. Millions of square kilometres of American land had been thus treated, with relatively few ill effects. In Vietnam, however, the use of Agent Orange had become unrestricted, with people becoming regularly sprayed by the 'Ranch Hand' planes. No one knew what the effects of such exposure would be. As it turned out, numerous cases of cancer in post-war Vietnam would be attributed to Agent Orange, as would the heartbreaking reports of deformed children.

The planes converted to spray the defoliants were C-123 Providers, slow and vulnerable transport aircraft that flew together in small numbers for greater coverage. An Air Force F-4 Phantom would often 'ride shotgun' with the Providers, ready and able to strafe, rocket and bomb enemy troops who opened fire on the planes. When defoliating a jungle trail for the first time, one Provider would go in low with its spray booms ready while a second would fly high above, able to see the trail through the forest canopy and correct the flight of the first. At a later stage, follow-up planes simply flanked the long corridor of dying jungle and widened the defoliated zone out to 250m on either side of the trail. In some instances, especially when cropland was being targeted for defoliation, a leaflet drop would precede the spraying operation to warn the local inhabitants. Many saw the entire defoliation campaign as just one weapon that could be used to destroy the South Vietnamese countryside. We have already discussed what this programme aimed to achieve (see Chapter 5), and Agent Orange provided a powerful lever with which to carry it out. Re-location of the peasant population away from the Viet Cong, who fed off them and hid amongst them, was made far easier when a village's entire cropland could be destroyed. Without food or livelihood, a peasant farmer had no choice but to become a refugee. Donald Hornig, one of President Johnson's advisers, declared that the 'Ranch Hand' operation was 'all geared to moving people'. Although roads and trails were exposed to cameras and bombers, the jungle refused to be beaten and eventually grew back just as thickly. It seemed that the main target of Agent Orange was to become the innocent South Vietnamese themselves.

At the war's end, over 20 per cent of South Vietnam's jungle and 36 per cent of its mangrove forests had been sprayed with chemical defoliants. Troops had also been accidentally sprayed, often on their own firebases while 'Ranch Hand' aircraft unloaded their defoliant on the surrounding jungle. As media awareness of Agent Orange gradually emerged after the war, a number of Vietnam veterans made disability claims against the manufacturers of the herbicide. More than a decade later there were tens of thousands of these claims outstanding. In the mid-1980s the manufacturers of the various herbicides acknowledged their responsibility in the affair and agreed to establish a $180 million fund for the payment of these claims. Today, the problems facing US troops who had been exposed to Agent Orange during their tour are more widely understood and recognised. For their Gulf War counterparts, the fight for recognition is being waged all over again. Reports of the mysterious 'Gulf War syndrome' began as soon as allied troops began coming home from the battle zone in 1991, and they were not restricted to US soldiers. Some British and French troops have also complained about a mysterious illness that affects coordination, muscle-mass, mental health and the health of their newborn children. At first there were few in Washington who believed that such a condition existed, but so widespread is the problem now that the authorities have no choice but to investigate the strange illness. Vietnam veterans battling for Agent Orange compensation from the government can sympathise with the Gulf soldiers' forlorn plight. As far as Washington is concerned, the Gulf War is over—cut and dried. Mounting evidence seems to suggest, however, that the allied governments blundered and are now highly reluctant to acknowledge any responsibility for their actions.

It now seems likely that 'Gulf War syndrome' is not the result of the toxic residue from the oil fires that raged on after the war, or of the anti-chemical warfare drugs that troops were required to take. It was, in some cases, caused by unreported gas attacks by the Iraqi Army, in others by the release of chemical weapons (nerve gases and blister and blood agents) into the desert air when allied planes bombed Iraqi weapons factories and chemical storage facilities. Chronic exposure to the very substances that the allied commanders feared most had been initiated by their own warplanes. Yet no one dare accept responsibility for such an act, however noble the intent. Agent Orange has been resurrected in another form, and government intransigence and obstinacy will ensure that the controversy continues to rage for many years to come.

The final word on Agent Orange should be given to the countless South Vietnamese (and Laotian) civilians who were indiscriminately sprayed with the herbicide and who have suffered in silence ever since. Disability payments from the chemical companies will never reach these unfortunates, people who suffer the same crippling illnesses and whose children exhibit similar birth abnormalities. Hospitals in modern Vietnam continue to treat Agent Orange victims and their children. At the close of the war, President Gerald Ford signed an executive order that formally renounced the use of herbicides in warfare. Fears were growing that academic opinion might lay charges of war crimes at the White House door. Did Agent Orange constitute a chemical weapon equal in stature to sarin or mustard gas? Had the United States contravened the Geneva Convention by targeting crops with defoliants, rather than troop concentrations with nerve gas? The fact that the herbicide was already being used in quantity back in the US further complicates the argument. The General Assembly of the United Nations made a ruling in 1969, however, that reinforced the Geneva ban on chemical weapons of *all* kinds. Accepted opinion today recognises that using the defoliant was wrong, on military grounds as well as moral, and may have amounted to ecological warfare of a kind never seen before.

Missing in Action

One aspect of any war that plays a vital role in American morale both in the field and at home is the abuse of prisoners or hostages. The massive aerial bombing campaign that was unleashed over North Vietnam, combined with the determined and extensive communist air defence system, virtually guaranteed that a number of American pilots would be shot down. These almost always fell into enemy hands. Many of these prisoners were held in Hanoi at the so-called 'Hanoi Hilton' (actually the Hoa Lo prison), while others were imprisoned at compounds elsewhere in Hanoi or North Vietnam. As the war progressed, the American prison population increased and more camps sprang up to accommodate the prisoners. Conditions in these Third World prison camps were truly appalling. Torture, threats of violence and continual demands for propaganda-type confessions were carried out. Meanwhile the prisoners lived amongst filth, insects, rats and their own excrement, they were often painfully bound and they suffered from debilitating illnesses.

As part of the Paris Peace Accords, the return of all US servicemen held by Hanoi was guaranteed, and by the summer of 1973 all 591 were returned to the United States. There were some who had not made it through the ordeal and had died or been killed in captivity. Less than a dozen of the returning prisoners had been captured by NVA units across the border in Laos to be passed on to Hanoi. They represented an entirely unseen and unreported war that had raged in parallel with the conflict in Vietnam. They also represented an undeclared and unwanted prison population over the Vietnam border, for there were hundreds of missing servicemen in Laos, some of whom were suspected to be still alive and imprisoned in communist camps. But in 1973 the Laotian conflict was still shrouded in secrecy, and Washington continually denied that America had violated that country's neutrality by prosecuting a war there. It could not now demand prisoners from a conflict that should not have existed. The Watergate affair began to obscure the end of the war, and, for much of America, the Vietnam War was at last over. However, the families of soldiers and airmen who were still classified as Prisoners of War or Missing in Action (POW/MIA) would not find it so easy to divorce themselves from the conflict.

In the late 1970s, reports of sightings of American prisoners who were still alive in Laotian prison camps surfaced infrequently. Most of these reports were unsubstantiated rumours, passed on from locals who told their story for US dollars. The families of these 'survivors' fought a losing battle in an attempt to spur the US authorities to take action. Diplomacy, rescue attempts or at least reconnaissance to counter or support the allegations were demanded. Nothing was done. An organisation had been formed during the war to unite these families and apply pressure to the government. It was called the National League of POW/MIA Families, and it wanted the unrecovered remains of American dead returned to the United States as well as information on living MIAs followed up. In response to this pressure, the Carter and Reagan administrations secured the return of numerous human remains from Hanoi. When missing Marine Bobby Garwood turned up in 1979, he was immediately (and bizarrely) arrested and charged with collaboration with the communists. He had gone missing at the very start of the war and had learned to speak Vietnamese to survive in the prison camp that was to be his home for the next nine years. What he privately told those who would listen (the authorities would not officially de-brief him) was that prisoners were still being held by North Vietnam. Some had even been sent to the Soviet Union ('Moscow bound'), Garwood alleged. More and more sightings turned up, as well as photos of what seemed to be actual US prisoners.

Congress would not take the POW/MIA subject seriously. The incumbent administration, meanwhile, pledged to do everything it possibly could to secure the freedom of extant prisoners, as and when concrete evidence could be furnished. The CIA thoroughly denied that any prisoners remained alive in Laos (or anywhere else) and had begun a fight in the 1980s to dissuade individuals and organisations from pressing the matter further. Limited access to the information that the CIA actually had available on the issue was maintained by a core of Vietnam veterans, mostly ex-intelligence operatives and Special Forces soldiers. Jerry Mooney, a former analyst with the National Security Agency, had tracked up to 600 American prisoners of war up until the last days of the conflict, and has sworn affidavits testifying to their existence after the war. Mooney is an expert in electronic and human intelligence-gathering and was tragically denied a chance to give evidence to the Senate Veterans Affairs Committee in 1986. The Committee aimed to shed light on a lawsuit brought by two Green Beret soldiers, Sergeant First Class Melvin McIntire and Major Mark Smith. Two years earlier they had initiated the legal proceedings in an honourable attempt to prove that the US government already knew about live prisoners but refused to act on the information that it had acquired. Unsurprisingly, the Committee's findings were inconclusive, garbled by intelligence denials and national security restrictions.

One agency, the Joint Casualty Resolution Center (JCRC), had been set up to monitor information concerning POW/MIA reports and to act on them. But it has made little progress—deliberately so, say the families of missing Americans. The JCRC has even been accused of suppressing evidence from POWs so that post-war covert activities within Indo-China can proceed without interference. This theme was picked up by journalists Monika Jensen-Stevenson and William Stevenson in their book *Kiss the Boys Goodbye*. There are various theories that explain US government intransigence in accepting and acting upon information about American prisoners. Perhaps the most common is that the government does not want the Vietnam War reopened and fears condemnation or ridicule if it becomes known that it abandoned men in South-East Asia for the sake of a speedy resolution to the war. A second asserts that Congress refuses to honour a pledge made by President Nixon to pay war reparations amounting to $3 billion. In return, Vietnam refuses to release its American prisoners, since they have become an insurance policy against a future payment of this vast sum. This theory gains plausibility when it is remembered that French prisoners held in Vietnam have often been bought back by their government over the intervening years. Why should Vietnam's approach to the United States be any different? However, ex-CBS reporter Monika Jensen-Stevenson, who worked as a producer on *60 Minutes* for six years, has come to a startlingly different conclusion. Her findings are backed by countless interviews and important documentation (often derided by the government) that link the suppression of prisoner intelligence with a secret war still being fought in South-East Asia. It is a war that was first begun in the 1950s by the French government as it fought for control of Laos.

Joining the French in their fight against the communist Viet Minh was a young Laotian tribesman called Vang Pao. As a lieutenant, he had marched his commando unit through the mountains to help relieve the French garrison at Dien Bien Phu but had arrived too late. With France gone after 1954, Laos became a nation on the edge, and it quickly became a staging post and conduit for the Vietnamese communists as well as the Laotian communists (the Pathet Lao). President Kennedy, interested only in counter-insurgency, not a Third World War, tasked the CIA to establish a highly secret presence in Laos and wage a proxy guerrilla war with local tribespeople. Meanwhile the US Army organised Operation 'White Star', the military training programme dedicated to turning the Royal Lao Army into an effective fighting force. Laos was seen as one of the dominoes in the dreaded line-up, and it had to be effectively neutralised in the war against the communists. China and North Vietnam had already fallen; Laos, South Vietnam, Thailand and Cambodia were thought to be next. At the heart of South-East Asia, Laos was a land-locked and mountainous cross-roads that had to be negotiated to reach the rest of the dominoes. Control of Laos became of vital importance.

Winding through the Laotian mountains, the newly established Ho Chi Minh Trail saw a massive influx of North Vietnamese units into the country. The southern half of Laos (the 'panhandle') became a virtual highway to South Vietnam, and the CIA's hill-tribe forces (mainly Hmong villagers) were directed to carry out spoiling attacks against communist rear areas. Vang Pao was recruited by the Agency as the leader of these Hmong guerrillas fighters. As General Vang Pao, he organised a campaign of covert warfare against the North Vietnamese units and the communist Pathet Lao. He headed an extensive intelligence network, rescued downed US air crews (flying in support of the CIA operations under the designation 'Barrel Roll') and provided defences for the crucial Site 85. Site 85 was a navigation guidance outpost, manned by sanitised (i.e., 'civilianised') US Air Force technicians, that allowed 'Rolling Thunder' bombers successfully to navigate their way into North Vietnam. It sat atop the sheer cliff faces of the Phou Pha Thi mountain and was surrounded by heavily jungled hills and opium fields. Colonel Gerald Clayton, head of operations at the top-secret site, told Monika Jensen-Stevenson that to get to it technicians 'had to walk through the dope they were growing'.

Opium played an important part in this murky undeclared war. Although the Royal Lao Army was trained and equipped with funds from Congressional appropriations, the CIA-backed army of Vang Pao had to rely on purely covert CIA funding. Like the French, the CIA had begun to utilise the extensive cultivation of opium in the Golden Triangle for the 'good' of the war effort. Drugs paid for more equipment, more food, more weaponry and more wages. Such funding did not need approval by Congress and could not be traced. It must have seemed the perfect source of revenue for a covert war. Air America, the CIA's own airline, shipped drugs out of the Laotian wilderness to local markets, and from there the heroin was trafficked across the globe. General Pao's 22,000 mercenary soldiers were being paid in drug money by the United States' foremost intelligence agency! Vang Pao was not just a military commander, he was a community leader who had to provide for the scattered half-a-million Hmong. Heroin money would have come as a blessing to these poverty-stricken hill people.

For ten years General Pao fought the communists to a standstill, personally defending his mountain-top base at Long Chieng from infantry assault in 1971. Three years before, Site 85 had actually fallen to the enemy in a surprise attack. And not all of the Air Force technicians made it off the mountain in time. Then there were the other servicemen, pilots, Army advisers and operatives who had also gone missing or been captured during the secret war in Laos. With continued denials of an American presence in the country, followed by Nixon's withdrawal from Indo-China, these prisoners seemed to have little chance of repatriation. But the families never lost hope of seeing their menfolk again. After the Vietnam War had officially come to an end with the North Vietnamese invasion of the South in 1975, communist groups also took over in Laos and Cambodia. The Hmong became a persecuted people and have been fleeing the persecution ever since. Along with refugee Vietnamese and Cambodians, the desperate Hmong have made for the Thai border. There they are resettled in overcrowded and ill-equipped camps. Many still remain behind, and some of these have organised a resistance movement against the communist government with aid from General Vang Pao, who had fled to America.

For a minority of intelligence operatives, however, the war continued. General Vang Pao's Hmong forces provided the opportunity for the CIA to continue covert action in Indo-China after 1975, and the heroin trade provided an ideal source of revenue. The illegal funding assured total independence from Washington, and it seems that a secret network within the Agency has been carrying on the fight against Indo-Chinese communism ever since. The stakes in this covert war were raised again with the Vietnamese invasion of Cambodia in 1978. Hmong networks, spy satellite photography, aerial surveillance and jungle-stomping patrols masquerading as JCRC or Drug Enforcement Agency teams provided an in-depth intelligence-gathering system. And part of this intelligence included the existence and location of American prisoners of war, still in captivity long after Vietnam had been united. After hearing of numerous official denials, of dark warnings and of obstructions placed in the path of every POW/MIA investigation, Jensen-Stevenson concluded that rogue elements in the CIA could not let the existence of US prisoners surface. Along with that information would come the full story of the Agency's illegal war in a neutral country, and the far more damaging revelations that it had funded a mercenary army with the proceeds of heroin. This was being sold on to dealers in (amongst many other places)

American cities. It seemed that this activity had not been terminated: it was not a closed chapter of the Vietnam War but a continuing and still highly sensitive covert operation. Presidential candidate Ross Perot told Jensen-Stevenson that 'guys got in the habit of using drugs to raise money to finance anti-communist operations'. He doubted that they had kicked the habit.

For the refugee population encamped along the Thai border region, the war against communism continues, and they have become recruits in this secret CIA conflict. It is well known that the United States had been clandestinely supporting the Cambodian Khmer Rouge guerrilla army against the Vietnamese-imposed government in Phnom Penh. Even the British Special Air Service (SAS) commando regiment was rumoured to have helped the CIA turn Indo-Chinese refugees into guerrilla fighters. Since 1989, when Vietnam could no longer afford the occupation of Cambodia and withdrew its forces, the situation has become more stable. But it is still unknown how many American prisoners have been sacrificed by an élite group for the pursuance of national interests, how many of the abandoned Hmong have been executed by the victorious Pathet Lao since 1975 or how much of the blame for the West's drug problems can be laid at the door of this shadowy group. Whatever the revelations of the future, the fate of these prisoners is far from fitting. Risking life and limb, and out of uniform in a wholly deniable role, they may have been sacrificed in an attempt to continue the war unbeknownst to the world at large. It is an ignoble ending to a controversial and inglorious war, a war that blurred the distinctions between combatant and victim, destruction and development, friend and foe.

Even though President Clinton has 'normalised' US trade relations with Vietnam, one is forced to ask whether the Vietnam War has ended. For most Americans, the war ended in 1973; for most South Vietnamese it ended disastrously in April 1975. How it ended, and what the United States learnt from this tragic conflict, was a drama that involved a drastic re-thinking of strategy, military development and the role of America on the world stage. Presiding over this transition from war to peace was President Richard Nixon.

Chapter 9

DEFEAT—AND LESSONS LEARNED

As United States units began pulling out of South Vietnam, North Vietnamese Army units also began withdrawing. Time was now on Hanoi's side. All the communists had to do was wait until the United States had fully redeployed its vast military machine back across the Pacific from where it had originally come. The venerable Ho Chi Minh died at the end of 1969, in time to detect a definite wavering of American resolve but with his countrymen still over five years away from total victory. From concerted large-scale sweeps and multi-division offensives into enemy-held base areas, the dominating strategy from 1970 onwards became one of small-scale patrolling. The new programme, 'Vietnamisation', was intended to replace the massive commitment in men and material that the United States had been supplying since 1961. 'Vietnamisation' was a plan to hand over American killing technology to the South Vietnamese and provide adequate training in its use. It also stressed the continuing application of rural pacification, which could fill the vacuum caused by the destruction of the VCI during the Tet Offensive. 'Vietnamisation' was a financially expensive option, but the mood of the American people, of Congress and of the media, was that the sacrifice of American lives would be the most expensive option of all.

Future manoeuvring would be carried out at the Paris peace talks, not on the battlefield. With Nixon had come a new era in the Vietnam War. He pledged to secure a 'victory with honour', a way out for American forces that did not cost lives (and, more importantly for Nixon, votes at home). But there was a strange paradox within the President's peace strategy: it was punctuated by some of the most intense destruction so far wrought by American forces. Part of the reason for this was that the out-going President, Johnson, had not left Nixon with many options. 'Rolling Thunder' had been terminated on 1 November, denying him the option of stepping up the bombing of North Vietnam, and troop levels had reached a ceiling beyond which the national mood would not let him rise. Negotiations had already been entered into by the Johnson administration, and yet Nixon found that he had few diplomatic levers at his command. And, at the heart of the matter, the difference that had brought Hanoi and Washington into open conflict in the first place still remained: North Vietnam wanted to invade and absorb South Vietnam while the United States wanted to prevent this happening. With such a fundamental stumbling block, negotiations would drag on for three years before peace accords could be signed.

President Nixon looked at the Vietnam War anew, and with help from his own Vietnam Special Studies Group reappraised predictions for the conflict's future. Was it victory or defeat that lurked in the middle distance? What time-scale was available for the defence of South Vietnam? And could that nation actively defend itself? What emerged from the study prepared by adviser Dr Henry Kissinger was that outright victory was impossible and that immediate withdrawal of all American assets would threaten US commitments across the globe. 'Vietnamisation' was to be Nixon's answer to the Vietnam problem. In essence it was a practical rendering of the new-found 'Nixon doctrine' that pledged to support allied nations from armed aggression, but in economic and military aid only. The burden of any fighting would have to be shouldered by the nation itself. This meant that there was now a limit to the extent America would fight communism overseas. Ironically, it was this approach that had been employed by both China and the Soviet Union throughout the war. These nations declined to fight the Vietnam War for Hanoi but provided extensive supplies of weaponry and funds with which North Vietnam could carry the fight southwards itself.

The Last Years of the Vietnam War

So ravaged were the communist forces by the 1968 Tet Offensive and its aftermath that there were no offensives launched into South Vietnam in 1969. In Cambodia and Laos, the North Vietnamese formations dug in and prepared for events that would not materialise. Operation 'Menu', the bombing of Cambodian border camps by B-52s, was designed to prevent NVA deployment and provide the 'Vietnamisation' process with a breathing space. Two years were needed, it was calculated, for pacification to neutralise what was left of the Viet Cong and restore national confidence. That would also allow time for the completion of ARVN mobilisation, training and rearming. These first years of 'Vietnamisation' seemed to be virtually free from large-scale NVA attacks, and whereas in 1965 allied patrols were hard-pressed to cope with the contacts they made, by 1970 units had to scour the bush for signs of enemy activity. Tet *had* made a difference. And 'Vietnamisation' succeeded almost beyond expectations, cutting Viet Cong activity measurably while providing a greater control of peasant communities. The Phoenix Program, instituted at this time, added to the gains and ensured that any viable guerrilla infrastructure would be struck a mortal blow.

A new strategy was formulated to deal with the massing North Vietnam Army over the border in Cambodia. President Nixon, taking advantage of a changing political climate in that country, authorised a military expedition across the border to strike at communist army bases. Previous military commanders had often dreamt of such a manoeuvre, but with Prince Sihanouk's desire for neutrality this had been an impossibility. In 1970, however, the NVA had become virtual feudal overlords in eastern Cambodia, closing roads, taxing peasants, drafting manpower and restricting the access of Cambodian officials. A new hard-line government ousted the prince and then proceeded to call for US help in removing the NVA. A decision was made to stage an incursion into that part of Cambodia known as the 'Fishhook'. Estimates put the communist troop total there at 7,000 and predicted that the Viet Cong central headquarters, the elusive COSVN (Central Office for South Vietnam), was also sheltering there. Highly mobile American and South Vietnamese army units moved into Cambodia on 1 May 1970, supported by firebase artillery and high-altitude bombing. Contact was initiated almost immediately, but the strength of the communist defence was not as great as had been expected. In fact, it seemed that most of the NVA had fled, along with COSVN. But, unfortunately for the enemy, its huge supply dumps had been abandoned. Nicknamed 'The City' by those on the operation, the supply complex astounded everyone by its sheer scale. Hospitals, ammunition, weaponry, clothing, explosives and everything else required to wage war was discovered there. Hundreds of bunkers and whole acres of jungle were levelled in an attempt to obliterate what remained of the enemy presence. After weeks inside Cambodia, the force pulled back into the relative safety of South Vietnam. Operation 'Toan Thang 43', as the incursion had been labelled, had been a decisive success. Although a full-scale engagement had not materialised and COSVN was never found, an important staging post and months of communist preparation had been destroyed. The ARVN had, for the first time, fought offensively, with the initiative, and with a new and rapidly maturing army. It had also helped to buy more time for both the 'Vietnamisation' process and the consolidation of the military.

If Cambodia had formed the supply depot for Hanoi's armies, Laos was at the same time the highway to it. And, despite several attempts to sever the highway with B-52 strikes, 'Igloo White' and General Vang Pao's guerrillas, it remained obstinately free-flowing. As 1970 came to an end, MACV received reports that supply dumps were being established around the Laotian town of Tchepone, those in Cambodia being, for the most part, out of action. Like a sword slash, the ARVN was to sweep into Laos to cut the Trail and prevent further build-ups. The force was to be given American artillery and air support but would fight the ground war itself. It would be a supreme test of maturity for the ARVN. On 30 January, using a reoccupied Khe Sanh as a forward base, the attack got under way. Despite poor weather and stiff communist resistance, Operation 'Lam Son 719' fulfilled its operational objectives, but the toll in human life was high. This time the NVA stood and fought, with artillery and even tanks. After destroying supply bases around Tchepone, the ARVN column made a withdrawal back over the border. But General Giap, coordinating things from Hanoi, realised how badly the ARVN as a whole would be hurt by a rout and sent everything he had against the retreating soldiers. With tremendous air support, the enemy forces (numbering perhaps 30,000) were pounded mercilessly and destroyed in Laos.

Fighting all the way, the beleaguered ARVN columns crossed the border and by the end of March the operation had ended. Many doubt the value of 'Lam Son 719', calling it a waste of men for a temporary foray. Others see it as another successful spoiling attack that cut the Trail and crippled the NVA supply line. In fact it threw back Hanoi's invasion plans by yet another year, since the vast military forces sent against the column had been devastated. More than 10,000 communist casualties may have been sustained, and the weaponry and equipment lost had also to be replaced. At some cost, the entire communist offensive had been sent reeling, gaining time for US withdrawal and South Vietnamese readiness.

Another year would pass before General Giap could muster adequate forces for his third invasion of South Vietnam (previous attempts had been the 1965 Ia Drang campaign and the 1968 Tet Offensive). Termed the 'Eastertide Offensive', the 1972 invasion was a bold and large-scale plan which aimed to suck the ARVN into border battles while other units severed the country through the Central Highlands. With a degree of surprise the NVA poured across the DMZ—surprise due not to the invasion's timing (intelligence reports had already predicted such an attack) but its tactics. Gone were fluid and fast-moving NVA units, attacking and disappearing at will: the Eastertide Offensive employed tank regiments, mobile anti-aircraft guns and towed artillery. The conventional invasion so feared in the late 1950s had eventually arrived. Nixon unleashed the entire fury of the US Air Force on North Vietnam and the attacking forces. It was Operation 'Linebacker', an air campaign with a purpose that lacked the self-imposed restrictions of President Johnson's 'Rolling Thunder'. Ports were mined from the air, rail lines into China were cut and the road network within North Vietnam (particularly just north of the DMZ) came under fierce attack. As the communist advances into South Vietnam encountered the tough opposition of the ARVN, weeks of very bloody fighting began. By June the NVA spearheads were being repulsed, suffering from both counter-attacks on the battlefield and logistical disruption in the rear. The invasion, strung out through Laos and extending deep into the South, withered on the vine. 'Linebacker' blasted its roots while a staunch and unyielding South Vietnamese Army plucked away at the fruit. Giap's invasion had failed.

For the rest of the year talks in Paris attempted to institute a plan for peace in South-East Asia, whilst the bombing of the North continued. In December, to punish Hanoi for extending the talks in an attempt to secure as much territory as it could before a cease-fire agreement, a new bombing campaign ('Linebacker II') blasted targets in the Hanoi–Haiphong area. Other locations in North Vietnam were also hit and the damage proved extensive. North Vietnam had not seen devastation on this scale before. The talks continued, and in January 1973 a peace agreement was signed by representatives of both Hanoi and Washington. The United States agreed to refrain from intervention in Saigon's affairs, although, with troop numbers now at pitifully low levels, that point was rather academic. With the signings, President Nixon could claim a 'peace with honour'. He had presided over the end of the war, and it had been a war that had not been lost. Neither had it been won, but, as we have seen, winning had never been a realistic option.

By the end of 1973 fighting between the NVA and the ARVN had reached serious levels once again. It was becoming clear that the peace agreement was little more than a sham that allowed the United States officially to disengage from the conflict in South Vietnam. Fighting continued throughout 1974, with President Thieu's forces standing firm. But with US aid reduced to a trickle, and Soviet aid increasing, the balance was being rapidly tipped in favour of Hanoi once more. Troops, supplies, tanks and artillery flooded south along the refurbished Ho Chi Minh Trail (now a virtual motorway, complete with hardened surface and fuel pipelines). As the new offensive broke in early 1975, ARVN units up against it crumbled and civilians and panicking soldiers rushed headlong towards the coastal enclaves. On 30 April NVA tanks entered Saigon, and, with little other option, the South Vietnamese government surrendered. With the fall of the Saigon regime, the Second Indo-China War had come to an end. Vietnam was reunited at last and the United States government and military reflected on a war that had cost them so much, not just economically but also politically and morally.

Secretary of Defense Robert McNamara has offered his own accounts, his reasons for failure and his apologies for the awful mismanagement of the Vietnam War. He has said, 'I criticise the president [Lyndon Johnson], his advisers, and myself as much as the chiefs [of staff] for this negligence', and his book *In Retrospect* abounds with 'we should haves'. After a catalogue of eleven major reasons for defeat in Vietnam, McNamara turns to the 58,000 American dead and asserts that, although 'our effort in Vietnam proved unwise', it did not 'make their sacrifice less noble'. For the Vietnamese, the toll was higher—absurdly so: there were perhaps 500,000 South Vietnamese soldiers and civilians killed, and anything from 600,000 to 1 million Viet Cong and North Vietnamese soldiers and civilians killed.

The Vietnam War Syndrome

Collective amnesia afflicted much of America following the end of the Vietnam crusade. No one wanted to see the country again embroiled in some nasty foreign war without a clearly defined purpose. The Nixon doctrine marked a new shift in international politics. From now on American soldiers would only go to war to preserve American freedoms on American soil. But weaponry, know-how and funding would still be supplied to nations that were battling communism; the next overseas conflict would be a 'proxy war'. This fear of failure in wars overseas would come to be known as the 'Vietnam syndrome'. It would mark a period of American foreign policy that shunned direct intervention and even tended towards isolationism.

With Nixon's remarkably successful moves to normalise relations with both the Soviet Union and Red China in the 1970s, the anti-communist zeal that had led to the Vietnam débâcle waned. It soon became clear that acts of communist aggression sponsored by the Soviet Union would be fiercely denounced, but that little overt action would be taken to prevent such aggression. In the Angolan civil war Cuban soldiers stepped in with Soviet backing, and communism became inextricably linked with the war between Ethiopia and Somalia. In Afghanistan a Soviet-backed government came to power and invited the Soviet armed forces to do battle against its Mujaheddin opponents. Back in South-East Asia, a reunited communist Vietnam invaded Cambodia and installed its own regime in Phnom Penh. But Washington declined to intervene directly in any of these important conflicts. Covert assistance would, however, be given. The Mujaheddin fighters were heavily supported by American military aid smuggled in over the Pakistani border, and in Cambodia Washington backed the Khmer Rouge extremists who had been ousted from the capital.

President Nixon seemed temporarily to have exorcised the demon of communism from the American psyche while reining in the military strategists who were committed to expunging it from the world, wherever it occurred and at whatever cost. Obviously there was a cost, and after Vietnam it was not a cost that most Americans and their Congressmen would willingly meet. Meanwhile the Soviet Union seemed to be enjoying a period of international freedom and political expansion, a trend that worried some in Washington who were beginning to believe that the United States had overreacted to the loss of South Vietnam. Clearly, to bury one's head in the sand, ostrich-like, did not lessen the dangers that seemed to imperil the Free World. A backlash was bound to follow.

Turmoil within Central America (considered to be the 'US backyard') in the 1980s proved to be a test of the Nixon doctrine as understood by the incumbent President, Ronald Reagan. Following the Vietnam War, the Special Forces units that had gained so much fame and notoriety in that conflict quickly lost their popularity with policy-makers in the Pentagon. Smacking too much of interventionism (and of the failed American hostage rescue attempt in Iran in 1980), the élite troops found themselves unwanted in the new political climate. Their time would come. In Central America, the escalating conflicts that wracked nations such as El Salvador, Nicaragua and Grenada deeply troubled the Reagan administration. The El Salvadorian government battled a plethora of communist guerrilla groups throughout the 1980s. In Nicaragua, following the 1979 revolution, the National Guard of exiled President Somoza re-formed along the Honduran border as the 'Contras' and began a war to topple the hard-line revolutionary government of the Sandanistas. Reagan was determined that, while El Salvador must not fall, the Nicaraguan government *must*. In an effort to apply leverage in this most important of geographical regions, the United States supplied the Contras with training and hardware from over the border in Honduras. Meanwhile it bolstered the flagging armed forces of El Salvador in an echo of the situation in South-East Asia of the early 1960s. Of course, interests in that region continued to be maintained through the Khmer Rouge. It was in these covert wars of training and advice that the Special Forces again found their services in demand. Reagan saw in them the perfect deniable lever that enabled him (as it had Kennedy) to participate in these conflicts without committing troops and simultaneously losing votes. The 'Vietnam syndrome' prevented him from mobilising the nation to defend yet another foreign government in trouble, however close it might be to the US border. Thus were the secret wars of the 1980s quietly declared.

By 1980 the 'Vietnam syndrome' was coming to be seen, not as a doctrine that would keep America out of other people's wars, but as a disability crippling its overseas influence. The invasion of Afghanistan, the invasion of Cambodia, the fall of the US-backed Shah of Iran and the Teheran hostage crisis all seemed to confirm the impression that America was a crippled superpower, unable to act decisively. From being a 'restraint', the syndrome became a 'constraint' to international relations, and a barrier that had to be breached. A sharp increase in terrorist attacks on American civilians overseas also heightened the impotent nature of US foreign policy. Riding on the outcome of the 'Vietnam syndrome' was the self-confidence of the entire nation. President Reagan reintroduced the black-and-white formula of the Cold War, since it had been President Carter's lack of forcefulness and direction that had brushed him from the White House. The East–West conflict could galvanise the nation and provide him with the support at home that he needed to carry out various overseas interventions. Hand in hand with the phrase 'no more Vietnams' went the description of the Soviet Union as the 'evil empire' by Reagan and his military chiefs. With the promise not to commit America to another never-ending war of attrition and broken trust, he was simultaneously squaring up against the Soviet Union. It was Reagan's mission to re-establish the nation as the pre-eminent superpower and the main arbiter of world events.

Reagan re-wrote the outcome of the Vietnam War, or, more accurately, he re-wrote the reasons for American failure in that war. Feeling the need to flex American muscle overseas, he had to convince the nation that the next military adventure would not be a re-run of Vietnam. This fear affected every decision made by the Pentagon throughout the decade. It was a ghost to be exorcised. And, to exorcise it, Reagan announced that he would never send American soldiers into battle overseas unless (in his words) 'we are prepared to win'. As part of a new 'revisionist' view of the Vietnam War, this statement appeared to set the stage for later wars, perhaps of a similar nature. A growing opinion amongst military apologists shifted the blame for the 'defeat' from the armed forces to the politicians and the anti-war movement. This mood was reflected amongst veterans' organisations, books and films. The sudden growth of Vietnam War movies in the mid-1980s carried the new interpretation to extremes. Charlie Sheen's character in *Platoon* contemplatively suggests that the enemy 'was ourselves'. Green Beret John Rambo prepares to return to Vietnam in search of POWs and asks 'do we get to win this time?'. In *Hamburger Hill*, the underlying commentary is of an honest, self-sacrificing army betrayed by the anti-war demonstrators.

A constant theme recurs—that of a crusade undertaken for legitimate reasons by a military that is keen to carry out the task but is let down by politicians and a vocal opposition to the war. Strict control of the war by Johnson and his advisers from the grand strategic to (in some cases) the tactical level hamstrung the war effort and wasted the energy and enthusiasm of a generation. So went the revisionist thinking, and underpinning it were academic works such as *On Strategy: The Vietnam War in Context*, written by Colonel Harry Summers in 1981. Seen by many as the US Army's 'official' analysis of the failure to secure South Vietnam in the 1960s and 1970s, it roundly criticises the civilian interference in military decision-making. Such critical self-assessment is typical of any defeated nation: the question 'What did we do wrong?' is often asked. Rather than admit that an enemy could outwit or outfight one's armed forces, it is often easier to blame oneself. The 'Vietnam syndrome', then, was essentially the stigma of a war fought against unnatural odds, hampered at home by politicians and demonstrators, and which blamed the war's veterans for its failures.* It characterised an open-ended military commitment in a protracted war that lacked a method for victory. Next time would be different, ran the argument. In October 1983 American forces deployed to the Caribbean island of Grenada, the first time they had entered a combat zone since Vietnam. Would this war be different? Could the Vietnam syndrome be cured for good?

When US Marines and Rangers were landed on to the island of Grenada to contest the ultra-left wing government that had recently staged a *coup d'état*, every possible attempt was made in Washington to ensure a victory. There would be a specific mission to be achieved, the political resolve to back it and forces sufficient to guarantee a victory. Cries of 'another Vietnam' were easily and expertly parried. In essence, the Grenadan invasion was a 'police action'—short, sharp and decisive. It was everything the Vietnam War was not. US casualties amounted to 18, and within three days most of the fighting had ended. That same month, in the Lebanon, 241 US Marines on a United Nations peacekeeping mission died in a terrorist car bombing. Within two months Reagan announced that the rest of this Marine force would be 'redeployed' back to the Fleet, and out of the conflict. The 'Vietnam syndrome' had reared its head: the American people and their government wanted no more part of an unending fratricidal war without clear boundaries or conditions for victory. Vietnams were everywhere: Beirut, Nicaragua, El Salvador and Angola all beckoned. The next

---

*After the war, many Vietnam veterans found themselves alienated and unwanted, a situation which led to incidents of Post Traumatic Stress Disorder (PTSD). Once controversial but now an accepted psychological illness, PTSD mixed feelings of guilt, rage, fear and confusion—without the cushion of thanks and gratitude that met returning Second World War veterans. It is a sad fact that more US soldiers have committed suicide since the war than were killed in it (58,000).

overt military attack by US forces came in 1986 when F-111 jets, flying from air bases in Britain, bombed selected targets in Libya. Again, like Grenada, the action was a surgical, short-duration, sure-fire combat mission. Reagan's successor, George Bush, similarly launched an overseas offensive with the Vietnam syndrome weighing heavily on his shoulders. His precision-guided invasion of Panama was designed to unseat and apprehend the CIA stooge Manuel Noriega, while proving once more that American forces *could* fight—and win. Operation 'Just Cause' was launched on the morning of 20 December 1989 and involved over 12,000 troops. It had definite mission objectives, namely the seizure of selected sites, the rescue of prisoners and the capture of Noriega. Again, within a matter days the fighting was over; 23 American soldiers had been killed, at a cost of 314 Panamanian soldiers and at least 250 civilians. But these tiny police actions were to be only a foretaste of what was to come. Operation 'Desert Storm', fought in 1991, would be George Bush's attempt finally to overcome the 'Vietnam syndrome'.

Iraq, under the leadership of President Saddam Hussein, had invaded the small monarchy of Kuwait and begun a campaign of arrests, looting, and murder. President Bush announced that Operation 'Desert Storm' would not be 'another Vietnam', and, as the plans for the liberation of Kuwait were drawn up, each element of the 'Vietnam syndrome' was countered. Hussein himself boasted that American attempts to recapture Kuwait would turn into a second Vietnam War, and the fear of re-fighting that war weighed particularly heavy on the US leadership. It soon became clear, however, that the Gulf War would again be a textbook police action in the mould of Grenada and Panama. For five weeks an allied bombing campaign destroyed virtually everything of tactical importance using both 'iron' bombs and updated Vietnam-era 'smart' bombs. Nothing had been seen on a similar scale since the massed attacks over Germany during the Second World War. On 23 February 1991 the allied ground offensive pushed into Kuwait and Iraq to engage Iraqi forces. Although some pundits had predicted monumental casualty figures, the advance was far easier than anyone had expected. President Bush was able to declare Kuwait liberated within four days of the beginning of the ground war.

The lessons of Vietnam were truly burned deep into the psyche of the political and military hierarchy. Each of the conditions of the Vietnam syndrome were again overcome to create the 'perfect' war. It had lasted 100 hours, had involved 6,000 allied armoured vehicles, had destroyed (or captured) 3,000 Iraqi tanks, had captured 65,000 Iraqi prisoners and had killed perhaps 100,000 of Hussein's soldiers. The cost had been surprisingly light, with American deaths (including 28 men killed by a 'Scud' missile at Dhahran) amounting to only 182 killed or missing in action. Victory had been guaranteed, the victory conditions were clear and unambiguous and the American people were wholeheartedly behind the President. It seemed as if the 'Vietnam syndrome' had been exorcised for ever. Who could now doubt that the United States again had the military might to effect political and military change anywhere on the globe? Bush bathed in the radiated glory of the war for a short period, until the political fall-out from the war began to seep on to the nation's nightly TV news broadcasts. President Hussein was still in power and his despotic government was now hunting down and annihilating the Kurdish and Shiite peoples in Iraq who had risen up against him. Perhaps there never *could* be a 'perfect' war. Despite the crowning achievement of the 1991 Gulf War, President Bush failed to win the next election, partially because the war had not really resolved the problems that had caused the conflict in the first place. His successor, Bill Clinton, would also discover that wherever military action overseas seemed inevitable, Vietnam would re-surface as a cautionary watchword against any intervention at all.

The Former Yugoslavia

Although President Clinton had promised the voters that it was 'the economy, stupid', that would occupy his time and energy once elected, he could not avoid the problems facing US troops in the African nation of Somalia. The country had been utterly destroyed by anarchic guerrilla groups, and in 1992 famine and disease gripped what remained of the population. Something *had* to be done. President Bush had already sent in US troops as part of a United Nations peacekeeping force, primarily to stabilise the situation and to allow aid to reach those who needed it.

Now Clinton had to pull a 'victory' out of the bag. Somalia broke the trend of two decades of interventionism and quickly overreached itself—to everyone's horror. There were no conditions for 'victory', no withdrawal date and no certainty that the military objectives could be achieved. As such, it became an 'African Vietnam', with US soldiers patrolling slum areas in the hope of forcing the armed gangs with their heavily armed pick-up trucks ('technicals') off of the streets. Firefights ensued, and gradually the exchanges became more heated, involving machine guns, rockets and helicopter gunships. Élite Delta Force rescue missions failed miserably, and when an attack on one of the chief warlords was staged, the American troops found themselves trading bullets with sympathetic Somali civilians. The situation degenerated rapidly, and several local leaders demanded an American withdrawal. When the corpse of a single US serviceman was dragged through the streets of the capital, Mogadishu, the American people demanded an immediate withdrawal. War had been declared on the people that the Americans had gone there to try and protect. Clinton got out fast, and Somalia remains as grief-stricken as it ever was.

But another overseas crisis beckoned, and promised to be yet another pitfall for American forces. That crisis was the civil war in former Yugoslavia. In the summer of 1991 the country split apart, and blood was shed almost immediately. Serbia, the largest and most affluent of the former republics, fought a war against Slovenia and Croatia, which countries will remain unstable at least until the end of the millennium. Accompanying that conflict was the gruesome and messy civil war that engulfed the former province of Bosnia-Hercegovina. There, a many-sided and always confusing battle involving Serbs, Croats and Muslims raged out of control. Guerrilla armies skirmished on hilltops and in streets, villagers were massacred by unknown gunmen, mortars pounded the larger towns and all sides gave no quarter. While GIs patrolling villages in South Vietnam had only one enemy, the UN peacekeepers assigned to Bosnia often had three. BBC correspondent Kate Adie recalled how she began interviewing a group of fighters engaged in a gun battle in Bosnia and had to first ask them who or what they were, and at which side they were shooting! When plans were put forward to send American soldiers to Bosnia with peacekeeping objectives, fear must have been struck into the hearts of every American Army commander old enough to remember Vietnam. Words used to describe the Vietnam War, such as 'nightmare', 'morass' and 'quagmire', apply more so to Bosnia. British, French and other forces have been on the ground under the United Nations banner for several years, escorting aid convoys (those that made it through the checkpoints), monitoring sporadic and short-lived cease-fires and dodging incoming mortar-fire on their bases. With the traumatic experience of Vietnam in mind, it was always doubtful that the American government would send troops to join their European colleagues. The outcome of the failed mission in Somalia was one that no one wanted to repeat.

Ominously, President Clinton made tentative moves towards military action in Bosnia, pushed, as was Lyndon Johnson thirty years earlier, by the fear of inaction. His gut reaction to stay out was tempered by his commitments to the NATO alliance. Congress, too, feared that Bosnia, was yet 'another Vietnam', and cautioned against military intervention. On 7 June 1995 a Congressional Hearing sat to debate the Clinton policy towards Bosnia, and members of both parties roundly criticised that policy. Vietnam hung in the minds of many. 'Vietnam still haunts and confronts us still,' said Senator James Exxon (Democrat). And, referring to the US air strike against a Serbian ammunition depot a few days before, Senator John McCain (Republican) voiced his worry that it 'smacks so much of the failed strategy of Vietnam'. He went on to declare that 'it gives me nightmares'. During the hearings there were continued references to Vietnam, and senators found it difficult to understand how Clinton, who had protested against the failed bombing of North Vietnam in his youth, could preside over the apparent failed bombing of a Serbian military target. Both were measures designed to replace a ground force with aerial force, and to limit any involvement to a series of high altitude, short-duration raids. But, as President Johnson discovered, even these commitments can get out of hand quickly. The nation was shocked to learn that an American pilot had been shot down over Bosnia that same week, and a vast armada of helicopters and fixed-wing aircraft was dispatched to retrieve him. Hundreds of people were involved in the rescue, putting further lives at risk and courting an escalation of American activity in the region.

As innocent civilians caught up within the Bosnian conflict suffered again and again, the call for intervention was continually being heard throughout the Western media. There was a great desire for something to be done, but no one, from seasoned politicians and Army Generals to the general public, really knew quite what. Some journalists (exposed to the sufferings of the refugee victims) openly commented on the bizarre media inversion that had taken place since the Vietnam War, with the bias leaning *towards* military intervention, not *against* it.

Sporadic air strikes against the Bosnian Serbs climaxed in mid-1995. Public outrage at the shelling of a Sarajevo market on 28 August 1995 by Serbian gunners spurred a NATO blitz of Serb positions. The attacks were a massive US-led show of force and were designed to quell the clamour for further military intervention. Clinton's fingers had been burnt once before in Somalia, and he made great efforts to sidestep the region's deepening crisis. But again, like his predecessors in the 1960s, he seemed to regard it wiser to do something rather than nothing. One commentator likened the intensive three-day bombing campaign to Nixon's 'Linebacker II' operation over North Vietnam—not the first strike of an unending commitment, but a final climax of force designed to prepare the way for disengagement and negotiation.

At the end of November 1995 an unexpected cease-fire became a peace agreement involving Serbia, Bosnia and Croatia, and Clinton was able to take the glory. His Secretary of State, Warren Christopher, had done the impossible at a closed summit at Dayton, Ohio. The way was paved for a massive influx of NATO troops (including 20,000 US soldiers) into Bosnia to secure the peace. However, the conflict will surely remain unstable, and the danger of another 'war without front lines' will continue to lurk for any nation willing to commit troops to the region. Had President Clinton learnt the ultimate Vietnam lesson? The Dayton Peace Accord can be seen as an affirmation of a new kind of foreign policy. Haiti, North Korea, Ulster, Bosnia and the Middle East were all diplomatic *coup d'états* that replaced the iron hand of the Cold War with the velvet glove. That Clinton is the first postwar US President not to have served in the military, and that he actively protested against the Vietnam War, may have a bearing on this new and successful approach. Somalia was Clinton's overseas failure, but many commentators have seen the last-ditch spoiling activities of George Bush behind the deployments: Somalia may well have been a move to discredit the incoming President.

Vietnam will continue to play a role in Presidential elections. As Bill Clinton found out in his electoral battle with Bush, to have spoken out against the controversial Vietnam War marked him (despite the passage of twenty years) as both a traitor and an unpatriotic subversive. In his defence, the 'draft-dodger' described himself as anti-Vietnam, not anti-American. Yet, to many American conservatives, the two are not mutually exclusive. These days the war is more of a political metaphor than a military object lesson.

It seems that the spectre of Vietnam will loom over every war, wherever and between whomever it is fought. Every Western nation has learnt something from the failures of America's South-East Asian war, and many more are learning by experience. Some, such as the Russian Federation, do not even learn from their *own* mistakes. Russia followed the abortive counter-insurgency war in Afghanistan sixteen years later with the bloody and open-ended war in the republic of Chechnya in early 1995.

There will be many Vietnams, each subtly different in setting, tone, vigour and outcome, but the United States cannot truly say it will never fight that war again. It lurks in many corners of the globe, and under many guises.

APPENDIX: KEY INDIVIDUALS

During a decade and a half of American intervention in Vietnam, the personalities in key positions periodically changed. The following lists the names of the most important Americans involved in the shaping of the Vietnam War.

US Presidents
1961–1963	John F. Kennedy
1963–1968	Lyndon B. Johnson
1969–1974	Richard M. Nixon
1974–1976	Gerald R. Ford

US Secretaries of Defense
1961–1968	Robert S. McNamara
1968–1969	Clark M. Clifford
1969–1972	Melvin R. Laird
1973	Elliott L. Richardson
1973–1975	James R. Schlesinger

US Ambassadors to South Vietnam
1961–1963	Frederick E. Nolting
1963–1964	Henry Cabot Lodge
1964–1965	Maxwell D. Taylor
1965–1967	Henry Cabot Lodge
1967–1973	Ellsworth Bunker
1973–1975	Graham A. Martin

Commanders of MACV
1962–1964	General Paul D. Harkins
1964–1968	General William C. Westmoreland
1968–1972	General Creighton Abrams
1972–1973	General Frederick C. Weyland

Chairmen of the Joint Chiefs of Staff
1960–1961	General Lyman L. Lemnitzer (Army)
1961–1964	General Maxwell D. Taylor (Army)
1964–1970	General Earle G. Wheeler (Army)
1970–1974	Admiral Thomas H. Moorer
1974–1978	General George S. Brown (Air Force)

BIBLIOGRAPHY

The Indo-China Wars encompassed thirty years of hostilities and had repercussions that were felt around the world. No bibliography can hope truly to do justice to the enormity of the subject. Many of the books listed below were valuable in forming ideas and opinions during the preparation of the present work, while others will provide readers with a more detailed discussion of certain aspects of the Vietnam War.

Allen, T. B. and Berry, F .C. *CNN: War in the Gulf*. London: Maxwell Macmillan, 1991.

Arnold, J. R. *Artillery: Illustrated History of the Vietnam War*. New York: Bantam Books, 1987.

Baker, M. *NAM*. London: Abacus, 1982.

Bonds, R. (ed.). *The Vietnam War: The Illustrated History of the Conflict in Southeast Asia*. London: Salamander, 1979.

Bowman, J. S. (ed.). *The Vietnam War: An Almanac*. New York: World Almanac, 1985.

Braestrup, P. *Big Story* (2 vols.). Boulder: Westview (in cooperation with Freedom House), 1977.

Burke, J. P., and Greenstein, F. I. *How Presidents Test Reality: Decisions on Vietnam, 1954 and 1965*. New York: Russell Sage Foundation, 1989.

Chomsky, N. 'The U.S. Media and the Tet Offensive', *Race and Class*, vol. 20. London: 1978.

Chomsky, N., and Herman, E. S. *Manufacturing Consent*. New York: Pantheon Books, 1988.

Doleman, E. C. *Tools of War*. Boston: Boston Publishing, 1985.

Donovan, D. *Once a Warrior King*. London: Weidenfeld & Nicolson, 1986.

Dorr, R. F. *Air War Hanoi*. London: Blandford, 1988.

———. *Air War Over South Vietnam*. London: Arms and Armour, 1990.

Dougan, C., and Weiss, S. *1968*. Boston: Boston Publishing, 1984.

Doyle, E., Lipsman, S., and Weiss, S. *Passing the Torch*. Boston: Boston Publishing, 1981.

Doyle, E., and Lipsman, S. *America Takes Over*. Boston: Boston Publishing, 1982.

———. *Setting the Stage*. Boston: Boston Publishing, 1981.

Ethell, J. L. and Price, A. *One Day in a Long War*. London: Greenhill Books, 1990.

Ezell, E. C. *The Great Rifle Controversy*. Harrisburg: Stackpole, 1984.

Fallows, J. 'M-16: A Bureaucratic Horror Story', *Atlantic Monthly*, June 1981.

Forbes, J., and Williams, R. *Riverine Force: The Illustrated History of the Vietnam War*. New York: Bantam Books, 1987.

Halberstadt, H. *War Stories of the Green Berets*. Osceola: Motorbooks, 1994.

Hamilton-Merritt, J. 'General Giap's Laotian Nemesis', *Vietnam*, vol. 8, June 1995.

Herr, M. *Dispatches*. London: Pan Books, 1978.

Jensen-Stevenson, M., and Stevenson, W. *Kiss the Boys Goodbye*. London: Bloomsbury, 1990.

Kamps, C. T. *The History of the Vietnam War*. London: Guild Publishing, 1988.

Karnow, S. *Vietnam: A History*. London: Century Hutchinson, 1983.

Lipsman, S., and Doyle, E. *Fighting For Time*. Boston: Boston Publishing, 1983.

Lipsman, S., and Weiss, S. *The False Peace*. Boston: Boston Publishing, 1985.

Luce, D., and Sommer, J. *Viet Nam: The Unheard Voices*. Ithaca: Cornell University Press, 1969.

Macdonald, P. *Giap: The Victor in Vietnam*. London: Fourth Estate, 1993.

Maclear, M. *Vietnam: The Ten Thousand Day War*. London: Thames Methuen, 1981.

Maitland, T. and Weiss, S. *Raising the Stakes*. Boston: Boston Publishing, 1982.

Mangold, T. and Penycate, J. *The Tunnels of Cu Chi*. London: Hodder & Stoughton, 1985.

Mason, R. *Chickenhawk*. London: Corgi, 1984.

McNamara, R. S. *In Retrospect*. New York: Times Books, 1995.

Morrocco, J. *Thunder From Above*. Boston: Boston Publishing, 1984.

O'Brien, T. *If I Die in a Combat Zone*. London: Panther Books, 1980.

Page, T. *Page After Page*. London: Sidgwick & Jackson, 1988.

Palmer, D. R. *Summons of the Trumpet*. Novato: Presidio Press, 1978.

The Pentagon Papers. Gravel edn. Boston: Beacon Press, 1971.

Powell, C. L. *A Soldier's Way*. London: Hutchinson, 1995.

Race, J. *War Comes to Long An*. Berkeley: University of California Press, 1972.

Rosenberg, M. J., Verba, S., and Converse, P. E. *Vietnam and the Silent Majority: The Dove's Guide*. New York: Harper & Row, 1970.

Rust, W. J. *Kennedy in Vietnam*. New York: Da Capo Press, 1985.

Sheehan, N. *A Bright Shining Lie*. London: Jonathan Cape, 1989.

Short, A. *The Origins of the Vietnam War*. New York: Longman, 1989.

Summers, H. G. *On Strategy: A Critical Analysis of the Vietnam War*. Novato: Presidio Press, 1982.

———. *Vietnam War Almanac*. New York: Facts On File, 1985.

Thomas, G. C. (ed.). *Guidebook for Marines*. Quantico: Marine Corps Association, 1990.

Thompson, L. *The U.S. Army in Vietnam*. Newton Abbot: David & Charles, 1990.

Thompson, Sir R. (ed.). *War in Peace*. London: Orbis, 1985.

VanDeMark, B. *Into the Quagmire: Lyndon Johnson and the Escalation of the Vietnam War*. New York: Oxford University Press, 1991.

Walsh, J. (ed.). *The Gulf War Did Not Happen*. Aldershot: Arena, 1995.

Westmoreland, W.C. *A Soldier Reports*. Garden City: Doubleday, 1976.

Williams, W. A., and McCormick, T. (eds.). *America in Vietnam: A Documentary History*. Garden City: Anchor Press Doubleday, 1985.

Wintle, J. *The Viet Nam Wars*. London: Weidenfeld & Nicolson, 1991.

INDEX